S...

Pla...ng

1968,1972,1976,1980,1984,1988, 1992, 1996

Human Kinetics

D1428684

238 107

Library of Congress Cataloging-in-Publication Data

O'Brien, Ronald F.
  Springboard and platform diving / Ron O'Brien.-- 2nd ed.
     p. cm.
Rev. ed. of: Ron O'Brien's diving for gold. c1992.
Includes index.
  ISBN 0-7360-4378-0 (softcover)
 1. Diving. I. O'Brien, Ronald F. Diving for gold. II. Title.
  GV837 .017 2003
  797.2'4--dc21

2002013393

ISBN-10: 0-7360-4378-0
ISBN-13: 978-0-7360-4378-6

Developmental Editor: Anne Cole; **Managing Editor:** Carla Zych; **Copyeditor:** Patsy Fortney; **Proofreader:** Jennifer Davis; **Indexer:** Sharon Duffy; **Permissions Manager:** Toni Harte; **Graphic Designer:** Fred Starbird; **Graphic Artist:** Tara Welsch; **Art and Photo Managers:** Carl D. Johnson and Dan Wendt; **Cover Designer:** Keith Blomberg; **Photographer (front cover):** Rob Tringali/Sports Chrome; **Photographer (author photo):** Judy Temple Schober; **Illustrators:** Mary Yemma Long and Roberto Sabas; **Printer:** Versa Press

Human Kinetics books are available at special discounts for bulk purchase. Special editions or book excerpts can also be created to specification. For details, contact the Special Sales Manager at Human Kinetics.

Printed in the United States of America   10   9   8   7   6   5   4

Human Kinetics
Web site: www.HumanKinetics.com

United States: Human Kinetics, P.O. Box 5076, Champaign, IL 61825-5076
800-747-4457
e-mail: humank@hkusa.com

Canada: Human Kinetics, 475 Devonshire Road, Unit 100, Windsor, ON N8Y 2L5
800-465-7301 (in Canada only)
e-mail: info@hkcanada.com

Europe: Human Kinetics, 107 Bradford Road, Stanningley
Leeds LS28 6AT, United Kingdom
+44 (0) 113 255 5665
e-mail: hk@hkeurope.com

Australia: Human Kinetics, 57A Price Avenue, Lower Mitcham, South Australia 5062
08 8372 0999
e-mail: info@hkaustralia.com

New Zealand: Human Kinetics, Division of Sports Distributors NZ Ltd.
P.O. Box 300 226 Albany, North Shore City, Auckland
0064 9 448 1207
e-mail: info@humankinetics.co.nz

This work is dedicated to my wife, Mary Jane, and my children, Anne and Tim. Their willingness to give me the freedom to pursue my career and their unselfishness in letting me help raise other people's children through sport have been truly remarkable.

Contents

Preface

This book is about all phases of diving skills and conducting or participating in a successful diving program. The first edition was purposely geared more toward beginning- and intermediate-level coaches and divers, with some information for advanced coaches and divers. This second edition is directed at all levels of coaches and divers.

By retaining necessary fundamental information while adding more specific and advanced nuances to the techniques, I have greatly expanded the technical material covered in this book. The new boardwork checklist in chapter 2 takes you through, step by step, the performance of a proper forward approach and backward press. Analyzing a diver's boardwork with this checklist will help you pinpoint any skills that are missing or deficient and explain how they should be performed.

Chapter 9, new to this edition, includes directions on how to plan for the training year and presents a six-week peaking-for-competition program. This information has been the basis of my preparation of divers for world and Olympic competitions for the past 20 years. It is information I have not readily shared in the past because, as an active coach, I wanted an edge.

Chapter 10 includes coaching techniques that have proven successful throughout my career. Additionally, the guidelines that I present for both divers and coaches are taken from my own experiences in interacting with divers in training and competition. These guidelines reflect the high standards of behavior I have always demanded of my athletes and myself. Finally, in this chapter I reveal the way my divers and I created a competitive advantage through special, and often overlooked, means of preparing for competition outside of the actual training program.

These new areas are the backbone of whatever success my diving programs and divers have enjoyed. I hope these additions are valuable to all who read them. Diving is a very complicated sport, and the only way to continue to improve as a coach or diver is to study constantly and work hard. So get going on the book; then take the information to the pool and put it to good use.

Good luck!
Ron O'Brien

Acknowledgments

My sincere thanks and deepest appreciation go to all the divers I have had the privilege of coaching in my career. Their cooperation with my experimentation and trial-and-error coaching methods made much of the information contained in this book possible. Their contribution has been invaluable.

© Jeff Shaw/SportsChrome East/West

Body Alignment

Correct body alignment is the key factor in performing an effective springboard approach, backward press, platform approach, and all takeoffs from the springboard and platform. Because elevation, distance, and rotation are all determined when the feet leave the takeoff surface, skill mastery in this area of a dive is paramount to success.

Body alignment begins with the stance assumed before beginning the dive and continues through the movements of the approach and takeoff. Especially important is the area from the hips to the head because this is where most errors occur. Correct positioning creates stability and leads to a more balanced, aesthetic, and powerful performance.

BASIC ALIGNMENT

Imagine the body as a column of building blocks. Such a column is certainly more solid, stable, and balanced when the blocks are stacked in a straight line than when each block is shifted slightly off center. A straight column is more resistant to outside forces that may threaten to topple it. This is significant when you consider that a great many strong outside forces work to move the body parts in various directions during a dive.

When springing the diving board, the poorly aligned body acts as a rubber tube; it is compressible and absorbs some of the energy of the board, thus reducing lift and spin. The correctly aligned body takes on the properties of a steel rod when the board is recoiling beneath it.

Figure 1.1 illustrates the typical body position of an untrained diver. The hips are rotated downward, causing a lower back arch. The rib cage is positioned downward and backward, resulting in a severely rounded shape in the upper back, and as a reaction to these positions the head and neck project forward. The center of balance is located back on the heels, and the overall effect is poor balance and appearance.

Figure 1.1 Incorrect body line.

The diver achieves correct body line by repositioning these areas, beginning with the hips and working upward. To experience the correct hip rotation, the diver can rotate the pelvis to an extreme downward or incorrect position (see figure 1.2a) and then move it in the opposite direction to achieve upward rotation (see figure 1.2b). The diver should easily feel the difference. This upward rotation should occur until the lower back is as straight as possible, but not to the extreme that a weakening or bending of the knees occurs.

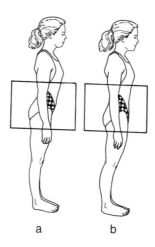

a   b

Figure 1.2 (a) Incorrect downward hip rotation and (b) correct upward hip rotation.

With correct hip position as the foundation, the rib cage can now be positioned to align directly over the hips. Notice in the untrained diver (figure 1.3a) that the center point of the shoulders is considerably behind the center point of the hips. In aligning the upper body, the diver should bring these two points into a straight line. In addition, as the rib cage is relocated, the alignment of the back should be straight or *slightly* round. In no case should this line be concave. To accomplish these goals, the diver elevates the rib cage slightly and positions the trunk to align with the hips, as shown in figure 1.3b. Elevating the rib cage allows muscular control to occur, which helps eliminate unnecessary movements in this area.

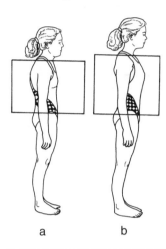

a   b

Figure 1.3 (*a*) Incorrect, depressed rib cage and (*b*) correctly elevated rib cage.

Just bringing the hips and upper body into line, however, does not always result in a straight or slightly round shape in the back. Some divers, when elevating the rib cage, develop a concave, or hollow, shape in the back; this is not a stable position and should be corrected. Other divers may have a pronounced convex, or round, appearance. A slightly round shape is acceptable if a straight line cannot be achieved, because it is a stable position, but a significantly rounded position is not aesthetic, and the diver should correct it as much as possible.

To alleviate the problem of the hollow back, the diver should move the rib cage upward and inward (ribs toward spine); to remedy the rounded back, the diver should move the rib cage upward and outward. The diver may need manual help to achieve the correct alignment by using one of two techniques to force the body into the right position.

To maneuver the diver from a concave to a straight position, the coach places one hand on the ribs, pushing them upward and backward to keep the rib cage elevated while it moves backward. The coach places the other hand on the lower back, spanning the low back area to keep the hips in their upwardly rotated position as the ribs are moved.

To remedy a rounded back position, the coach places one hand on the diver's abdominal area, pressing this area toward the spine. The palm of the other hand is on the diver's low back area with the fingers spread so that the thumb can press the rib cage forward to straighten the upper back, while the little finger presses down on the pelvis to keep it in the upwardly rotated position. The combination of these forces will help the diver find the correct body alignment.

As the rib cage and spine are aligned, the shoulders should be positioned so that they are in line with the trunk or in a slightly closed position (toward the front of the body). The shoulders must not be in an open (backward) position because this contributes to instability and lack of balance.

Maintaining muscular control of the rib cage during all diving movements is critical to good performance. This is the area of the trunk where stability and balance are most affected. Unnecessary movements (especially an outward projection of the rib cage) cause unwanted reactions in other areas of the body, and a "disconnect" between the upper and lower body occurs.

The last area of alignment is the head and neck. Many divers have "forward head syndrome," which means the head and chin protrude forward (see figure 1.4a). To correct this, the diver needs to draw the chin in toward the spine without dropping it below horizontal (see figure 1.4b). The head should align with the rest of the body, but not to the point where it appears stiff.

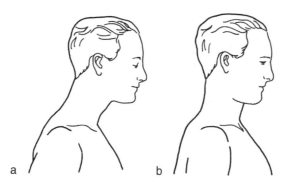

Figure 1.4 (*a*) Incorrect, forward head position and (*b*) correct head position.

Finally, it is very important to maintain the weight forward over the balls of the feet in the stance and in all phases of the approach and takeoffs from the springboard and platform so that the toes can be used to maintain balance. When the weight shifts backward, a loss of balance control occurs.

When the diver integrates all of these movements, he or she will achieve correct body alignment, as shown in figure 1.5. Because of variations and restrictions imposed by different body builds, not everyone can achieve an absolutely

Figure 1.5 Correct body alignment.

straight line, but constant training and practice can result in significant improvement for all divers.

To maximize progress in body alignment, the diver must work to make the correct posture a part of daily life. Constantly carrying the upper body in this position not only benefits diving but also is healthier than the common slouched posture most people have. Consistent work on these posture skills, and the help of a coach in correcting and commenting on them and giving a verbal reward when they are done properly, needs to be part of the training process.

Training Methods for Body Alignment

1. **Lying on the floor.** By lying face up on the floor and pressing the lower back toward the floor to eliminate any space in that area, the diver can practice and feel proper alignment. Because the head and upper back rest on the floor, they will automatically align correctly.

2. **Standing against a wall.** Keeping the heels one inch from the wall and the head and upper back straight against it, the diver rotates the hips upward and presses the lower back as close to the wall as possible. Eliminating the space between the wall and lower back is ideal. The coach can assist the diver in achieving correct position by pressing the abdominal area toward the wall.

3. **Using a full-length mirror.** Positioning and relocating various body segments in front of a mirror offers immediate feedback as to what is correct and incorrect. This method also gives the diver a chance to see how much better he or she looks and reinforces continued practice. Practicing armswings, the forward approach, and backward presses while maintaining correct alignment helps the diver transfer these techniques to the pool.

Stance

The stance a diver uses before the forward approach or backward press may seem simple and inconsequential, but it is crucial to good performance and good scores. There are two reasons for this:

1. The impression a diver's stance gives to the judges and spectators bears on how that diver is perceived and received even before he or she makes a move.

2. Errors in stance set the stage for errors in the movements to follow.

Obviously, correct body alignment is the foundation of the forward and backward stance, but other factors must also be considered. In order to achieve proper stance, the diver must pay careful attention to his or her shoulders, arms and hands, hips, legs and feet, and balance.

The diver should keep the shoulders in a downward position, not elevated as shown in figure 1.6a. Elevated shoulders create tension in the muscles of the neck and shoulders, which spreads to other muscle groups and makes physical and mental relaxation before performance difficult. When most of us are under stress, we have elevated shoulder positions and tension without even being aware of it. The correct downward position for shoulders is shown in figure 1.6b.

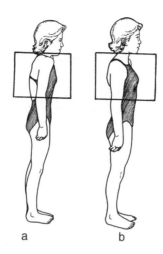

a   b

Figure 1.6   (*a*) Incorrect, elevated shoulders and (*b*) correct, downward shoulders.

The arms must be straight but not rigid, and each hand should be held with the palm in on the center of the leg, with the fingers together but relaxed in a normal, partially curled position. Abnormal hand and wrist variations are unaesthetic and distracting. Keeping the hands and fingers in a rigid state causes tension to radiate up the forearms to the upper arms and shoulders, again impairing proper predive relaxation.

The diver must align the hips with the upper body. A twisted hip position is unattractive and can lead to an uneven forward approach, hurdle, and takeoff or to a twisted, sideward, or backward takeoff.

The diver should keep the legs straight but not stiff, with the feet placed evenly to keep the legs from twisting. The feet should be positioned with the heels together and the front of the feet rotated outward, especially for backward and inward takeoffs, so that the toes are aligned directly under the hips. This creates a triangular base for more stability. Also, this allows the feet and legs to align under the hips during the extension phase of takeoff, which is the most efficient jumping position.

As mentioned previously, the diver should maintain the center of balance over the front half of the foot. Here is a teaching cue to determine whether the diver has proper balance: The diver should lift the toes up while keeping the rest of the body still. If the diver does not begin to fall forward, his or her balance is not in the right place. The diver should achieve the balance position by leaning the whole body slightly forward as a unit, not by bending at the waist.

Alignment in Movement

Correct alignment in the stance is the starting point. Then, as the diver walks, jumps, swings the arms, squats down, springs the board, and initiates the takeoff, he or she must maintain this alignment and balance over the toes. Misalignment in the movements leading up to and including the takeoff, which results in poor balance and performance for the rest of the dive, usually occurs in one of two ways:

1. The rib cage projects forward, causing the hips to rotate downward, the shoulders to move backward, and the back to change to a concave shape.

These movements create an arched trunk position, and maintaining balance and stability becomes very difficult (see figure 1.7).

2. The head moves forward and downward, either shifting the balance point too far forward or causing the body to compensate by moving backward (see figure 1.8).

These misalignments can also occur simultaneously (see figure 1.9).

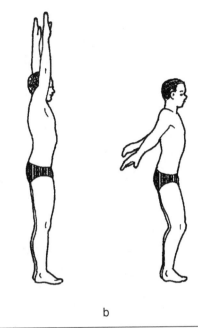

a   b

Figure 1.7 Open trunk position (*a*) arms overhead and (*b*) arms down behind the body.

a   b

Figure 1.8 Head forward and down at (*a*) the top of the hurdle and (*b*) squatting down.

Figure 1.9   The top of the hurdle with head down and trunk open.

When Misalignment Commonly Occurs

Misalignment errors generally occur in the following situations during the approach (springboard and platform), backward press, and all takeoffs:

1. The arms swing backward behind the body, either while at the sides or from an overhead position.
2. The diver is applying force to the springboard or platform.
3. The springboard is applying force to the diver.
4. The diver's arms are in an overhead position.

The coach and diver need to check alignment constantly at these critical points to achieve good, consistent takeoffs for all dives. This is the area of performance in which most of the errors that manifest themselves in poor results later in the dive occur.

SUMMARY

Correct body alignment in the stance and movements leading up to and including the takeoff allows a stable and balanced performance to take place. Alignment also gives the diver greater control of movements and an aesthetic appearance. These factors add up to an improved performance overall, resulting in higher scores. That extra half point or point more per judge on each dive adds up.

© Sport The Library/SportsChrome

Armswing, Boardwork, and Takeoffs

Proper use of the springboard is a goal all competitive divers continuously pursue no matter what their level of performance. The importance of correct and efficient use of the springboard is monumental because height, distance, and amount of rotation are already established by the time the diver leaves the board. However, the skills involved in performing the forward approach, backward press, armswing, and the four types of takeoffs are the most difficult to master.

Before beginning work on the forward approach, backward press, and takeoffs, the diver must learn to swing the arms correctly. An ineffective armswing technique negatively affects all other movements. An incorrect armswing reduces the amount of board depression that occurs before takeoff, thus reducing the force of the board recoil. This is translated into less elevation from the board, less time in the air to perform the dive, and reduced somersault rotation. Also, an incorrect armswing makes getting the arms into the proper position for the take-off very difficult.

Boardwork, armswing, and takeoff are all interdependent. Once the diver masters the fundamentals of boardwork and armswing, the takeoffs are a matter of balance and position on the tip of the springboard, and knowing which movements to make and when.

ARMSWING

The armswing consists of two phases, the descent and the ascent. The descent phase begins when the arms begin a downward and backward movement. The ascent phase begins when the arms pass the legs and start an upward movement in front of the body. In each phase, certain principles must be followed to perform a correct armswing:

1. The shoulders should stay relaxed, as tension in this area reduces the ability to accelerate the swing.
2. The shoulder joint and shoulder girdle should both be used to create the swing.
3. The elbow, wrist, and finger joints should be kept straight.
4. The arms should make the biggest circular path possible.
5. The area of acceleration of the arms should begin at approximately shoulder level behind the body and continue to shoulder level in front of the body.

Performing the Armswing

The armswing begins from an overhead position in both the hurdle and the backward press. The arms are in a Y position, in line with or slightly in front of the bodyline, with the palms facing outward (see figure 2.1a). The descent phase begins as the arms move relatively slowly in a downward and backward path,

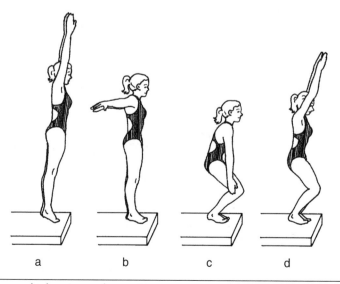

a   b   c   d

Figure 2.1   Armswing path showing palm position.

as far as shoulder flexibility will allow, so the biggest circular path possible is performed. If shoulder flexibility restricts backward movement when the arms are overhead, then the arms should be moved to a lower lateral position before beginning the backward movement. Each diver will have to find the least restricting path to getting the arms behind the body. As the arms move from the overhead location to shoulder level, the palms rotate from an outward to a downward-facing position (see figure 2.1b). At this point the diver begins accelerating while keeping the shoulders relaxed. As the arms pass the legs, the palms face inward and acceleration continues (see figure 2.1c). During the ascent phase the diver must keep the elbows straight and the palms facing inward until the arms move above shoulder level (see figure 2.1d).

Legs-arms-legs is the movement sequence that is used when performing the armswing in coordination with the legs. When dropping to the springboard from the hurdle or backward press, the legs begin to bend before the arms accelerate. However, this does not mean that the arms cannot be moving into position to accelerate before the legs bend. After the legs bend and the arms accelerate, the legs do not fully extend before the arms swing to an overhead position. This sequence takes place in all springboard takeoffs.

Practicing the Armswing

Which method you use to practice the armswing movements and coordination with the legs depends on what training equipment is available. If a trampoline or dryland board is not available, the drills will have to move from the ground to the springboard in the pool. As stated in chapter 1, alignment errors frequently occur when the arms are in a swinging movement. It is important that proper alignment be maintained during the following drills. The diver should do the following:

1. Standing with the legs straight and together, do the armswing technique with one arm several times, then the other arm. Start the armswing from a lateral position 45 degrees above horizontal.

2. When the technique in step 1 is good, do the same with both arms (no leg movements).

3. The start position is with the arms lateral in a Y shape.

4. From the start position, bend the legs first so the body drops down six to eight inches; then perform the armswing. At the end of the armswing keep the legs bent.

5. Repeat steps 1 through 3, and after the arms have swung overhead, stand up. This is the pattern to be used on the springboard—legs-arms-legs!

6. If a mirror is available, perform steps 1 through 5 in front of it.

7. If a trampoline is available, practice the armswing technique, first bouncing with the legs straight and only the arms moving. Keep the bounces low and swing the arms on every second or third bounce to give time to prepare. As the skill improves, begin swinging on every bounce.

8. Using low bounces, begin bending the legs, then swinging the arms, then finishing with leg extension. Keep the legs-arms-legs sequence from step 5. At first, swing the arms every second or third bounce; then progress to every bounce.

9. When step 8 is done well, begin bouncing with moderate height.

10. Stand on the end of the one-meter springboard facing forward with the arms in the overhead Y position. Bend the knees; then accelerate the arms, and as they pass overhead, perform a front jump straight into the water.

11. When step 10 can be performed well with good alignment, repeat it with a small bounce preceding the armswing.

When the diver can perform the armswing technique well, it is time to begin the first step in learning the forward approach, the hurdle jump. This skill allows the diver to learn the basic movements of jumping to the end of the board and to gain a feel for the hurdle position without the complicated legwork of the actual hurdle.

HURDLE JUMP

A hurdle jump is performed from a distance of two-foot lengths from the end of the board. It is a two-foot takeoff, jumping upward and forward to the end of the board, landing on two feet, and then performing whatever jump or dive is desired. The hurdle jump is a preliminary skill to learning the approach and hurdle. Practicing this simplified version of the hurdle allows the beginning diver to learn the feeling, position, and balance of the descent phase of the one-leg hurdle before actually performing this more complex skill. The hurdle jump also lets the diver work on balance and distance from the board in a more controlled way. Correct body alignment and armswing technique must be strongly emphasized while practicing this skill.

Learning the Hurdle Jump

There are three progressions to follow in learning a hurdle jump. The diver must show correct balance, body alignment, armswing, and distance from the board before moving to the next step.

STEP 1   Stand at the starting point with the arms straight and overhead. Without using the arms, jump from both feet up and forward to the end of the board and, without an armswing, spring the board and perform a front jump.

STEP 2   Repeat step 1, using an armswing when landing on the end of the board.

STEP 3   Repeat step 2, starting with the arms down, straight, and held in parallel alignment behind the body. Swing the arms forward and upward to an overhead position as the hurdle jump begins. See figure 2.2.

In step 3 it is important that the diver learns to hold the arms still in the overhead position in the ascent phase of the hurdle jump before beginning the armswing in the descent phase. The arms should be aligned as described for the hurdle in the next section (see figure 2.5).

When the hurdle jump is mastered into a forward jump straight, practice can begin with a jump in tuck and pike positions, then a forward dive in tuck position. As the forward approach is learned, practice should continue on the hurdle jump, with jumps and dives, to keep reinforcing proper fundamentals.

a   b   c   d

Figure 2.2 Hurdle jump.

BOARDWORK

Because of the importance of boardwork, the diver must practice the movements involved until they are mastered before attempting to perform them with any kind of difficult dive. Using the training methods described in this chapter, the diver can develop correct techniques first in slow motion and then gradually at normal speed as suggested. The diver can then take the boardwork to the springboard and practice diligently with jumps and basic simple dives. The more difficult dives will be much easier to learn with this slow practice as a foundation.

It is futile for the diver to follow the frequently used system of learning the basic motions of boardwork, learning dives, learning more difficult dives, and then trying to correct and improve boardwork at a later date. Many bad habits learned in the beginning because of lack of patience, practice, and attention to detail become ingrained and uncorrectable and remain throughout the diver's career. Practice doesn't make perfect; perfect practice makes perfect!

Forward Approach

The overall effect of the forward approach should be a smooth, even flow of motion. No one part of the movement pattern should stand out. At the same time, the diver needs to attain excellent height and balance in the hurdle and takeoff. Divers can achieve this by following certain guidelines in constructing the approach. The diver should do the following:

1. Use a moderate rate of speed in the steps.
2. Determine the length of the steps and hurdle relative to his or her size.
3. Eliminate unnecessary movements by establishing a consistent timing pattern between the arms and legs.
4. Apply force within the boundaries of smoothness.

For each part of the approach, the diver should adhere to these guidelines. The result will be an appealing, efficient, effective blend of motion. The forward approach is illustrated in figure 2.3, a through q. Refer to this figure as each segment of the approach is described in the following sections.

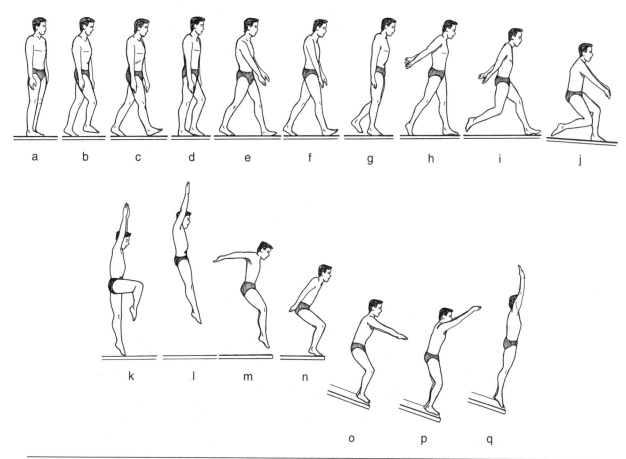

Figure 2.3 Forward approach.

Number and Speed of Steps

Divers normally use three, four, or five steps in the approach. I recommend the four- or five-step approach because it gives more time to establish a good rhythm before taking the faster and stronger step before the hurdle. Beginning divers using the three-step approach tend to walk too fast and rush the hurdle. Two factors will dictate the number of steps taken:

1. Which leg the diver uses to begin the approach
2. Which leg the diver uses to lift into the hurdle

If the diver uses the same leg for the first step as is lifted into the hurdle (the hurdle leg), then a four-step approach must be used. If the diver uses one leg to start the approach and the other as the hurdle leg, then a three- or five-step approach must be used. The reason for this is simple. When the same leg is used for both the first step and the hurdle, the hurdle can occur only after the second or fourth steps. When opposite legs are employed for the first step and the hurdle, the hurdle can occur only after the third and fifth steps. Therefore, diver preference, based on what feels best with regard to the starting leg and hurdle leg, determines the number of steps to be taken.

The speed of the steps needs to be moderate so the diver appears to be neither rushed nor lacking in continuity. Experimentation with various speeds as measured with a metronome has shown that a speed of 75 to 90 beats per minute, depending on the size of the diver, best accomplishes this result. By performing the approach using a metronome set to different speeds, the diver and coach can determine the speed that is best for that individual. Obviously, 75 to 90 beats per minute is a target area you should use as a starting point. Each diver will have his or her own comfortable rhythm; however, if this rhythm is 50 or 120 beats per minute, the net effect is probably not going to be good.

Constructing the Approach

When the diver or coach is left to design a forward approach with few or no parameters, the results are extremely diverse. Certain physical measurements applied to a formula can be used to develop a very specific approach. With this as a beginning point, the coach and the diver can then adopt changes to meet the diver's individual needs.

You need three diver measurements to begin constructing the approach:

1. Distance in inches from the bottom of the kneecap (patella) to the ground

2. Length of the foot in inches

3. Standing height

Measuring foot length and standing height are no problem; however, determining the distance from the bottom of the kneecap to the ground is trickier. Without shoes, the diver stands with the legs straight. At the front of the knee, using the index finger, feel the location of the bottom of the kneecap. Slide the finger straight across to the side of the leg and measure the distance from that point to the ground.

Add this length to the foot length to determine the basic step length of the approach. Then establish the size of the steps and hurdle as follows:

Hurdle = 80% of basic step length

Last step (step before hurdle) = 60% (plus or minus 5%) of standing height

Intermediate steps = basic step length (distance from knee to ground) + length of foot

First step = 90% of basic step length to the nearest half inch

When marking off this approach on a board or on the ground, begin from the tip of the board and work back to the starting point. After the diver practices with this for a reasonable time, determine whether he or she has great difficulty performing a good approach, and make adjustments as necessary to fit the diver's needs.

The basic principle here is that the approach is a function of certain anatomical measurements with adjustments in various areas for specific reasons. The diver should take the first step with less leg swing than the intermediate steps because he or she initiates that step with the legs together rather than swinging them from a position behind the body. Thus, the first step is calculated as 90 percent of step length. The last step before the hurdle is performed as a faster, stronger step than the intermediate steps; therefore, a longer length is designed to accommodate this. Observation and experimentation with various-sized divers has shown that a hurdle 80 percent of the basic step length provides sufficient horizontal velocity to the end of the board but does not make the hurdle so long that horizontal velocity is too great. Figure 2.4 illustrates this formula mapped out on a diving board.

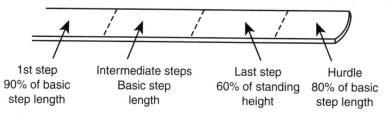

1st step
90% of basic
step length

Intermediate steps
Basic step
length

Last step
60% of standing
height

Hurdle
80% of basic
step length

Figure 2.4   Approach formula mapped out on a diving board.

During the steps before the last step, the foot should strike the board in the normal heel-to-toe walking action. In the last step, either a heel-toe placement or a whole foot placement of the foot can be used. These two methods more effectively allow the diver to transfer body weight over the pushing leg into the hurdle, and provide better balance. Placing the foot down with the ball of the foot first impedes the body weight moving forward and tends to create a backward lean in the hurdle.

Armswing and Timing With Steps

Using armswing in the approach is important to help the diver achieve rhythm and timing as well as to increase the amount of lift into the hurdle. By developing a simple but concise timing of the armswing with the steps in the approach, the diver can establish a pattern of movement that he or she can repeat consistently.

Other than the use of the arms in the walk, there is no difference among the three-, four-, and five-step approaches. In the three-step approach the arms swing forward on the first step, in the four-step approach they swing forward on the second step, and in the five-step approach they swing forward on the third step. The key factor in all the approaches is the point at which the arms begin to swing forward in relation to the leg action. The diver can adapt the basic timing principle from the four-step method described here.

In the four-step approach, the arms hang naturally at the sides during the first step. The instant the heel contacts the board in the second step, the arms swing forward one to one and a half feet in front of the body, depending on the diver's preference. When the heel contacts the board in the third step, the arms swing backward one and a half to two feet behind the body, with the palms facing backward. The diver should finish this backward swing with the arms starting the final forward swing into the hurdle *just before* the foot is placed on the board in the last step.

It is very important for the diver to be concise in starting the forward and backward armswings the instant after the foot contacts the board in the second and third steps. If the armswings are too early, the arms either will have to hesitate, thus ruining the rhythm and flow of motion, or will be too early into the hurdle, causing poor height and balance. Should the arms start late, they will not be behind the body and ready to start the hurdle at the right time, which results in a very fast backward-forward motion of the arms during the fourth step. Again the rhythm and flow are disrupted, and poor balance (usually a backward lean) occurs in the hurdle. The timing of the arms swinging forward just before the foot strikes the board in the last step is also very important to a smooth arm lift into the hurdle and aids tremendously with being in time with the rhythm of the board.

Throughout the armswing movements, the diver should relax the muscles in the arms and hands with the exception of the triceps, which is the muscle located on the back of the upper arm. The triceps, when maintained in a mildly contracted state, keeps the elbow extended so no arm bending can occur. This is most important during the forward swing of the arms into the fourth step in preparation for the hurdle, and during the hurdle, press, and takeoff.

Balance

Throughout the steps of the approach, the body weight is kept forward over the front part of the foot (an alignment described in chapter 1). This is especially important when taking the last step. Since the arms are in a backward position while stretching out for the longer last step, this will create a strong tendency for the balance to fall backward. To counteract this, as the last step begins, while the leg is behind the body, the whole body leans forward. As the leg passes the support leg and begins stretching out in front of the body, the trunk moves to a vertical alignment and remains there as the jump into the hurdle takes place. Refer back to figure 2.3, g, h, and i on page 14.

Hurdle and Press

As the foot is placed on the board after the last step, the knee and hip joints of that leg (the "drive" leg) flex and the body weight drops. The arms begin their swing forward and up; then the other leg (the "hurdle" leg) starts its forward and upward lift. A great aid to attaining good balance into the hurdle is to make sure the knee of the drive leg aligns over the toes before beginning extension into the hurdle. If the knee is significantly behind the toes when extension begins, a backward lean or piked body position is likely to occur. Conversely, if the knee is significantly ahead of the toes, a forward lean or overjumping the end of the board may occur.

The diver should keep the arms straight and parallel with the wrist, elbow, and shoulder joints in a neutral, natural position. No unusual rotation of these joints in the inward or outward direction should occur. As the arms and hurdle leg approach their final positions for takeoff into the hurdle, the drive leg extends to a straight line at the hip, knee, and ankle joints, propelling the body upward. In the takeoff position for the hurdle, the diver holds the arms straight, parallel, and slightly overhead in front of the body with the palms facing forward; the head should be tilted slightly forward with the chin drawn in so the diver can see the tip of the board. The hurdle leg should be positioned with the thigh horizontal and the lower leg vertical, causing a 90-degree angle in the knee joint, and with the ankle and foot pointed. The diver should be able to sight down the inside of the lower leg and foot to the tip of the board when the hurdle leg is lifted; this will help the diver make sure the position is correct. Study this position in figure 2.5; it is critical to a balanced and controlled hurdle and takeoff.

As the body rises from the board, the knee of the hurdle leg begins a smooth and gradual extension so the legs are together with toes pointed at the peak of

Figure 2.5   Hurdle takeoff position.

the hurdle while the arms remain in the hurdle takeoff position. The diver must lift the knee into the hurdle and extend the knee without any hesitation or detectable change in speed. If a jerky high-speed drop of the hurdle leg occurs while the body is in the air, a backward movement of the torso will occur.

When the body starts its descent from the top of the hurdle to the board, the arms begin to move backward and downward. The knee and hip joints begin to flex, so the diver is in a deep squat when first contacting the board. The arms begin to accelerate as they pass shoulder level behind the body. Variation in arm timing is required for different types of dives. In general, the arms are in an area from behind the hips to slightly in front of the hips as the feet land on the board. If the arms remain straight, the hands will pass the legs at the level of the knee joint or lower.

The toes are drawn up so the landing occurs on the balls of the feet, hip-width apart. As the body weight drops onto the board, the heels will come down to make contact with the board. While the arms continue their path past the legs and up to the overhead takeoff position, the body extends and the recoil of the board propels the diver into the air. The diver must bring the feet and legs back together tightly when leaving the board.

Visual Focus

Throughout the approach, the diver should focus the eyes on the tip of the board to ensure the best chance of hitting the mark and to aid in keeping the balance point over the toes on landing. Just before landing on the board, the diver should shift the focus of the eyes to the far side of the pool in front while the head lifts to a level position for the landing. The diver should not see the feet make contact with the board.

Training Methods for the Forward Approach

1. Floor work. The diver should accurately measure his or her approach on the floor, marking with tape or sidewalk chalk the points at which each step should occur and the point at which the hurdle should land on the tip of the board. The diver should then slowly walk through the movements of the steps, hurdle, and front jump, stopping after each step to check balance, body alignment, and arm position. After performing the fourth step and lifting the arms and leg into the hurdle motion, the diver should stop and hold the correct hurdle position while balancing on the drive leg. By learning to perform the perfect hurdle takeoff position in this way, a diver greatly increases his or her chance of transferring this position to an actual approach on the springboard. After balancing in the hurdle takeoff position for two to three seconds, the diver should place the toes of the hurdle leg on the mark indicating the end of the board and bring the legs together, standing up on the toes while holding the arms still. This simulates the drop of the knee that occurs during ascent and the top of the hurdle position. Next the diver flexes the knees and then the hips while balancing on the balls of the feet. The arms move backward and downward as the body drops and the heels drop to the floor, then the arms accelerate. As the arms swing upward in front of the body and to an overhead position, the diver performs a front jump.

As the diver's movements and positions become more accurate, the speed of the practice can be increased gradually. However, the diver should continue to practice holding the hurdle takeoff position for two to three seconds before he or she continues the press and takeoff. When the diver can balance the hurdle takeoff position consistently and in the proper position, he or she should practice the walk-through with a jump into the hurdle.

2. Mirror work. The diver can perform the same drill in front of a full-length mirror. The hurdle takeoff, holding for two to three seconds, can be practiced from both a front and a side view to monitor all aspects of the correct position.

The importance of extensive, continuous practice of the approach at slow and then faster speeds on the floor and in front of the mirror cannot be overemphasized. Great patience and perfectionism here can ensure a great forward approach, hurdle, and takeoff.

3. Metronome. A metronome set to the desired speed of the approach can help tremendously in developing a consistent rhythm of steps and hurdle. This can be used not only for floor and mirror work but also during actual diving practice. For most divers, 75 to 90 beats per minute works well as a target speed.

4. Length of last step. Most divers tend to make the last step of the approach too long and the hurdle too short. To correct this problem, a four-foot length of surgical tubing can be tied around the board at the point where the fourth step should end. The diver can then practice both on the dryland board and in the pool with the tubing in place. Each time the diver oversteps the mark, contact with the tubing will instantly indicate that the step was too long. This also gives the diver a visual cue as to where to place the foot correctly. Eventually, the diver will no longer need the tubing, but whenever the problem recurs, the rubber tubing should be put back on the board. If the diver takes too short a last step, the rubber tubing can be placed in a position that forces him or her to step over the tubing and thus take a longer last step.

5. Knee extension timing. The knee action of the hurdle leg should be continuous and smooth so that there is no noticeable stop of the hurdle leg in the lifted position. As soon as the leg reaches its proper position at the point of takeoff for the hurdle, it should immediately begin to extend as the body rises to the top of the hurdle. To emphasize and learn this motion, the diver should practice taking the fourth step of the approach and the hurdle from the ground or deck onto a bench or stair step, landing with the arms overhead, the legs straight, and the feet together, standing up on the toes. The height of the landing platform can be adjusted to the strength of the diver so the feet come together just before landing.

6. Arm timing. Divers often tend to hold their arms in position too long at the top of the hurdle and then have trouble getting the arms down, past the hips, and back overhead in time for the takeoff. To alleviate this error, the diver can practice stepping off a platform or step with the arms in the position desired at the top of the hurdle. As soon as the body begins dropping to the landing spot, the diver should begin to circle the arms backward and downward. The diver should land on the toes, with feet hip-width apart and the shock of landing absorbed in the knees and hips. The arms should be timed so they are just beside the hips at the point of contact with the ground.

Common Forward Approach Mistakes and Corrections

Mistake	Correction
The approach is too fast.	Roll the fulcrum back several inches beyond the normal setting. As you see the speed slowing down to accommodate the slower board movement, place the fulcrum back to the original position. Repeat the process until a change occurs. The diver can practice the approach in time with a metronome set to the desired speed.
The foot is placed down toes first going into the hurdle.	The diver should concentrate on placing the heel down first. This is easier than concentrating on placing the whole foot at one time.
The elbows bend excessively in the hurdle and press.	The diver can practice approaches while wearing manufactured or homemade elbow braces that prohibit bending.
The hurdle is too long or short.	If using rubber tubing doesn't work, adjust the diver's approach length. Divers who have practiced the approach for a year or more may find it almost impossible to change the length of the last step to adjust hurdle length. Therefore, if the hurdle is too short, lengthen the approach by the distance you wish to lengthen the hurdle, and vice versa for a hurdle that is too long.
The arms swing down too early from the hurdle (typical of young divers and gymnasts).	The diver should touch the sides of the knees with the fingertips when landing on the board. This cannot be done when the arms swing too early.
The arms swing down too late from the hurdle.	Same method as for early armswing.
The diver constantly over-jumps the end of the board.	If the diver is using correct hurdle technique, lengthen the approach. If this doesn't work, the diver should walk more slowly.
The diver lands short of the tip of the board.	If the diver is using correct hurdle technique, shorten the approach by the distance the diver misses the end of the board. Walking slightly faster can also help.
The diver constantly misses the timing of the board on takeoff.	This can be caused when the diver swings the arms and lifts the knee too fast into the hurdle. It occurs frequently during difficult optional dives and in competition. The diver should take a longer backswing of the arms in the next-to-last step, which will cause him or her to take more time to complete the movements. If this doesn't work, roll the fulcrum forward slightly. Mistiming of the board can also occur when the diver swings the arms forward after the foot strikes the board in the last step. Work on timing this so the arms start forward just before the foot strikes the board.

Backward Press

The backward press is much less complicated and demanding than the forward approach. For this reason it very often doesn't command as much attention and practice as it should. Depending on dive selection, 40 to 50 percent of all dives in the competitor's program begin with the backward press, so effective performance of it is extremely important.

Even though there are many variations of this skill, only two methods are included here: the two-part backward press and the four-part backward press. The first is recommended for beginners and beginning competitive divers because of its simplicity. Once the diver attains a suitable level of balance and skill, he or she should use the second, and more complicated, four-part backward press.

Proper body alignment and stance, as mentioned in chapter 1, are essential to successful performance of the backward press; the diver must possess all the elements of proper alignment and stance before starting the first motion.

Two-Part Backward Press (Beginning Divers)

The diver stands with the heels slightly above horizontal. The two parts of this press are described here and illustrated in figure 2.6, a through g.

Part number	Description
1	The arms lift laterally to a position 45 degrees above horizontal and slightly in front of the bodyline. The diver then lifts the heels to their highest position. This is called the top of the press.
2	As the arms begin to circle down and back, the heels drop partially. The knees bend, then the hips bend as the body crouches into the springing position. As the arms pass shoulder level, they begin to accelerate. At the end of the squatting movement, the heels are in a horizontal position. As the arms pass the hips and begin their upward swing in front of the body, the arms are parallel and straight. During the upswing of the arms, the legs begin to extend and the board depresses and recoils to propel the diver upward.

a   b   c   d   e   f   g

Figure 2.6 Two-part backward press.

Four-Part Backward Press

The starting position for this press is the same as for the two-part press; the heels are just above horizontal. The four parts of this technique are described here and shown in figure 2.7, a through j.

Part number	Description
1	Without any other motions, the diver lifts the heels to their highest point.
2	The diver brings the heels down to the original starting position while lifting the arms laterally and slightly in front of the bodyline to shoulder level. (This is called opposition, because the heels and arms move in opposite directions.)
3	As the arms continue to move upward to a position 45 degrees above horizontal or higher and slightly in front of the body, the heels again rise to their highest point. The top of the press positions in the two-part press and the four-part press are identical.
4	The arms begin to circle back and down, and the heels drop partially. Then the knees bend, then the hips bend as the body crouches into the springing position. As the arms pass shoulder level, they begin to accelerate. This follows the same sequence of movement as that of the two-part press.

a　　b　　c　　d　　e　　f　　g　　h　　i　　j

Figure 2.7 Four-part backward press.

Note: The speed of the ankle movement dictates the speed of the arm motions in parts 2 and 3. Because a quick movement of the arms is not desired, it is important for the diver to keep the ankle motions moderate in speed.

The two-part press is simple and relatively easy for the beginner to learn while still struggling with maintaining balance and distance from the board. To introduce the four-part press at this point would tremendously complicate the situation. However, even though the two-part press is simple, it tends to make the diver move too quickly in springing the board. For this reason, the diver should move on to the four-part press as soon as he or she is ready.

The four-part press has the advantage of allowing consistent balance and good resulting lift from the springboard. During this press the heels lift initially in an upward motion, which helps keep the body weight over the front of the feet, where the toes can create pressure on the board to adjust balance and control. A downward ankle motion in the starting movement tends to drop the body balance backward.

By using opposition of arm and ankle actions in part 2 of the four-part press, a slower arm motion is achieved because the arms must wait for the heels to go down and then back up as they lift to an overhead position at the top of the press. When the arms and heels lift simultaneously, this generally creates a much faster movement, making balance more difficult. Also, by keeping the arms slightly in front of the bodyline at this time, the diver stays balanced on the board while the heels drop and the board moves downward (both motions can cause the diver to fall backward).

All movements made in reaching the top of the press serve to establish a rhythm and balance as well as to elevate and stretch the body in preparation for the drop of the body weight and the acceleration of the arms into the press. Excessive rocking of the board does not result in more spring; it merely increases the chance of losing balance. More forceful upward movements of the arms and body also make balance more difficult.

Additional Elements for Successful Performance

In both the two- and four-part presses, other points should be considered. Visual focus and resulting head position, armswing path, and foot and ankle placement, when performed correctly, add balance and stability to the press and take-off.

- **Visual Focus.** The most important factor here is not so much the point on which the diver focuses but rather the position of the head, which should be erect and in line through the backward press. However, the point of focus does play a part: If the diver focuses on a point somewhere between the fulcrum and the back of the board, the correct head position is easier to achieve than if looking down at a point more forward on the board.

- **Armswing Path.** Throughout the press, the diver should use the armswing technique described earlier. As the arms circle back and down from the top of the press, the diver's shoulder flexibility dictates the distance behind the body that the arms travel. If the diver swings the arms back until the shoulders and upper body are pulled backward or a misalignment occurs, an off-balance takeoff will result.

- **Foot and Ankle Position.** One-third to one-half of the foot surface is kept on the board to aid in balance and to prevent slipping. The heels are kept slightly elevated to compensate for the downward angle of the board from the diver's weight. Standing very high on the toes is an unstable and difficult balancing position. At no time during the backward press should the heels drop below the board level. For lateral balance and good jumping position, the diver should use a triangular placement of the feet with the heels together and the front of the feet aligned hip-width apart.

Training Methods for the Backward Press

1. Floor work. The diver goes through the movements of the backward press slowly, pays attention to detail, and makes sure that each action is correct. As the motions become more natural and consistent, the diver can gradually increase the speed until he or she is performing the motions at the speed to be used on the springboard. Then the diver can practice the backward press with a jump. As the arms pass the legs at the bottom of the press, the diver should continue to swing upward in front of the body to a position 45 degrees above horizontal, as he or she initiates a backward jump with the arms moving to an overhead reaching position.

2. Mirror work. Using a full-length mirror, the diver goes through the backward press motions in the same manner as described in the section about training methods for the forward approach, from a forward and side view.

3. Bench work. The diver stands on a low bench or step to practice the movement pattern slowly and precisely, then gradually increases the speed of execution until it is the same as that to be used on the springboard. This allows accuracy of movement and balance with the foot in the same position as when on the springboard.

4. Side of pool. The diver performs the press at the same speed as on the springboard and does a backward jump.

Common Backward Takeoff Mistakes and Corrections

Mistake	Correction
The diver bends forward and shifts the balance forward.	A coach or helper holds a stick or pole across the front of the diver a few inches from the chest during the press. As soon as the arms swing down near the hips, the helper removes the pole.
The diver circles the arms back and down too early or excessively bends the arms.	The diver should touch the sides of the knees with the fingertips at the bottom of the press.
The arms are too late getting through the pressing motion.	Check the armswing technique; the diver should stay in the sitting position longer as the arms swing upward.
The distance from the board is too great.	See if the heels drop below horizontal in the preliminary rocking motion or at bottom of the press. A coach or helper can hold a pole across and in front of the board a foot farther away from the board than the diver should land. The diver does the press and whatever dive desired between the pole and the board. Obviously, the helper should move the pole if the diver is going to hit it, but should not tell the diver he or she intends to do that. The coach or helper could also hold the pole across the diver's shoulders until his or her arms reach the top of the press, then remove the pole. This ensures that the diver does not lean away early or move the arms back too far in the upward movement. This also works great for keeping inward dives in good balance.

FULCRUM SETTING

For the beginning diver the fulcrum should be set at the midpoint for all takeoffs to allow for easier balance and control. When balance and distance are good at this setting, the fulcrum should be moved back. In the forward takeoffs, move it back as far as possible while still allowing a soft landing on the board after the hurdle. This means that as the feet make contact with the board, it is starting its downward motion.

The backward press creates a different problem when determining where to set the fulcrum. Because the feet do not leave the board during the springing motion, finding the point where the diver is not in rhythm with the board is more difficult than in the forward approach. However, the ideal fulcrum setting for the backward press is the setting at which the greatest height from the board is achieved. This point can be found by moving the fulcrum to various settings and observing the diver performing a back jump.

The earlier a diver is forced to use a slower board, the easier adaptation will be. Periodically test to find out if the board can be used effectively with the fulcrum set farther back. Divers can learn to adjust to a progressively slower motion of the board, but must be challenged to do so.

SPRINGBOARD BOARDWORK CHECKLIST

Table 2.1 is a checklist of points that should be evaluated in the forward approach and backward press. The type of forward approach intended for this checklist is the traditional walking steps with either a nonairborne (continuous contact with the board) or airborne (loss of contact) last step. The airborne last step is characterized by a leaping or hopping action before contact with the foot of the drive leg, in preparation for the hurdle.

By studying the checklist, the elements of the forward approach and backward press can be learned and used to construct a correct performance. Improvement in a diver's boardwork can be achieved by checking each point in the list against the diver's performance. For most of the items listed, this can be done best by videotaping the skills and replaying the tape while following the checklist. For the step and hurdle segments, actual measurements may have to be taken.

TAKEOFFS

The takeoff period occurs in forward approach dives from the time the toes make initial contact with the board, after the hurdle, until the toes have last contact with the board. In backward takeoff dives, the takeoff begins when the diver's body begins to drop down from the top of the press and continues until the toes have last contact with the board.

Before addressing the execution of the takeoffs applying to the four different directions of rotation (forward, backward, reverse, and inward), some techniques common to all of these should be discussed.

Boardwork Checklist

Skill	Explanation	Yes	No	Comments
Stance: Forward and Backward	1. Feet even			
	2. Heels touching and feet in "V" shape			
	3. Legs straight			
	4. Hips square (no turn)			
	5. Hips (pelvis) rotated			
	6. Rib cage slightly elevated			
	7. Rib cage closed (drawn toward spine)			
	8. Abdomen drawn in			
	9. Shoulders slightly closed			
	10. Head in line, chin in			
	11. Balance on balls of feet			

Steps are measured from toes to toes.

Skill	Explanation	Yes	No	Comments
Forward Approach: Step and Hurdle Segments	1. Hurdle = 80% of step length			
	2. Last step 60% of standing height. This is a starting reference point; adjust as needed.			
	3. Intermediate steps equal to the distance from the bottom of the kneecap to the ground + foot length			
	4. First step 90% of step length			
	5. All steps heel/toe contact			
Armswing	6. Swings arms with hurdle leg in a forward-backward-forward pattern			
	7. Arms forward on next to last step			
	8. Arms back on last step			
	9. Palms facing backward			
	10. Armswing starts forward in last step; begins just before the drive leg contacts the board.			
	11. Arms kept straight swinging into the hurdle			
	12. Arms kept parallel swinging into the hurdle			
Vision	13. Point of focus on tip of board throughout walk and hurdle until just prior to contact out of hurdle, when the head levels and line of sight moves to the water.			

Skill	Explanation	Yes	No	Comments
Last Step	14. Heel-toe or whole foot method of contact			
	15. Knee of drive leg flexes before contact			
	16. Center of gravity drops prior to foot contact			
Hurdle Ascent	17. Knee of drive leg moves in line with toes before extension begins			
	18. Arms swing to a position approximately 10° in front of vertical overhead			
	19. Arms parallel with palms facing forward			
	20. Shoulders touching ears at last contact into hurdle			
	21. Arms and shoulders remain in this position to the top of hurdle			
	22. Chin in, head tilted forward with eyes looking at the tip of the board			
	23. Thigh lifted to horizontal			
	24. Knee flexed between 45 and 90°			
	25. Hurdle leg ankle extended and toes pointed			
	26. Rib cage slightly hollow			
	27. Shoulders slightly closed			
	28. Hip on drive leg side locked into straight line			
	29. Knee begins extension immediately after last contact with the board			
	30. Legs straight, feet together by top of hurdle			
Top of Hurdle	31. Chin in, head tilted down			
	32. Arms still approximately 10° in front of vertical			
	33. Shoulders against ears			
	34. Rib cage slightly hollow			
	35. Hips straight			
	36. Legs straight and together			
	37. Ankles extended, toes pointed			
	38. Body angle approximately 5° behind vertical			

The following movements must be done in the sequence listed.

Skill	Explanation	Yes	No	Comments
Hurdle Descent	39. Arms begin to spread laterally and down to a "Y" position			

(continued)

Boardwork Checklist *(continued)*

Skill	Explanation	Yes	No	Comments
Hurdle Descent *(continued)*	40. Palms rotate to face outward			
	41. Arms begin to circle down and backward			
	42. Palms rotate to face down when the arms move behind the body			
	43. Arms move behind the body as far as shoulder flexibility will allow			
	44. Knees begin to flex			
	45. Hips begin to flex			
	46. Arms accelerate quickly			
	47. Arms swing in as big a circle as possible			
	48. Deep squat position achieved on contact			
	49. First contact made with balls of feet			
	50. Head level at first contact			
Backward Press: Stance	1. See the items listed under "Stance" at the beginning of this checklist			
Starting Position	2. Arms at the sides or lateral at shoulder height			
	3. Ankles slightly above board level (board is angled down) and horizontal or slightly down			
Initiating Board Movement	4. Ankles move first in an upward direction			
	5. Board is ocillated 2-3 times			
	6. On final board rock, the sequence of movement is ankles drop, arms begin to lift, then the ankles lift			
Press Ascent	7. Arms lift laterally and slightly in front of the body line			
	8. Palms face down			
	9. Rib cage slightly hollow			
	10. Shoulders remain slightly hollow			
	11. Hip and knee joints straight			
	12. Head remains still and level			
Top of Press	13. Arms stop between 45 and 90° above shoulder level and slightly in front of body line			
	14. Shoulders touch ears			
	15. Palms face outward			
	16. Shoulders slightly hollow			
	17. Rib cage slightly hollow			

Skill	Explanation	Yes	No	Comments
Top of Press (continued)	18. Hip and knee joints straight			
	19. Highest arm and ankle positions reached simultaneously			
	20. Ankles extended (plantarflexed as high onto the toes as possible)			

Movements #21-25 are done in the sequence listed.

Skill	Explanation	Yes	No	Comments
Press Descent	21. Ankles drop partially			
	22. Knees begin to flex			
	23. Hips begin to flex			
	24. Arms move down			
	25. Arms move backward as far behind the body as shoulder flexibility allows			
	26. Palms face down as arms pass behind body			
	27. Arms accelerate from shoulder level as squat movement continues			
	28. Arms make a big circular path			
	29. Palms face inward as they pass the legs and swing upward			
	30. A drop to a deep squat occurs as the arms accelerate (90° knee angle if leg strength allows)			
	31. Ankles drop to horizontal			
	32. Rib cage slightly hollow throughout descent and beginning of upswing			
	33. Legs begin to extend as arms swing upward			
	34. The whole sequence of movements in the press is legs (flex)-arms (swing)-legs (extend)			
Vision	35. Focus on any point on the board throughout the press as long as the head stays level			

Preliminary Takeoff Position

One basic preliminary takeoff position of the body and arms is common to all takeoffs regardless of the direction of rotation or the number of somersaults or twists to be performed. The diver flexes the knees and hips and initiates a jumping movement while holding the arms above and in front of the body. This position is illustrated in figure 2.8, a and b, for the forward approach and backward press takeoffs. Note that they are identical except for the direction the diver is facing.

Figure 2.8   Preliminary takeoff position for (a) the forward approach and (b) the backward press.

This preliminary takeoff position occurs just before the springboard begins its recoil. What happens after this point is determined by the dive to be performed. These body motions, positions, and balances will be described in detail as the dives are explained.

The most important point to remember is that not only are the arms above and in front of the body before the board propels the diver upward, but they are also in this position before the diver fully extends the legs in the jumping action. This arm timing in relation to the movement of the legs causes most divers trouble in takeoffs. In the vast majority of cases, the arms are late getting to this position and therefore cannot assist correctly in the remaining part of the takeoff.

This arm timing is difficult to achieve because it is an unnatural jumping motion, contrary to all the basic jumping activities we learn as children. When jumping to grab a bar overhead or to catch a ball, the arms and legs move simultaneously. This is illustrated in figure 2.9, a through d; in a normal jump, the arms swing upward as the legs extend to thrust the body into the air. In contrast, during all diving takeoffs the arms swing upward before the legs extend to begin the jump (see figure 2.10, a-d).

Figure 2.9   Normal jump.

Figure 2.10 Diving jump.

This difference is extremely important to understand as early in training as possible. Practice for this arm timing is incorporated into the floor work exercises described under the sections "Training Methods for the Forward Approach" and "Training Methods for the Backward Press" earlier in this chapter. It's critical that this correct but unnatural jumping action be practiced at all times during dryland boardwork drills and while doing forward and backward jumps from the springboard.

Basic Takeoffs

Before discussing specific takeoffs, we must understand the principle of action–reaction. Newton's third law of motion states that for every action there is an equal and opposite reaction. Applied to diving, this means that if a diver pushes against the board in one direction, a resultant equal force from the board will occur in the opposite direction. If in midair the diver rotates the head in one direction, the feet and body will rotate in the opposite direction. Although explaining the physics of diving is not the purpose of this book, a general understanding of this concept is needed for this section, as well as some other areas of discussion.

In springboard diving, there are four basic takeoff directions: forward, inward, backward, and reverse. The coach and diver must understand how these are performed to obtain good balance and distance and create adequate rotation to complete the dive.

Forward Dive Takeoffs

As the diver lands on the board from the hurdle, the body should be positioned with the center of balance over the front of the feet and the arms swinging through in the area of the hips. To aid in proper balance, the shoulders should be aligned over the knees as the squat takes place. This balance should be maintained until the arms swing to the overhead position.

The armswing accelerates through earlier in forward takeoffs than in reverse takeoffs. This is due to the fact that the arms must change direction after completing the armswing to initiate forward dives. After the diver completes the press and the board begins its upward movement, the body extends to a straight line, with the center of balance forward so the body leaves the board at an angle slightly forward of vertical. This position provides proper distance from the board (three to four feet) and adequate rotation for the basic dives. Figure 2.11 illustrates how the upward thrust of the board (A) causes the diver to travel away from the board (B) and creates rotation in the forward direction (C).

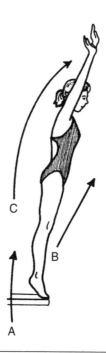

Figure 2.11   Forward straight-line takeoff.

When using the one- and three-meter boards, some divers who lack height in the air or who lack strength may need to create more rotation to complete the dive than occurs in the takeoff just described. A sequential forward motion of the arms, head, and torso into a pike position before takeoff will create this rotation. As illustrated in figure 2.12, the forward motion of the upper body (A) as the legs extend causes a forward push of the feet into the board (B); the board then pushes backward against the feet (C), creating a forward rotational movement (D). Because of the direction of the resultant force of the board against the feet, the diver's body will travel backward (E) as the body rotates forward. Therefore, the more forward rotation the diver creates, the more forward balance of the body is necessary to compensate for the increased backward travel and to achieve good distance. This direction of body movement is minimal in the basic dives because the rotational force needed is small. Thus, a diver need use only a slight forward lean in basic dives to compensate for the backward body movement and to assure good distance.

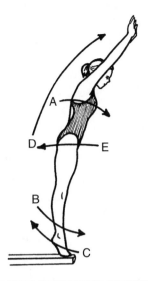

Figure 2.12 Forward pike action takeoff forces.

Inward Dive Takeoffs

Proper balance at the beginning of the inward press is crucial to successful performance. As the drop from the top of the press occurs, the shoulders should be aligned over the knees throughout the squat; this balance is maintained until the start of the throwing motion to initiate rotation. If the shoulders are aligned over the thighs or hips, a strong tendency to fall backward occurs; if the shoulders are positioned forward of the knees in the squat, a tendency to fall forward occurs.

The motions needed to achieve good distance and rotation from an inward takeoff position are the same as those needed in the forward dives. As in forward takeoffs, the arms swing past the hips as the diver completes the squatting movement into the press. The arms accelerate earlier in the inward takeoffs than in the backward takeoffs for the same reason cited in the forward versus reverse takeoffs. Figure 2.13 shows that the piking movement of the body (A) occurs

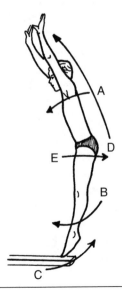

Figure 2.13 Inward takeoff forces.

before takeoff, causing the feet to push forward against the board (B) and causing the board's force to be backward against the feet (C), creating rotation in the inward direction (D).

As explained in the discussion of the forward takeoff, the direction of force from the board causes the diver to travel backward (E). With the inward takeoff, however, this means that the forces that create rotation also push the diver away from the board. For this reason balance must be maintained over the toes until these forces are applied, which occurs very late in the press, just before the diver leaves the board. Notice in figure 2.13 how the upper body is over the board as the feet are just about to lose contact with the board.

If the diver loses balance in the backward direction before the rotational force and resulting movement away from the board occur, two things will happen:

1. Little rotation or elevation will result because the weight of the body will not be over the legs and in line with the force of the board at takeoff.

2. The diver will be too far away from the board due to the combination of backward lean and backward movement from the rotation actions.

To further ensure good distance and rotation, the diver should think of keeping the upper body stationary while developing the piking motion before takeoff by driving the hips up and back with the legs, rather than keeping the hips stationary and driving the upper body forward and down. This is a major difference between the actions of the inward and forward takeoffs; the latter requires the diver to move the upper body forward when piking to develop more lean.

Backward Dive Takeoffs

To develop good initial balance for the backward takeoff, the shoulders should be aligned over the middle of the thighs as the diver drops from the top of the press into the squat position. This balance should be maintained until the arms begin to pass head level in the upswing.

As the squat into the press takes place, the arms swing backward and downward in a big circular pattern. The timing of the acceleration of the arms is later than in inward takeoffs. As the diver reaches the bottom of the squat position, the arms are swinging through from a position somewhere behind the hips to slightly below shoulder level, depending on the diver. The reason for this later acceleration of the arms is that they can make a continuous swinging motion to the overhead takeoff position.

To achieve good distance in the backward takeoff dives, the center of balance should move backward in the press and extension before the takeoff. This motion should not occur at the top of the press; if it does, the dive will be initiated with the whole body falling back too early and the dive will be out of control. Instead, as the arms move above head level in the upswing, the balance should shift backward by pushing forward on the board with the feet. As the diver extends up to a straight bodyline for takeoff into the backward dive (see figure 2.14), this shift of balance should result in an angle of takeoff sufficient for good distance and adequate rotation, the same as illustrated for the forward takeoff.

If added rotation is needed to complete the back dive (especially in the straight position), the body should be arched before takeoff. As shown in figure 2.15, the backward motion of the body (A) as the legs extend causes a backward push of the feet into the board (B); the board pushes forward against the feet (C), creating

Figure 2.14   Backward straight-line takeoff.

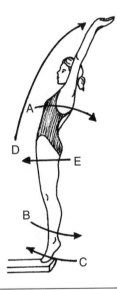

Figure 2.15   Backward arched takeoff forces.

a backward rotational motion (D). This forward pushing force of the board also causes the body to travel toward the board (E). Because developing backward rotation causes the diver to move toward the board, the more rotation that is created, the more a backward balance of the body is needed to overcome this movement toward the board and to obtain proper distance.

Reverse Dive Takeoffs

As the diver drops from the hurdle to the board, the body should be positioned with the shoulders over the middle of the thighs and the balance maintained over the front of the feet until the arms are in an overhead position before the board's recoil.

As the diver makes initial contact with the board, the arms are swinging through from a position somewhere behind the hips to slightly below shoulder level as in the backward takeoffs. The arms may be farther behind the body in the reverse takeoff than in the backward takeoff. There is more time to complete the armswing in the reverse takeoff due to a deeper depression of the board as a result of the hurdle.

The movements and direction of forces needed to create rotation in reverse dives are the same as those needed for the backward dives. Figure 2.16 illustrates these forces. The arch of the body created as the diver pushes the hips up and forward (A) as the legs extend causes a backward push of the feet against the board (B) and an equal force from the board pushing forward against the feet (C). The force of the board creates reverse rotation (D), and the body travels forward in the direction of that force (E).

The diver should execute the arching movement as the arms pass overhead by keeping the upper body still and driving the hips upward and forward. The opposite action of keeping the hips still and pulling the upper body backward and downward will shift the center of balance back over the board, resulting in insufficient distance.

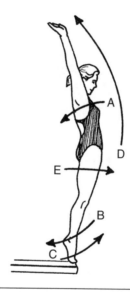

Figure 2.16   Reverse takeoff forces.

SUMMARY

Armswing technique, boardwork, and takeoffs are the most difficult skills in diving. Success in any one of these areas depends on correct performance in the others. Therefore, extensive dryland and pool practice must take place to allow the diver to master the movement patterns, positions, and balance. Bad habits acquired in these areas will affect every dive attempted. Patience and training for excellence are required here before moving on to the performance of the basic dives presented in the next chapter.

© Rob Tringali/SportsChrome

Basic Dives

Once the diver has learned the correct techniques of the forward approach and backward press, he or she should spend considerable time practicing forward and backward jumps. Then the diver should learn the four basic dives (forward, inward, backward, and reverse) in the tuck position before doing these dives in the pike and straight positions.

The training program for all levels of divers, not just for the beginner, should include work on these skills throughout the diver's career. These jumps and dives form the foundation for sound takeoffs and effective board use in all other dives. A diver who cannot perform an optional dive with the proper angle of takeoff, elevation in the air, and distance from the board most likely cannot execute a good jump or tuck dive in that direction of rotation.

FORWARD AND BACKWARD JUMPS

When performed in the straight position from the one- and three-meter springboards, the forward and backward jumps provide excellent training in achieving full use of the board, good balance, and control of distance from the board.

The objective after completing the press and extension from the board is to leave the board with a small angle of takeoff in the direction of the jump, with the body in a straight line and the arms straight and parallel overhead, in line with the body (see figure 3.1, a and b). The balance and angle of takeoff should be such that the diver can hold this position without movement during the flight of the jump. A diver performing a proper forward jump should enter the water three to four feet out from the board, while one performing a proper backward jump should enter the water at arm's reach of the tip of the board. Poor boardwork will make it hard for the diver to perform these jumps well.

a   b

Figure 3.1   Straight-line takeoff in (*a*) forward and (*b*) backward directions.

BASIC DIVES IN TUCK POSITION

The diving table used in competition assigns the forward, backward, reverse, and inward dives in tuck position lower degrees of difficulty than the same dives in pike or straight position. This would seem to indicate that tuck dives are easier to perform; however, these dives are really much more demanding. The tuck dives require more effective balance, body control, and use of the springboard than the other dives.

To perform the tuck dives well, the diver must have complete body extension and arm reach, excellent body alignment, and near-perfect angle of takeoff. These dives are so delicate that the slightest out-of-control position or movement will result in poor execution.

Forward Dive

The takeoff for the forward dive is performed with the body straight and the arms extended overhead shoulder-width apart, in line with the body. The head is level and the eyes look straight ahead. The correct angle of takeoff will allow for good distance and proper rotation without any arm, head, or body motion in the forward direction during takeoff. The diver merely needs to stretch upward in a straight line and let the springboard do the rest.

After the feet leave the board, the tuck position is gradually assumed by bending at the waist and knees, drawing the thighs to the chest, bringing the heels to the buttocks, bending the elbows, and bringing the arms down to grasp the midpoint of the lower legs (shins). The chin drops slightly, and the eyes begin to focus on the entry point. The completed tuck position should be achieved just prior to the peak of the dive.

At the top of the dive the body begins its gradual opening. As the descent to the water begins, the body extends to a straight line and the arms straighten and move laterally in line with the body to the overhead entry position (see figure 3.2, a-f).

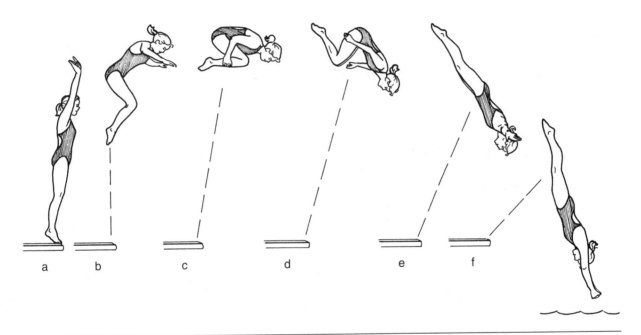

Figure 3.2   Forward dive tuck with lateral come-out.

Inward Dive

The actions in the air of the inward dive tuck are the same as those for the forward dive tuck. Because the inward dive tuck uses a different takeoff, different motions are made while leaving the board to achieve proper distance and rotation. As the arms complete their overhead reach and the body extends from the board, the diver first moves to a straight line of the body and arms. Then the arms and trunk move forward while the hips are driven backward and upward, causing a pike position just before takeoff. This motion moves the body away from the board and begins the inward rotation. The head is kept level and still during the takeoff, and the eyes focus on the back end of the board or the wall behind the board.

Unlike the forward dive tuck, in which the diver can keep the body and arms in a straight line and let the angle of the takeoff bring about good distance and rotation, the inward dive tuck requires a change in body shape to accomplish distance and rotation (see figure 3.3, a-f).

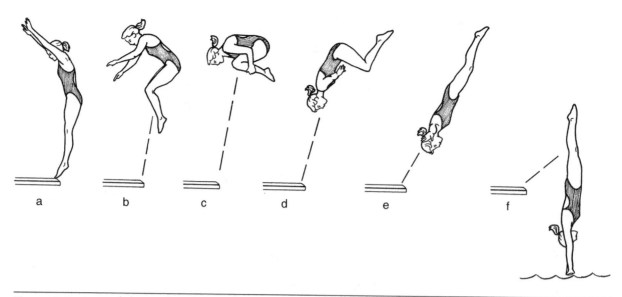

Figure 3.3 Inward dive tuck with lateral come-out.

Backward Dive

Most beginning diving students learn a basic backward dive first in the straight position. For ease of teaching, to reduce fear, and to eliminate the possibility of landing flat on the water, a coach will usually teach a diver initially to put the head back, look for the water with the eyes, and arch the back (see figure 3.4, a and b). There is nothing wrong with this method; it does get the student to perform the dive more readily. However, as soon as the diver passes this initial learning stage, he or she must learn a new technique of performing the backward entry, with the ultimate goal being a good backward dive tuck.

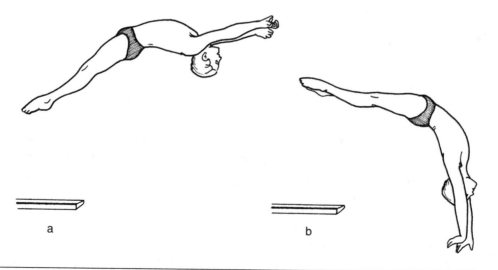

Figure 3.4 Arched backward dive.

Backward Slide-In (Straight)

To begin this process, a folding floor mat or exercise mat five or six feet wide is needed. Fold this and place it lengthwise on the end of the one-meter board. Throw some water on the mat to make it slippery.

The diver lies face up on the mat with the head toward the pool and the arms extended overhead in line with the body, hands together. The head must be slightly tilted upward with the eyes looking toward the water. The diver lifts the heels slightly off the mat, keeping the legs straight, as the coach lifts the foot-end of the mat high enough (approximately 45 degrees) to slide the diver into the water. The diver must hold the starting position throughout this dive, with no movement of the head backward or any arch in the body (see figure 3.5, a-c). The diver will not be able to see the water at the point of entry but should see the water as close to the entry point as possible without tilting the head back extremely. This is true of all the backward and reverse entries, from the basic through the optional dives.

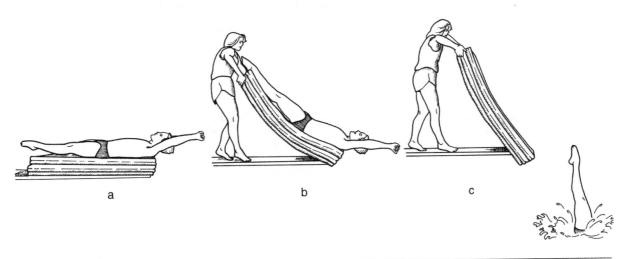

Figure 3.5   Backward slide-in.

Backward Slide-In (Lateral Arms)

When the bodyline can be held straight throughout the dive, try the slide-in with the arms straight and lateral at shoulder height in the starting position. The diver tilts the head forward with the chin in, the upper body slightly curled, and the eyes looking down the body to the elevated toes. The diver watches the toes as the slide begins. As the diver leaves the mat, the arms are brought laterally to the entry position while the head moves to a slightly tilted upward position and the eyes look back toward the water (see figure 3.6, a-d).

Repeat this drill frequently so that this body and head alignment becomes the "natural" way to enter the water backward. Even the highly skilled diver can benefit from periodic practice of this drill to maintain good backward and reverse entry technique.

Performing this drill from the three-meter board is an excellent way for more advanced divers to practice a straight line of entry for the backward and reverse dive. It is impossible to enter the water vertically from this height if any arch in

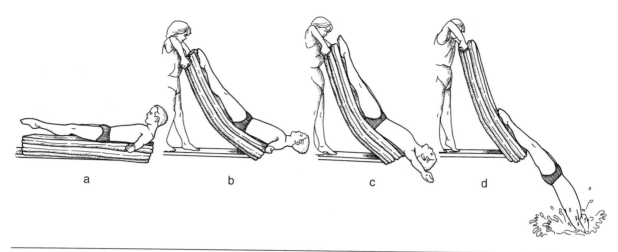

Figure 3.6   Backward slide-in with lateral arms.

the body occurs or if the head is moved backward prior to leaving the mat. Sliding in from this height also forces the diver to hold the correct position (slightly piked at the hips, the upper body curled, with the head forward looking at the toes) for a longer time in the drop before preparing for the entry.

Backward Slide-In (Tuck)

Again using the one-meter board, the diver lies face up on the mat in a tuck position. When the mat is lifted and the diver slides to the edge, the body is opened for the entry. The body position should be straight, as in the backward slide-in. When opening from the tuck, the arms move from their position on the middle of the lower legs up the midline of the body; the elbows bend and the hands stay close together. Then the arms extend for the entry as they pass head level (see figure 3.7, a-e).

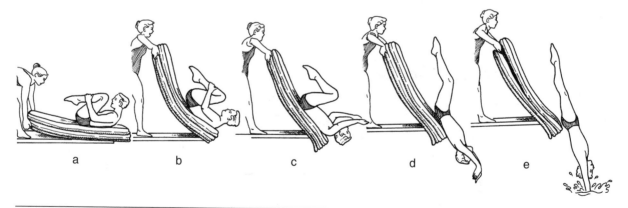

Figure 3.7   Backward slide-in in tuck position.

Backward Roll-Off (Tuck)

The mat should overhang the end of the one-meter board a couple of inches. The diver sits in a tuck position, with the back facing the water and the hips at the edge of the mat. After rocking backward, the diver opens for the entry when leaving the mat (see figure 3.8, a-e). The diver should take care to kick the legs up toward a vertical line. The same entry position and arm stretch is used as in the slide-in in tuck position.

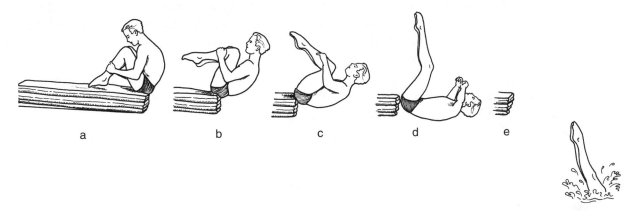

Figure 3.8 Backward roll-off in tuck position.

Backward Dive Tuck

Once the diver can perform the backward roll-off in tuck position well and can do a backward press with a jump an arm's length from the board, it is time to perform the backward dive tuck. This is the most difficult of the tuck dives to master because there is a strong tendency for divers to have too much angle of takeoff (backward lean) or too much arch in the body on takeoff. Both of these situations cause excessive rotation, and a lack of control results.

As the diver leaves the board, the body should be in a straight line with the arms straight, parallel, and overhead in line with the body (see figure 3.9). A slight angle of takeoff is needed to provide safe distance and proper rotation. In order to control the jump and counteract the tendency to rotate too fast, the head should be kept level but pushed forward of the body and arm line.

Figure 3.9 Takeoff position for backward dive tuck.

When the feet leave the board, the upper body and head are kept still, while the legs and arms bend and move to a tuck position during the ascent to the peak of the dive. Just before starting the drop to the water, the legs and arms are extended to a straight line for the entry. In this beginning stage, the arms should be brought up the midline of the body, with elbows bent and hands close together, then should straighten as they pass the head (see figure 3.10, a-f).

Figure 3.10   Backward dive tuck with straight-line come-out.

After the diver gains good control of the takeoff and dive rotation, another more advanced method of coming out of the tuck position needs to be learned. The lateral come-out method relates to the backward slide-in, in straight position, performed from the three-meter board. This drill will help most in perfecting this backward dive tuck technique.

At the top of the backward dive tuck, when the opening begins, the legs are straightened at the knee joint while the hips are not fully extended, and the body is in a slightly piked position. The arms straighten simultaneously with the legs, and the diver moves the arms to a lateral placement at thigh level. The upper body remains curled just as it was in the tuck position, and the head stays forward with the chin in, eyes looking at the toes (as with the backward slide-in from a three-meter board). When this position is established, the body extends at the hips to a straight line, and the arms begin to move laterally to the overhead entry position while the head tilts back to a slightly tilted upward position and the eyes look back toward the water (see figure 3.11, a-f).

Reverse Dive

The mechanics of execution for the reverse dive are exactly the same as for the backward dive tuck. Once the backward dive tuck is performed well, the reverse dive tuck should be no problem. In fact, with the exception of the takeoff, the reverse dive tuck is much easier to control.

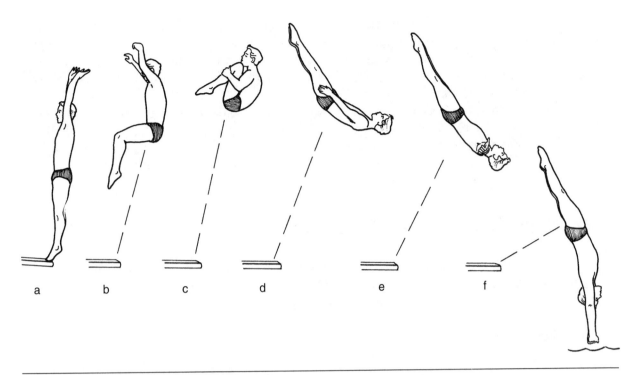

Figure 3.11 Backward dive tuck with lateral come-out.

Proper distance from the board during the backward dive tuck is achieved by having a slightly backward angle from the board. For the reverse dive tuck, the diver moves to a distance of three to four feet from the board by pushing the hips forward and upward, causing a body arch as he or she extends and reaches up with the arms after the press. This hip motion moves the center of gravity forward, and therefore the body moves away from the board. The body arch that occurs while the diver is still in contact with the board also helps create rotation for the dive (see figure 3.12, a-g). Obviously, too much hip and body motion will cause the diver to move too far out and rotate too fast. Consult the section on reverse dive takeoffs for a more extensive explanation of this technique.

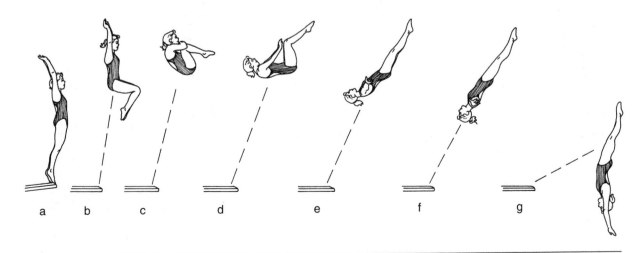

Figure 3.12 Reverse dive tuck with lateral come-out.

Unfortunately, other than practicing on a trampoline or dryland board with an overhead spotting apparatus, there are no feasible drills for practicing this dive. Learning a good backward dive tuck and a good forward approach with front jump and reverse directed angle of entry, and then combining the two, is the best method of learning this dive.

When the tuck dives can be executed with balance and control, it is time to learn the remaining basic dives. It is best to progress from tuck to pike and then, when the pike dives are done well, to straight position. Attempting the straight dives too soon can cause the loss of good takeoff and bodyline techniques. For this reason, the pike dives are presented next.

BASIC DIVES IN PIKE POSITION

The techniques for takeoff and initiating rotation are the same for the tuck and pike dives. Because the diver rotates more slowly in the pike position, more rotational force will be needed to complete these dives.

Forward Dive

The takeoff position for this dive is the same as for the forward dive tuck. When leaving the board, the eyes focus on a point at the far end of the pool. Just after the takeoff, the legs are straight, and the arms begin moving down the front of the body. The body bends at the waist so that at the peak of the dive the hands touch the feet in a pike position. When moving into the pike position, the eyes change focus from the far end of the pool to the entry point. At the beginning of the descent, the body opens in preparation for the entry by extending at the hips to achieve straight alignment and moving the arms laterally to the entry position (see figure 3.13, a-e).

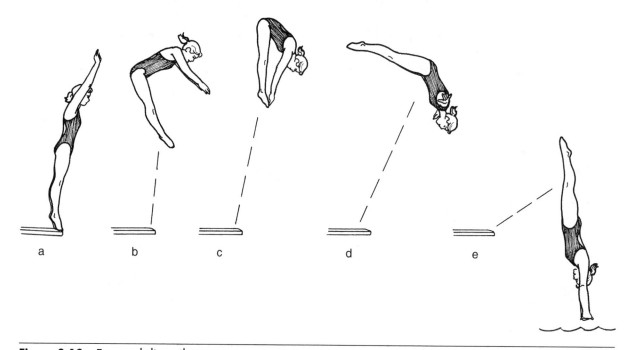

a   b   c   d   e

Figure 3.13   Forward dive pike.

Inward Dive

The movements of this dive in the air are the same as those for the forward dive pike. As noted for the inward dive tuck, just before leaving the board, the legs push the hips upward and back, causing the body to pike; this moves the body a safe distance away from the board and creates rotation for the dive (see figure 3.14, a-e).

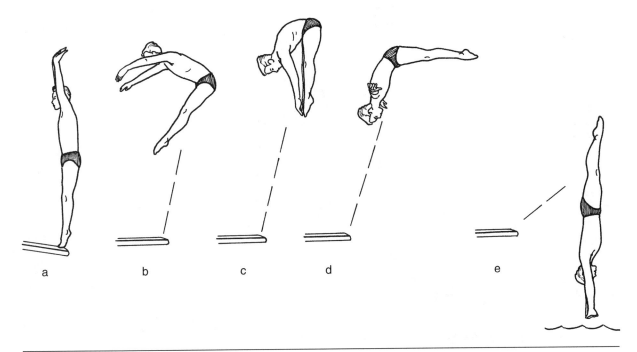

a   b   c   d   e

Figure 3.14 Inward dive pike.

Backward Dive

At the takeoff point, the body extends to a straight line at an angle slightly backward of vertical. The arms are straight, parallel, and stretched at the shoulder joint so they reach overhead in line with the body. The head is level but pressed forward, as described for the backward dive tuck, for balance and control. The eyes look straight ahead, waiting for the legs to come into view as they are lifted into the pike.

Immediately after leaving the board, the legs begin to lift into a pike position as the arms move forward in front of the body to touch the feet at an angle short of vertical. The angle of touch varies depending on the amount of rotation, the height from the board, and whether the dive is done from the one- or three-meter board. As the arms and legs come together, the eyes follow the feet to the touch position, and the head is positioned between the arms so the tops of the shoulders are pressed against the ears.

Following the touch, the arms move laterally (palms facing the feet) in line with the body as the body begins to open from the pike at the hip joint. The upper body remains in a concave, curled position, with the eyes focused on the feet. This is the same opening position described for the backward dive tuck. As the body reaches full extension of the hip joint, the back straightens, and the head moves back to a slightly tilted upward position, with the body in a straight line. The lateral movement of the arms is timed so they are at shoulder level when this occurs. At this point, the body is in a T shape.

As the descent continues, the arms move laterally overhead for the entry while the body maintains a straight line (see figure 3.15, a-f).

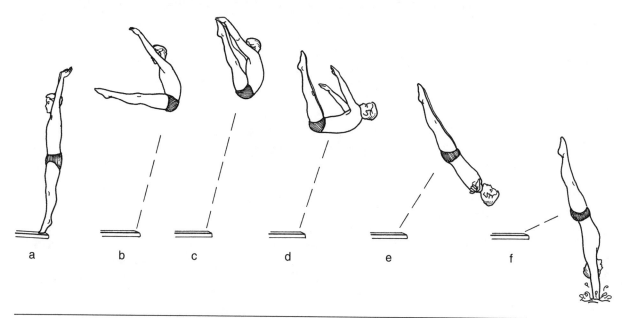

Figure 3.15   Backward dive pike.

Reverse Dive

The reverse dive pike is executed much like the backward dive pike. The difference occurs during the reverse dive pike takeoff, when a forward and upward motion of the hips causes a slight body arch at the point of takeoff. This arch enables the diver to move to the correct distance and develop the rotation needed to complete the dive (see figure 3.16, a-f).

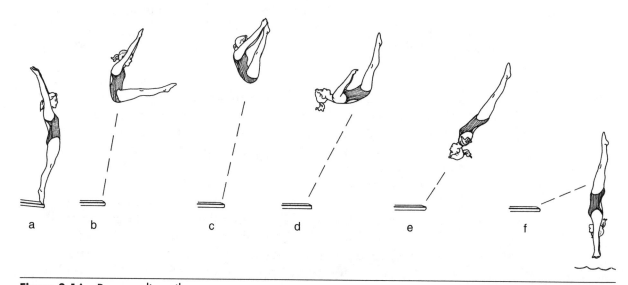

Figure 3.16   Reverse dive pike.

BASIC DIVES IN STRAIGHT POSITION

After the tuck and pike dives can be executed well, the diver should easily be able to learn to perform the straight dives correctly, with good balance, control, and most important, a straight bodyline throughout the dive.

Forward Dive

The takeoff position for this dive is the same as for the forward dives tuck and pike, except that the body is angled slightly more forward from the board to create the added rotation needed to complete the dive. A diver using the one-meter board, and especially a smaller, young diver who doesn't go as high in the air, may need to develop more rotation than is obtained with the body straight. If, just prior to leaving the board, the diver presses the arms and upper body slightly forward, causing a pike at the hips, added rotation will result. As soon as possible after leaving the board, the body must be straightened. In order to keep the head level, the eyes are focused on the far side of the pool while the diver rises to the top of the dive. A common tendency is to look at the entry point during this phase of the dive, which causes the head to drop. This head position doesn't look good, and it may create a pike in the body.

As soon as the feet leave the board, the arms move laterally in line with the body down to shoulder level. This position should be reached as soon as possible, but not in a rushed or jerky movement. Certainly this T alignment should be established before reaching the top of the elevation.

From the time just before reaching the top of the dive until the descent to the water begins, there should be no movement of the body parts, only rotation of the body forward as a single unit. At the peak of the dive, the eyes move from their focus on the far side of the pool to the entry point on the water, with no head motion. As the diver drops to the water, the arms move laterally to the overhead entry position (see figure 3.17, a-e).

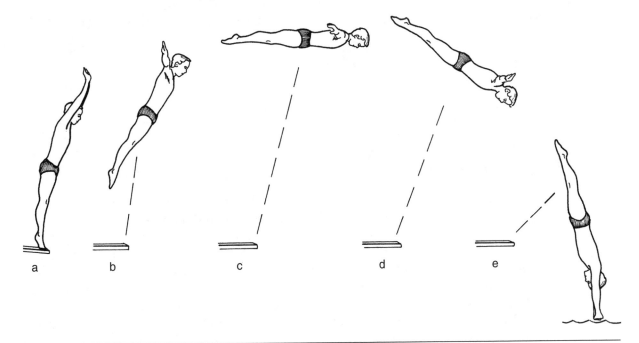

Figure 3.17   Forward dive straight.

Inward Dive

This dive is best learned from the three-meter board first. The added height makes it easier to complete the dive using good technique. Once the diver establishes the correct execution pattern, the dive can be transferred to the one-meter board.

The basic movements of this dive in the air are the same as for the forward dive straight. In order to move the dive to safe distance and develop the necessary rotation, as in the inward dives tuck and pike, the legs must push the hips up and back causing a slightly piked body position prior to takeoff. As soon as the feet leave the board, the body extends to a straight position as the arms begin their lateral motion (see figure 3.18, a-e).

Divers who are very young, who do not possess good strength, or who cannot maintain proper balance during the takeoff develop a pronounced pike for a considerable time period after leaving the board. These divers also tend to drop their heads very low throughout the flight of the dive. The overall result is a poor dive. A diver who has such a problem should not perform this dive until the factor causing the problem is corrected. For the balance problem, more work on backward jumps and the inward dive tuck is indicated. In the other cases, maturation, an exercise program, or both are needed.

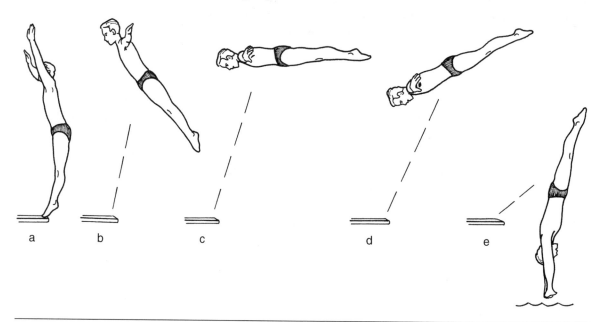

a   b   c   d   e

Figure 3.18 Inward dive straight.

Backward Dive

The takeoff position for this dive is a straight line through the body with the head level, eyes looking up, and the arms straight and shoulder-width apart in an overhead position in line with the body. Some divers may find a slight arch necessary in order to complete the rotation easily. The angle of the body during takeoff should be slightly more than that for the backward dive pike. When the feet leave the board, the arms move laterally down to shoulder level before the diver reaches the top of the dive.

As the arms move to the lateral position, the head tilts slightly backward and the eyes look upward. The diver should maintain a motionless T position through the middle third of the dive, that is, from before until after the peak of the dive.

During the drop to the water, the arms close laterally to the overhead entry position. Throughout the flight of the dive, the eyes should not focus on any one point because this will cause a head movement. Instead, the eyes should look up until the diver can see the water as he or she approaches the entry (see figure 3.19, a-e). As noted before, the diver should sight the water as close to the entry point as possible without tilting the head back extremely.

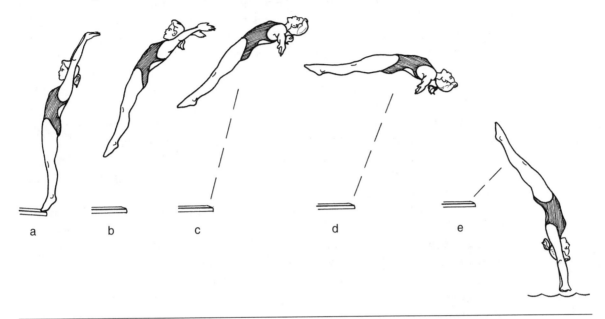

Figure 3.19 Backward dive straight.

Reverse Dive

As with the reverse dives tuck and pike, this dive is performed much like the backward dive. The difference is that during the reverse dive straight, the hips push forward and upward, creating a slightly arched body position on takeoff for distance and rotation purposes (see figure 3.20, a-f).

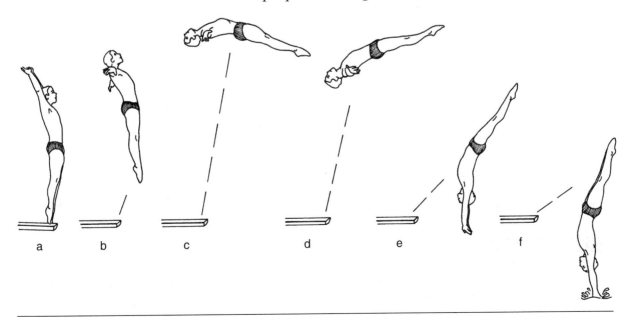

Figure 3.20 Reverse dive straight.

Forward Dive With Half Twist

Although this dive is not a basic requirement in most levels of diving, a diver faced with a lack of other twisting dive choices may elect to use it.

Just before the feet leave the board, the body is kept straight and the arms reach overhead; the shoulders begin a gradual turn in the desired direction of twist. Assuming the diver is twisting left, the right shoulder moves forward and the left one backward, initiating the twist from the board. As the feet leave the board, the arms move laterally down to shoulder level and the eyes focus on the far side of the pool. The arm position is achieved prior to the peak of the dive. The speed of twist should be such that at the top of the dive the leading arm (right arm in this case) points at the entry spot and the other arm points at the ceiling directly above the entry spot; the diver is in a quarter-twist position. When this position is established, the chin moves down and in line with the right shoulder, with the eyes sighting down the arm and hand to the entry point.

As the legs rotate upward and the body continues to twist, the right arm and the eyes continue to point to and focus on the entry point, while the left arm remains still. In holding this position, the diver will complete the half twist and the right arm will close overhead while the head rotates back to a slightly upward tilted position. Prior to closing for the entry, the right arm stretches overhead and the left arm is held lateral at shoulder level. Then the left arm is brought laterally overhead to join the right arm. This means preparation for the entry is done one arm at a time; the right arm closes overhead, then the left arm.

It is extremely important that the right arm point at the entry spot and the eyes maintain sight of the arm on the entry point (see figure 3.21, a-e).

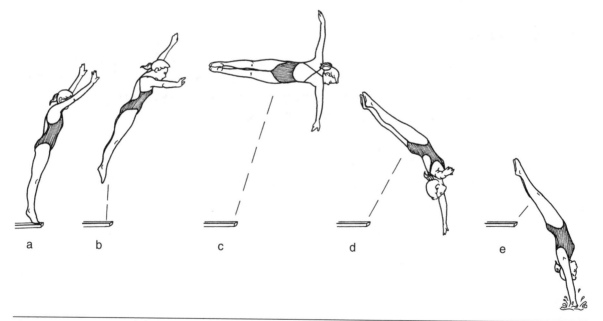

a   b   c   d   e

Figure 3.21   Forward dive with half twist straight.

SUMMARY

Practice on the basic dives in the tuck, pike, and straight positions should take place at the same time as training on the skills presented in the next chapter. Effective entry, lineup, and come-out techniques complement the basic dives well.

© Tim O'Lett/SportsChrome

Headfirst Entries, Lineups, and Come-Outs

Why discuss entries before considering any of the optional dives? The reason is that correct headfirst entry technique and methods of practice should be learned as soon as possible after learning the basic dives. Diligent, long-term training for good entries brings about better body alignment in all phases of diving, a keen sense of vertical completion of dives, and an opportunity to practice the various methods of coming out of basic and somersaulting dives.

Divers seem to enjoy practicing entries because they require less energy than the dives themselves; entries focus on one particular skill, and improvement can be rapid. It is important to devote some portion of daily practice to entry work, and on some days it is worthwhile to devote the whole practice to this skill training.

COMMON ELEMENTS

There are two types of headfirst entry: forward and backward. The forward entry is used for all forward, inward, and multiple-twisting dives, whereas the backward entry is employed in all backward and reverse dives. Regardless of the dive or the direction of the entry, certain fundamentals are common to all entries.

Body Alignment

Control of the hip, trunk, and head positions form the foundation of good forward and backward entries. This alignment provides stability through the body when the force of entry impact occurs. Without good alignment, movement in these body areas takes place in the first three to four feet of entry, which results in a whiplash series of movements. Figure 4.1, a and b, shows the correct basic dive entry position; note the arm alignment.

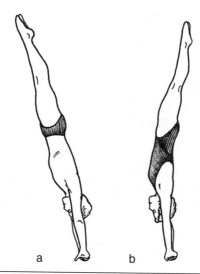

a   b

Figure 4.1   Correct basic dive entry position: (*a*) shows the forward inward stretch, and (*b*) shows the backward reverse stretch.

Hand Position

There is one element of hand position all experts agree on: The palm of the hand should make contact with the water first to initiate a good entry. Although there are variations, the most common and successful way to achieve this is to grab the back of one hand in the palm of the other with the thumbs interlocked and flexed so they are not sticking out for the water to pull on them. The lead hand (the one entering the water first) is open, with fingers extended and together and the palm area flat. The fingers of the grabbing hand are together and securely wrapped around the back of the lead hand (see figure 4.2).

Figure 4.2   Entry hand position.

Stretch Position

The lead hand should be positioned so that the palm is horizontal and the fingers point in a line parallel with the line of the shoulders. Impact should be felt with the water "dead center" on the palm of the lead hand. The shoulders are elevated and held tightly against the ears, and the elbows are locked. No movement in either the shoulder or elbow joints should occur during impact. A diver with hyperextended elbows can hold this position much more easily than one with a straight elbow joint, or worse, an elbow joint that does not straighten completely. When doing dives with a lateral line of closure for the entry, the palms are pronated (facing the feet) during this movement. This eliminates the need to rotate the palms in preparation for the correct hand position. Figure 4.3, a through c, illustrates this closing method and the correct stretch position.

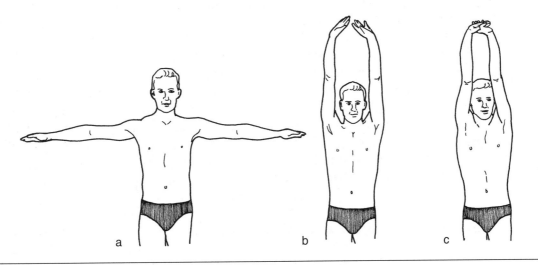

Figure 4.3 Entry stretch position.

Head Position and Vision

The head is held in a level position for forward entries and tilted slightly upward for backward entries. No head movement should occur during the entry.

In forward and inward rotating dives and twisting dives, the entry point can be seen at the beginning of the stretch because this point is located in the line of sight. However, after sighting this point, while dropping to the water, the diver must keep the head in a level position. The eyes should look through the eyebrows to see as close to the entry point as possible without lifting the head.

In the backward and reverse entry, the entry point cannot be seen because it is behind the line of sight. The head is tilted slightly upward, looking as close to the actual entry point as possible.

Body Shape and Angle of Entry

Because the direction of rotation and the direction of stretching for the water are opposite for the forward and backward entries, the body shape and the way the arms stretch must change to account for the differences.

"Go with the flow of the dive" best describes the most effective way to enter the water from any entry direction. This means that the diver must use the arms, the body shape, and the direction of stretch through the shoulder joint to keep the body rotating through the water in the same direction as the dive rotation.

Arm Movements

As the arm movements to the entry stretching position are made in the various come-outs and lineups, the arms and shoulders should be kept relaxed, while the body is kept firm. Tension in the arms and shoulders while moving to the entry position can cause undesired movements in other body areas.

FORWARD ENTRY

Due to the direction of rotation of forward entries (i.e., forward, inward, and multiple twists), a pressure is created as the hands contact the water. This pressure tends to push the arms back overhead to a position behind the ears, which pulls the trunk out of its body alignment to a position with the rib cage protruding forward. This causes an arch in the back and hyperextension across the hip joint. To compensate, the shoulder joint stretches upward and with a forward pressure. Depending on the speed of rotation of the dive and the angle of entry, the diver must assume a "hollow" body configuration. This hollow position means that a line drawn from the hands through the body to the feet will be curved, because the body is in a concave alignment (see figure 4.4).

In the basic forward and inward dives, the amount of rotation at entry is very small, and thus the angle of entry is close to vertical at impact. This means that a small amount of forward stretch pressure through the shoulder joint and a minimal or even imperceptible degree of hollow body position is needed in order to "go with the flow."

The optional dives, however, have far greater rotational force at entry, and the angle of initial entry can be far short of vertical at times. These conditions dictate not only a strong forward direction of stretch at the shoulder joint, but also a slightly downward position of the head, with the arms stretching in front of the bodyline. Also, the amount of hollow body configuration is significant (see figure 4.5).

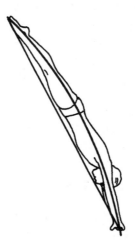

Figure 4.4   Forward dive with hollow stretch.

Figure 4.5 Forward two-and-a-half somersault with hollow stretch.

Forward Versus Inward Entries

The stretch and body alignment for these two entries are the same; however, the directions in which the diver moves in relation to the water are opposite, causing different actions on the body.

In the forward dives, including forward and backward twisting dives, the body travels across the surface of the water in the same direction as the rotation of each dive (see figure 4.6). This means that as the body contacts the water, its forward travel slows, causing a transfer of momentum through the upper body and to the legs. The result is a movement of the body toward overrotation.

In the inward dives, including reverse twisting dives, the body travels across the water in the opposite direction of the dive's rotation. Thus, when the body enters the water, the transfer of momentum through the body causes a movement toward underrotation (see figure 4.7).

This difference means that in order to achieve a vertical finish, the inward dives and reverse twisting dives must line up closer to vertical than is necessary for the forward dives, forward twisting dives, and backward twisting dives.

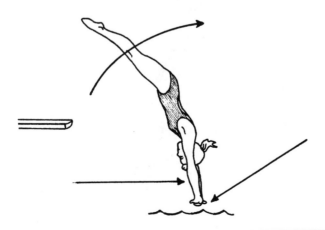

Figure 4.6 Forward entry rotational force.

Figure 4.7   Inward entry rotational force.

BACKWARD ENTRY

The backward and reverse rotating entries present the same set of circumstances as the forward entry, but forces occur in the opposite direction. When entering the water, pressure pushes the arms forward. This can move the arms out of line in front of the face and throw the body into a pike action. To counteract this, the diver should stretch the arms backward at the shoulder joint and use a curvature of the bodyline or arched position on the back side of the body. The diver must achieve the arched position through a stretching action across the hip joint while maintaining good body alignment in the upper body.

Arching the body backward by moving the rib cage off alignment causes the body to lose its rigidity on impact, resulting in a series of uncontrolled movements. This means that in addition to keeping the body arched, the diver must be sure that the muscles that maintain body alignment remain contracted.

As with the forward entry, the basic backward and reverse dives create a small amount of rotational force, and the angle of entry to the water is almost vertical. Therefore, the amount of backward stretch at the shoulder joint and the degree of body arch are minimal (see figure 4.8).

Figure 4.8   Backward entry for basic dives.

The optional dives, due to their greater amount of rotational speed and resultant greater initial angle of entry short of vertical at impact, require a stronger backward stretch of the arms and more body arch. It is important that the amount of body arch does not become excessive because when this occurs the appearance of the entry is poor and the diver loses control of the body during entry (see figure 4.9).

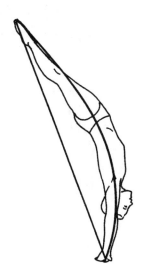

Figure 4.9 Backward entry for optional dives.

Backward Versus Reverse Entries

In the backward entry dives, the body travels across the water surface in the same direction in which the dive rotates; therefore, as in the forward rotating dives, the water pressure on the body causes a transfer of momentum through the trunk and legs, which results in a movement toward overrotation (see figure 4.10).

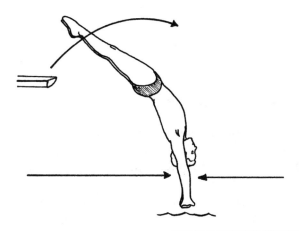

Figure 4.10 Backward entry rotational force.

The reverse dives are similar to the inward dives in that they travel in a direction opposite the rotation of the dive, thus causing a force on impact that moves the diver toward underrotation (see figure 4.11). The reverse dive entries, therefore, must be lined up closer to vertical than the backward entry dives in order to achieve a vertical finish.

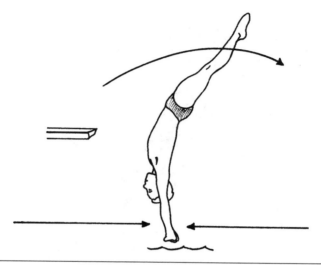

Figure 4.11 Reverse entry rotational force.

UNDERWATER ENTRY TECHNIQUES

The beginning- and intermediate-level diver should practice the basic stretch position, holding it throughout the entry period and going to the bottom of the pool without any other movements. Before moving to the more advanced entry techniques presented here, the diver should be able to demonstrate a good angle of entry in all directions along with a correct bodyline while doing the basic dives and lineup drills.

With a good bodyline and control of entry angle as the basic foundation, the diver can begin to change body shape and maneuver underwater to achieve a more consistent entry with less splash and to produce an accompanying unique sound. This type of entry is called a rip because the sound is similar to that of ripping a piece of fabric. Even though some divers can rip an entry using only the fundamental stretch described previously and the flat palm position, most divers are more successful at mastering this skill with the following methods.

Forward Swim and Save

During the first foot of penetration into the water, the diver releases the grasp of the hands and begins a breaststroke-like swimming action in a direction 30 to 45 degrees in front of the bodyline. During this motion the arms must remain straight. If this swimming motion is performed at the correct time and speed during the entry, the hands will stay very near the surface of the water as the body passes through. This will create a distinctive area of air and bubbles on each side of the entry.

As the hips pass through the surface, the head moves down, and a pike occurs at the hips, causing a rollover with the back to the bottom of the pool. This movement, called the forward somersault save, helps the legs enter the water on a vertical line. As the pike is performed, the legs draw toward the trunk to prevent overrotation. The speed and force of the pike action depend on the angle of entry and the amount of rotation of the dive. Only through practice and experience can the diver learn to match the amount of "save" with the various dives and entry situations.

Backward Swim and Save

As soon as the entry impact occurs, the diver releases the grasp of the hands and begins the swimming action of the arms during the first foot of entry. The swim is done with the arms straight and moving in a lateral direction from the body. When this is timed correctly, the hands will stay very near the surface of the water for the first part of the entry. As the hips pass through the water, the backward knee save starts as the head tilts backward and the body arches. When the knees pass through the water, they are bent, and the heels are pressed toward the hips while the body increases its arch and the head lifts toward the surface. The speed and force of the knee save depend on the angle of entry and amount of rotation of the dive. Experimentation with the different dives and experience gained over time will allow the diver to become very adept at keeping the angle of the legs and feet vertical at the finish of the entry.

TRAINING METHODS FOR ENTRIES

- **Shallow water drills.** The easiest place to practice the movement pattern of the forward and backward saves is chest-deep water. This can be done by assuming a vertical handstand entry alignment position with the hands on the bottom. The diver then pushes off in an upward direction with the hands and arms. As the descent to the bottom begins, the diver can practice the movements of either the forward or backward saves. The pushoff for the forward swim and save is done so that the body is angled in an overrotated (toward the back side of the body) direction. The pushoff for the backward save is done so that the body is angled in an underrotated (toward the front side of the body) direction. The diver can practice various angles of entry in each direction until the save movements are correct and he or she can make the legs enter the water vertically from many different angles of approach. The diver can then practice these save movements by falling in forward and backward from the one-meter board.

- **Hand position.** Dryland training drills can improve consistency in obtaining the correct hand position for entry. The diver first performs the grabbing motion at a slow speed by holding the arms laterally at shoulder height with the palms facing backward. Keeping the arms straight, the diver brings the hands together at shoulder height in front of the body. When the diver practices this way first, the coach and the diver can both visually check to see that the position is correct. As skill and familiarity with the correct grab increase, the speed of the closing movement can be increased. Next, the diver can practice the same drill to the overhead stretching position, making sure to maintain good body alignment, keep the head level, and look toward the hands.

When the diver is proficient with this drill, he or she can practice the dives from the pool deck with the hands initially placed in the flat palm stretching position, which aids in giving the feeling of the flat-hand entry. In the initial stages, the force on the hand created because of the larger landing surface may feel strange, and unstable movements of the body may occur, but both will pass in a short time. When accustomed to the feel of this entry, the diver can start the dive with the arms lateral at shoulder level and the palms down and close for the entry in midair. After several repetitions, the diver can try some dives from the one-meter board.

Using the hand-grab dryland drills in a daily warm-up routine will help the diver effectively and consistently achieve the correct hand position, which will be reflected in better entries.

• **Swimming.** The diver stands in the entry stretch position, with a partner standing behind. The partner reaches up and taps the flat palm of the diver's leading hand in the same spot where the diver should feel the water contact the hand (center of palm). As quickly as possible, the diver performs the swimming motion described previously. The participants repeat the drill several times, with the partner varying the time interval between taps so the diver cannot anticipate when to swim but must rely on feeling the contact on the palm before reacting.

• **Stability.** The participants start in the same position as the previous drill, except the partner stands on an elevated area (e.g., bench). The partner places both hands, one on top of the other, on the palm of the diver, then pushes down quickly and forcefully to simulate entry impact. The diver's goal is to hold the shoulders up tight against the ears and maintain alignment so that the impact force does not cause any movement in the back, hips, or knees. If such movement does occur, the bodyline is not straight and needs to be adjusted.

PRACTICING ENTRIES (LINEUPS)

Lineups are drills used for practicing the entry techniques just described without having to deal with the additional distracting influences of takeoffs and somersaulting momentum. They allow the diver to focus solely on achieving correct angle of entry, correct bodyline, and control of the entry path while performing a variety of movements that directly relate to those needed in the basic and optional dives.

There are three types of lineup drills:

1. Entry (forward, backward)
2. Basic dive (forward, inward, backward, reverse)
3. Somersault come-out (forward, inward, backward, reverse)

The diver should become proficient at each one, in the order presented here, before progressing to the next. Until the diver reaches an advanced level of entry skill, all three types of lineup should be practiced regularly. The advanced diver can be more specific by practicing the lineups that relate to the dives being done in competition.

Entry Lineups

The purpose of these lineups is to isolate the forward and backward entry skills by making the movements involved as elementary as possible. These entries can be practiced from the three-meter springboard or platform. However, if neither is available, a one-meter springboard can be used. By generating a small spring with the legs only, the diver will have enough time to enter the water vertically. After gaining experience at the three-meter height, the diver can practice these drills at the five-meter level.

The forward entry technique is best practiced with a lineup named the forward hollow fall (see figure 4.12, a-c). The diver stands on the end of the three-meter board, maintaining a straight line at the hips with the upper body curled into the hollow position. The arms are placed in the entry stretch overhead with the hands in the entry grab position and the head level with the chin down and in. The

diver then stands up high on the toes and falls forward into the water with no spring or body movements. When entering the water, the diver holds the hollow position and maintains a forward direction of stretch through the shoulder joint. This drill is designed to teach how to enter vertically while moving through the water smoothly in the direction of rotation (i.e., going with the flow).

a, b

The diver can practice the backward entry from the three-meter board while performing a backward fall. The diver stands backward on the end of the board with the arms overhead and the hands clasped in the entry position. The chin should be tilted slightly upward, with the eyes looking up. The body should have a slight arch at the hip joint, with the upper body kept in alignment. The diver then falls into a backward dive while holding the initial alignment (see figure 4.13, a-d).

At first, this lineup may cause the diver to enter the water short of vertical, but after practicing the falling speed from the board, the diver will achieve a vertical finish. This drill helps diver learn the proper arm, head, upper body, and body arch positions without any movement except the fall.

c

Figure 4.12 Forward hollow fall from three-meter height.

a, b, c

d

Figure 4.13   Backward fall with arms overhead from three-meter height.

Basic Dive Lineups

When the forward and backward entry techniques consistently line up vertically, the body is controlled throughout the entry, and the amount of splash is not excessive, the diver can move to the next level of practice.

The basic dives (forward, backward, reverse, and inward) done in any of the positions are all completed with a lateral close of the arms to the overhead stretch for the entry. A diver needs to know how to line up correctly when rotating in the different directions and moving from the various body positions to the entry. These lineups are presented in the order in which they should be learned and practiced.

Forward Lineup

The best way to learn a basic forward dive lineup is to practice the forward hollow fall in the straight position from the three-meter board, with the arms held lateral during the fall and closed laterally for the entry during the drop to the water. When the diver can do this effectively, he or she can begin practicing for the pike and tuck dives. The pike lineup is learned first, because it involves fewer movements and is therefore easier.

Initially the diver performs the pike lineup from the one-meter board by standing on the end, bent over into an open-pike position. The diver stands up on the toes, falls forward, and opens to the straight position while closing the arms laterally to the entry stretch position (see figure 4.14, a-d). The diver can then practice the same drill from the three-meter board. When the diver can do this effectively, he or she can perform the same dive standing with a spring from the one-meter and then the three-meter board.

Forward tuck lineups are done standing and are performed with a spring. Using the one-meter board, the diver performs a forward dive tuck with a lateral arm path while stretching for the entry. A tuck lineup from the three-meter board can also be performed. The diver sits forward in a tuck position on the end of the board (see figure 4.15, a-e). Staying in the tuck position, the diver rocks forward and begins rotating to the front dive position. As the hips leave the board, a kick-out and lateral lineup with the arms is done, just as described in chapter 3 for the forward dive tuck.

Lining up from the straight position is best practiced by using the three-meter board. The diver stands forward at the end of the board with the arms held lateral at shoulder height; this is similar to the hollow fall dive described earlier, only now the body is held in a straight alignment as in a forward dive straight. The diver stands up on the toes and falls to a forward dive entry.

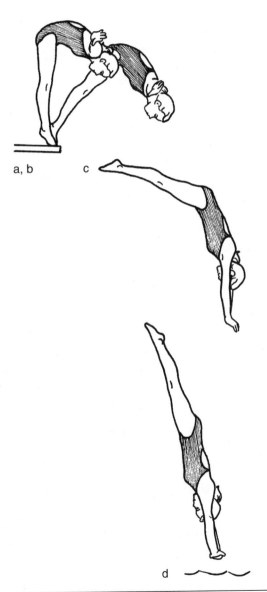

a, b   c

d

Figure 4.14 Forward open-pike fall from three-meter height.

Figure 4.15   Forward tuck roll-off with lateral come-out from three-meter height.

Inward Lineup

Because of the need to create rotation and move a safe distance from the board, inward lineups should be practiced with a backward press and spring. In addition, all should be done with a lateral stretching path for the entry. The sequence of drills to be practiced is as follows: inward dive in the open-pike position from the one-meter board, inward dive tuck position from the one-meter board, and then both dives from the three-meter board.

Backward Lineup

The easiest method to practice the backward lineup is to perform a standing backward fall from the three-meter board with the arms held laterally at shoulder height. No spring is used. After the feet leave the board in the fall, the diver closes the arms laterally overhead for the entry and tilts the head slightly backward as the eyes look back for the water. The body should have a slightly arched shape, with the arch at the hip area and not from the rib cage. This curved position allows the diver to slide into the water smoothly (see figure 4.16, a-d).

The same drill can be practiced from the one-meter board by taking a small spring with the legs into the takeoff; this allows the diver to complete the necessary rotation (see figure 4.17, a-f). The three-meter drill is preferred, especially

Figure 4.16 Backward fall with arms lateral from three-meter height.

Figure 4.17 Backward lineup with arms lateral and with spring from one-meter height.

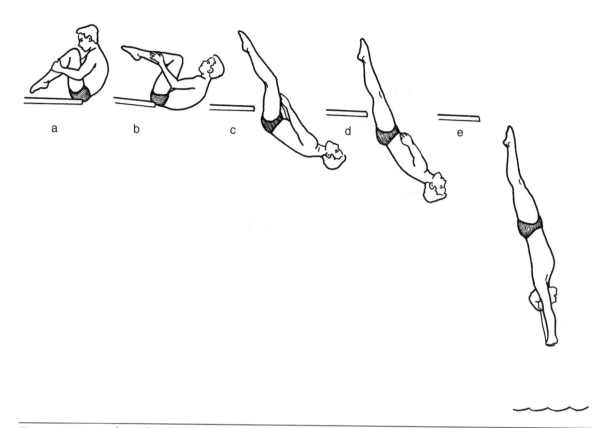

Figure 4.18   Backward tuck roll-off with lateral come-out from three-meter height.

for the less advanced diver, because less movement and rotation are involved, making concentration on body position and accuracy of entry easier.

When the diver can perform the back fall well, he or she can move on to the sitting tuck and pike roll-off from the three-meter board. The tuck position should be learned first.

The diver sits in a tuck position backward on the end of the board with the hips two to three inches from the tip (see figure 4.18, a-e). Sitting this distance from the tip of the board aids in the rotation of the dive because the board holds the hips up as the diver rotates backward. The diver rocks backward, staying in the tuck position until the hips leave the board. At this point, the diver kicks the legs and performs a backward dive tuck come-out action as described in chapter 3. This same drill can be done in the open-pike position, although balancing and holding the legs up in position requires more skill and strength than needed for the tuck roll-off.

If no three-meter board is available, the backward lineup from the one-meter board can be practiced by doing a backward dive tuck as described earlier, or a backward dive open pike as shown in figure 4.19, a through e.

Reverse Lineup

Unfortunately, as with the inward lineup, these entries must be practiced with a spring. However, if a good backward lineup is first mastered in various drills, these entries will be relatively easy.

From the one-meter board, the diver should first practice a standing reverse dive tuck and reverse dive open pike with a spring and then with a full forward approach. The same can be done from the three-meter board.

Figure 4.19 Backward dive open pike.

Somersault Come-Out Lineups

Somersault come-out lineups are performed to simulate methods of coming out of somersault spins for a headfirst entry; they also serve to teach good entry technique. During the come-outs the diver must keep the shoulders and arms relaxed until they are in position for the entry stretch. Tension in these areas during come-out can cause unwanted reaction movements in the body.

Forward and Inward Come-Outs

For forward and inward somersault optional dives in tuck or pike position, two come-out techniques are used: the straight line and the pike-out.

In the straight-line method, the legs and arms move sequentially to a straight line, with the legs beginning to extend first, then the arms straightening. The sequence of movement is from the bottom of the body to the top and is performed as quickly as the dive dictates. In the tuck position, the knees begin to extend first, followed by the hips; in the pike position, the hips extend to begin the come-out. After the legs or hips begin to extend, the trunk moves from a hollow shape to a straight line, the hands and arms move upward from their position near the thighs or lower abdominal area, and the head moves to a neutral position. The arms move to the overhead stretch by keeping the elbows bent as the hands pass up the center of the body. When the arms pass head level, they start to straighten and the hands are grabbed in the entry position (see figure 4.20, a-d).

Using the pike-out method, the legs extend at the knee joint while remaining in a tight pike position at the hips. As the legs straighten at the knees, the arms straighten and move from the shins to a lateral position in line with the level of

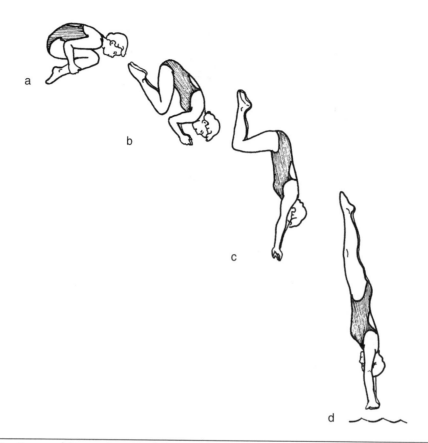

Figure 4.20 Forward/inward optional dives with straight-line come-out.

the knees. This arm location assists in keeping the pike position as tight as possible and allows greater control of the opening phase that follows. Following the move to this open-pike position, in a sequential pattern, the hips begin to extend, the trunk straightens, the arms begin to move laterally upward to the overhead stretch, and the head moves to a neutral alignment with the eyes focusing on the entry point (see figure 4.21, a-d).

Because the straight-line kick takes much less time to perform than the pike-out method, divers use it when they don't have a lot of time to prepare for the entry. Divers usually prefer the pike-out when they have enough time to use it because it allows more time to see the entry point and more opportunity to adjust the entry when the body is straightened and the arms are brought overhead.

For a forward come-out from the three-meter board, the diver sits facing forward in a tuck position at the end of the board and rolls forward into a dive. While leaving the board, the diver does a lineup using either the straight-line (see figure 4.22, a-e) or pike-out (see figure 4.23, a-d) come-out method. The same drill can be done in the closed-pike position.

On the one-meter board, the diver performs a forward dive tuck either from the standing position or with an approach to practice both come-out methods and the entry. The forward dive is usually not performed in closed-pike position because this tends to cause the diver to overrotate and not effectively practice a correct entry.

For an inward come-out either from the one- or three-meter board, the diver practices an inward dive tuck using the two come-out methods. Again, an inward dive closed pike should not be attempted because of likely control problems.

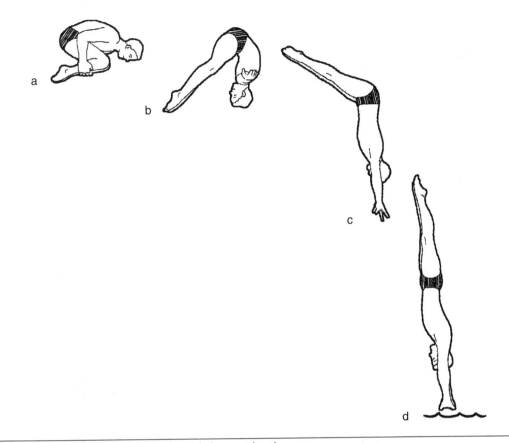

Figure 4.21 Forward/inward optional dives with pike-out.

Figure 4.22 Forward tuck roll-off from three-meter height with straight-line come-out.

Figure 4.23   Forward tuck roll-off from three-meter height with pike-out come-out.

Backward and Reverse Come-Outs

Backward and reverse somersaulting dives in tuck and pike position also have two methods of come-out: the straight line and the kick and stretch.

Using the straight-line method, the diver follows the same method used for forward and inward somersaulting dives, except in the backward direction. The speed with which the movements occur depends on the time available to prepare for the entry. In a sequential pattern, the movements occur from the bottom of the body to the top. In the tuck position, the knees begin to extend and then the hips; in pike position, the hips begin the come-out. After the knees and/or hips begin to extend, the trunk moves from a hollow shape to a straight line, the hands and arms begin to move from their location near the thighs or lower abdominal area upward to the overhead stretch, and the head moves to a slightly tilted upward position with the eyes looking toward the water. As the arms move upward, the elbows are bent, and as the hands pass head level, the hands are grabbed in preparation for the entry (see figure 4.24, a-d).

The kick-and-stretch method has a two-part movement pattern. The first part consists of opening from the knees or hips first while the arms, trunk, and head hesitate until this phase is completed. Part 2 is the sequential opening of the trunk, arms, and head. In tuck spinning dives, the legs extend at the knees while the diver maintains a slight pike at the hip joint. In pike spinning dives, the body opens at the hip joint and the diver maintains the same slight pike. In either case, as the opening takes place, the trunk is in a hollow shape with the head tilted forward and the eyes looking over the toes. Then the same sequential movement pattern occurs as described for the other come-outs. After the knees and/or hips

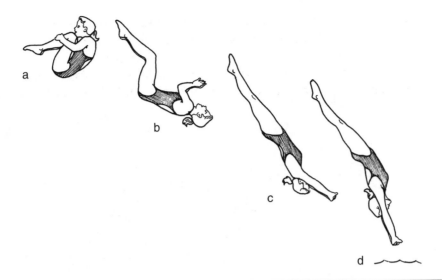

Figure 4.24 Backward/reverse optional dives with straight-line come-out.

begin to extend, the trunk moves from its hollow shape to a straight line, the hands and arms begin to move from their location near the thighs or lower abdominal area, and the head tilts slightly upward with the eyes looking toward the water. As the arms move up the midline of the body to the overhead stretching position, the elbows are bent, and as the hands pass head level, they are grabbed in preparation for the entry (see figure 4.25, a-d).

Divers use the straight-line come-out when they do not have much time to prepare for the entry. They use the kick-and-stretch method when time permits. An overly arched body position during entry can be avoided more easily with the kick-and-stretch technique because there is more time to develop a firm body position before the stretch begins.

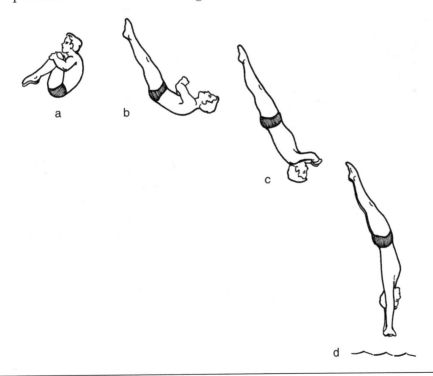

Figure 4.25 Backward/reverse optional dives with kick-and-stretch come-out.

Tuck and pike roll-offs from the three-meter board are good ways to practice the two backward somersaulting come-out actions (see figure 4.26, a-e, and figure 4.27, a-d). Because the roll-off method has been previously described, it will not be explained again here. The diver can also practice come-out techniques for tuck spinning dives from the one-meter board while doing a backward dive tuck.

Figure 4.26 Backward tuck roll-off from three-meter height with straight-line come-out.

Figure 4.27 Backward pike roll-off from three-meter height with kick-and-stretch come-out.

The diver can practice the kick-and-stretch come-out actions while doing a backward dive pike, with some variations from the usual mechanics. As the take-off occurs, the jump and reach are the same as for a normal back dive pike; however, as the diver rises and the pike position is achieved, the hands are placed in front of the lower abdomen. At the peak of the dive, when the body begins to extend to a straight position, the kick-and-stretch come-out actions are performed (see figure 4.28, a-f). As in all the other backward and reverse lineups, the head tilts slightly forward as the opening occurs and then tilts slightly backward with the eyes looking back toward the water.

For reverse come-outs, the reverse dive tuck, which can be done either standing or with an approach from the one-meter board, affords the best method of practicing the tuck somersault come-outs. As for the backward lineups, the same type of modified reverse dive pike is used to practice the pike somersault come-out movements.

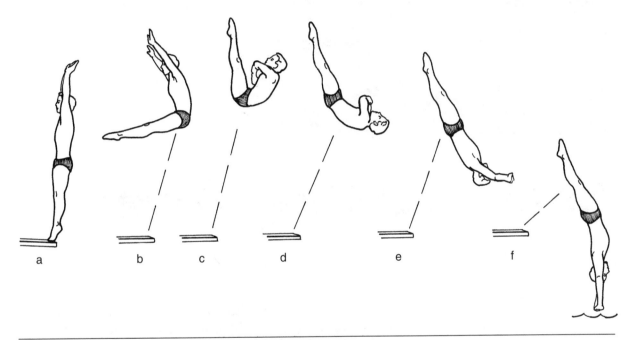

a   b   c   d   e   f

Figure 4.28 Backward dive open pike with kick-and-stretch come-out.

SUMMARY

There are many ways to practice entries and the various types of movements needed for different types of dives. No diver has the time to practice all of these drills. Divers should learn all the methods described here and then choose the drills that produce the best results and best fit their needs. These needs may change as dives are eliminated from and added to the diver's list; consequently, the entry drills that are practiced should be adjusted accordingly. The more proficient a diver becomes at come-outs, lineups, and entries as practiced in these drills, the easier it will be to finish the basic and optional dives with control and accuracy.

Somersaulting Dives

Somersaulting dives are performed in four directions: forward, inward, backward, and reverse. Because the methods of initiating rotation in the forward and inward dives are similar, as are those in the backward and reverse spinning dives, this is the order of presentation. However, all of the dives differ in the point at which balance is maintained and in the way the takeoffs are performed due to the way the forces involved in creating the rotation affect the distance from the board. The forward flying somersault dives are also presented in the forward and inward somersault section.

FORWARD AND INWARD SOMERSAULTING DIVES

The forward and inward somersaulting dives are similar in how the rotation is initiated. However, they differ in balance and how proper distance from the board is achieved. In forward somersaulting dives, when landing on the board out of the hurdle, the center of balance is maintained over the front of the feet. To aid this balance, the shoulders should be aligned over the knees during the squat and initial extension phases of the press. The sequence of arm and body motions used to depress the springboard are the same as described in the section concerning boardwork in chapter 2. The arms should swing up to a position overhead so they are in line with the head and upper body. Even though most divers have some elbow bend during the upswing of the arms in the press, the arms should return to a straight and elbow-locked position when they reach the overhead position. At this point, the arms may be deliberately bent at the elbows, with the hands located above and slightly behind the head. This allows the diver to snap the arms from a bent to a straight position to develop more arm speed and transfer of momentum to the rotational force. This aid to rotation, however, is not aesthetically pleasing and should be used only when (and to the extent) needed to perform the dive effectively.

As the arms complete their upswing, the center of balance is shifted forward when the board begins its upward thrust and just before the rotational forces are initiated. If the weight moves forward before the arms swing up and before the board begins its upward movement, the takeoff will be out of balance and the dive will lack elevation and move too far away from the board. Conversely, if the weight is located too far back at this point, the dive will be too close to the board and will spin more slowly because the board will not aid rotation as much.

Once the takeoff position is reached, with the arms overhead and the weight shifted forward, somersault rotation can be created. This is initiated by moving the arms in an upward-forward-downward pattern while holding them straight and parallel. As soon as the arms begin the throwing motion, the head moves downward and inward; then the rib cage moves inward to a hollow shape, and the hips begin to flex. While the arm, head, trunk, and hip movements occur, the legs, ankles, and toes are extending, and the board is recoiling. The amount of hip flexion that takes place depends on the number of somersaults to be performed. Note the differences in trunk positions during takeoff in figure 5.1, a through c, for forward one-and-a-half, two-and-a-half, and three-and-a half somersaults in the pike position.

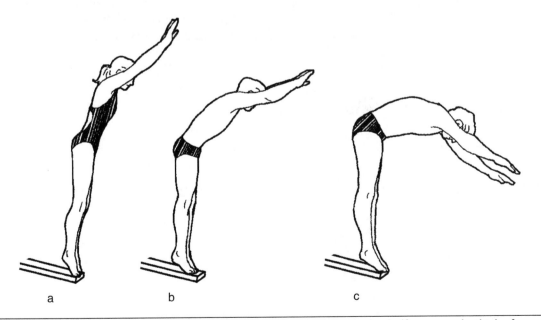

a   b   c

Figure 5.1 Comparison of takeoff positions for (a) the forward one-and-a-half somersault, (b) the forward two-and-a-half somersault, and (c) the forward three-and-a-half somersault.

In order to initiate spin effectively, the movements described earlier should take place in a sequential pattern from the top of the body to the bottom. This means that the arms begin to move, then the head, the rib cage, the hips, the knees, the ankles, and the toes. One movement is not completed before the next begins; rather, they flow in a domino effect. Variations from this sequential movement pattern will cause a loss of rotation. Finally, just before the feet leave the board, the arms move down in front of the body and begin to reach for the tuck or pike position. Figure 5.2, a through d, illustrates the correct technique of beginning forward rotation.

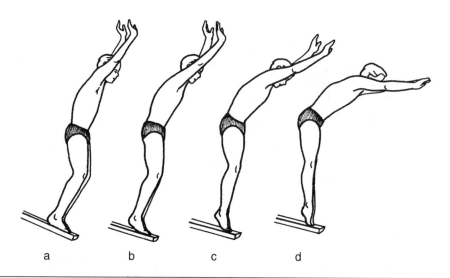

a   b   c   d

Figure 5.2   Forward sequential movement.

The method of creating rotation is the same for inward somersaulting dives as for forward spins. The sequential movement of the arms, head, and upper body, timed with the extension of the legs and the upward thrust of the board, is essential. Notice in figure 5.3, a and b, the comparison of takeoff position between the inward one-and-a-half somersault dive in tuck position and the inward two-and-a-half somersault dive in pike position.

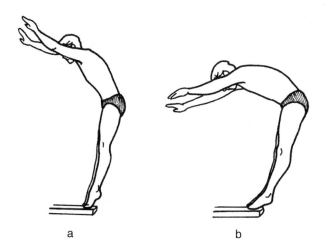

a   b

Figure 5.3   Comparison of (*a*) the inward one-and-a-half somersault in pike position and (*b*) the inward two-and-a-half somersault in pike position.

The key to performing good inward optional dives lies in how balance is maintained during the press and initiation of the somersault. Because developing the rotation causes the board to push the diver away on takeoff (review figure 2.13 in chapter 2), any lean or movement of balance backward prior to the somersaulting action will cause the diver to be too far from the board. A loss of balance backward also prevents the thrust of the board from aiding rotation and inhibits the diver's ability to get full extension from the legs and ankles. To aid in maintaining this crucial balance, the diver should align the shoulders over the knees when dropping from the top of the backward press into the squat position. This will result in a balanced position before the body begins to extend. This balance point should be maintained until the throwing motion for rotation occurs, at which time the forces of the takeoff will push the diver upward and backward.

The Right Feeling

When the forward and inward somersaults are executed correctly, it feels as though the motion is in an upward and forward direction. There should be little sensation of a downward throw. If the somersaulting motion feels predominantly downward, the movements to create spin are occurring too early and before the "kick" of the springboard. When performing the forward and inward somersault takeoff, divers should feel as though they are rolling over a barrel before moving to the tuck or pike position.

Visual Cues

Some visual cues will help to ensure that the correct movements are made at the right time. As the board is depressed and the somersaulting action begins in the forward or inward takeoff, the head should remain level. The eyes should focus wherever is comfortable as long as the head position is maintained. After initiating the somersaulting movement, the eyes should look at the legs just as they come off the board. These visual cues will help keep the head up in position during the throwing motion while getting the proper timing of the rotational force, and will also ensure that the head and body move down into the somersault action at the correct moment. These visual cues are illustrated in figure 5.4, a and b.

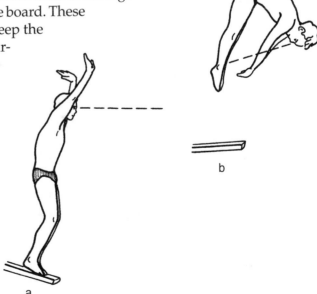

Figure 5.4 Visual cues for forward/inward optional takeoffs.

Getting Into Position

Just as the feet leave the board, the arms move down in front of the body to assume either the tuck or pike position. In the tuck position, the thighs are drawn to the chest while the hands grasp the shins midway between the knee and ankle and pull the heels to the buttocks. The head should be positioned with the chin in tight and tilted down so the line of sight is over the top of the knees. If the head is down too far and the line of sight is through the upper thigh area, spatial orientation (the ability to visually spot and see the entry point clearly) can be negatively affected. There will also be a strong tendency to overrotate. No matter where the head is positioned, the eyes must be kept open throughout the spin.

The pike position can best be accomplished by moving the arms so the elbows are at the knees while the arms are straight and the hands are well past the legs. At this point, the arms wrap around the back of the knees so the forearms hold the legs with each hand touching the outside of the opposite leg and each palm facing forward (see figure 5.5, a-d).

This method of assuming the pike allows the diver to assume a very compact position quickly, resulting in greater early acceleration. An alternate technique is to grasp the back of the knees with the hands and then to begin pulling into a tight position. Although many divers use this, it is not as effective for multiple somersault dives.

When in the pike, the diver can use one of two techniques for head position and line of sight. The head can be positioned so the eyes sight between the lower legs. This produces a tighter pike and therefore a faster spin. However, if the diver has trouble with orientation in this position, the chin can be tilted upward slightly so the eyes sight over the toes. It is important that the head not be moved inward so far that the knees, the thighs, or nothing at all can be seen, leaving the diver to guess when to come out of the spin.

Figure 5.5   Forward/inward pike position.

Coming Out

Regardless of whether the diver is in a tuck or pike position, the headfirst-entry somersaulting dives are completed using either the straight-line or pike-out somersault come-out techniques discussed in chapter 4. If there is adequate time, the diver should use the pike-out method (see figure 5.6, a-f); if there is little time to complete the dive, the diver should use the straight-line come-out (see figure 5.7, a-f).

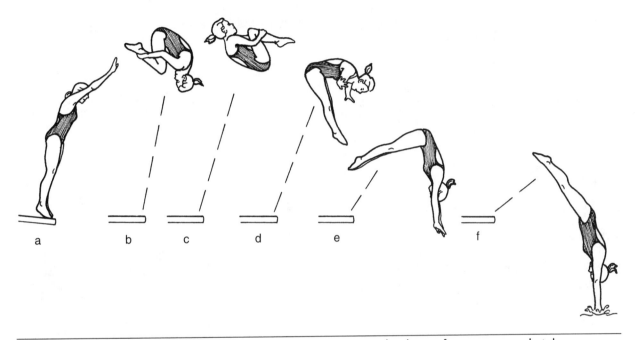

Figure 5.6 Forward one-and-a-half somersault in tuck position with pike-out from one-meter height.

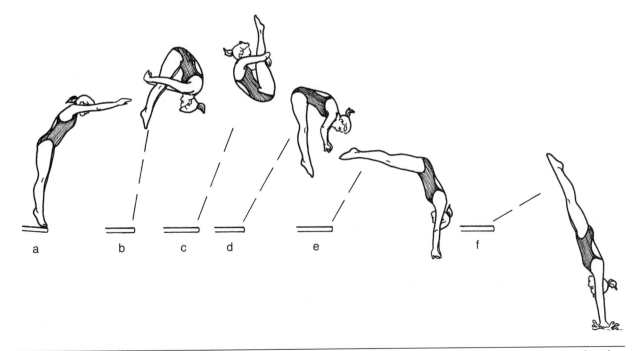

Figure 5.7 Forward one-and-a-half somersault in pike position with straight come-out from one-meter height.

In feetfirst entries, the body moves from the tuck or pike position directly to a straight line with the arms at the sides, palms on the side of the upper leg, and toes pointed. Throughout this opening, the head remains still. The diver will learn to recognize the proper point in the spin to start the opening through repetition.

As a general rule for the headfirst-entry dives in the tuck position, the kick-out begins as the head passes through the vertical position in the last rotation of the dive (see figure 5.8, e-f); for the pike position, the opening occurs at the quarter somersault position in the last somersault of rotation (see figure 5.9f).

Study the forward and inward somersaulting dives in figures 5.6 through 5.13 to get a visual picture of the correct takeoff, somersault position, and come-out technique for these types of dives.

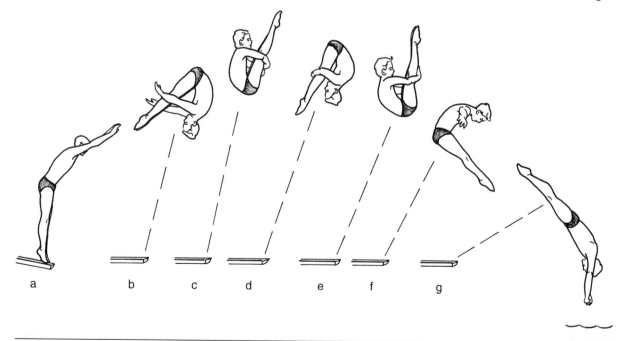

Figure 5.8   Forward two-and-a-half somersault in tuck position with straight come-out from one-meter height.

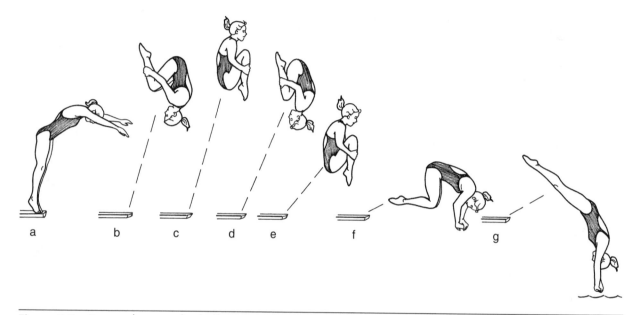

Figure 5.9   Forward two-and-a-half somersault in pike position with pike-out from one-meter height.

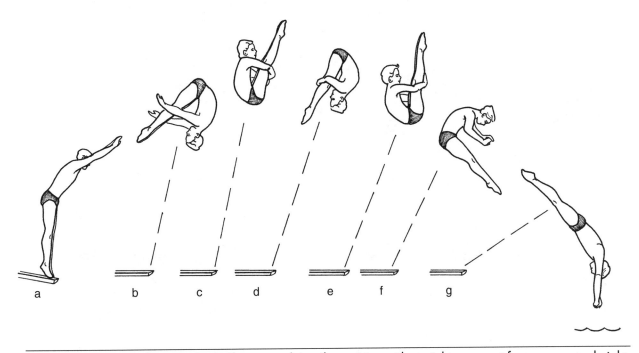

Figure 5.10 Forward two-and-a-half somersault in pike position with straight come-out from one-meter height.

Figure 5.11 Inward one-and-a-half somersault in tuck position with straight come-out from one-meter height.

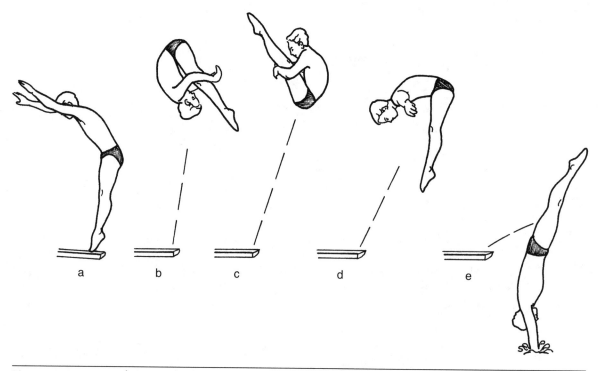

Figure 5.12 Inward one-and-a-half somersault in pike position with pike-out from one-meter height.

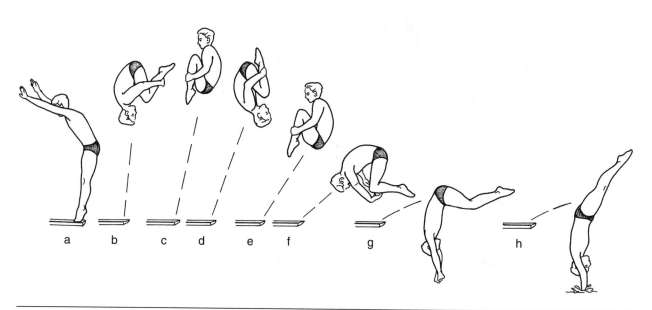

Figure 5.13 Inward two-and-a-half somersault in tuck position with straight come-out from one-meter height.

Flying Somersault Dives

The flying forward and inward somersault dives start like strong forward or inward dives in the straight position. The arms are straight and parallel overhead at takeoff, and the head is in a neutral position with the eyes looking somewhere out in front. At takeoff, more pike at the hips is needed than in the straight dives to create greater rotation from the board. As soon as the feet leave the board, the arms move laterally to shoulder level while the body moves from pike to straight as soon as possible. This position is held until a half somersault point, when a move to a tuck or pike position occurs to complete the desired amount of rotation. During the rotation from takeoff to the half somersault, the eyes gradually shift focus to the entry point in order to keep the head in a neutral position. In the tuck position, the hands grab the legs at midshin level, but in the pike dives, either a closed- or open-pike position can be performed.

If only one somersault is being done, the body straightens for the entry with the arms at the sides. For one-and-a-half or two-and-a-half somersault dives, the come-out is the same as for the other forward and inward somersault optional dives: either straight line or open pike.

Flying inward somersault dives are rarely performed due to the difficulty of holding the straight position to the half somersault point. The forward flying two-and-a-half somersault dive is also seldom done in competition. Therefore, only the forward flying one-and-a-half somersault closed-pike position is illustrated in figure 5.14, a through f.

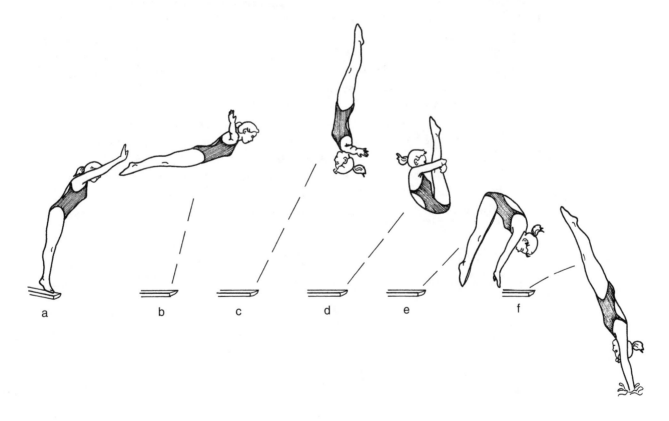

a b c d e f

Figure 5.14 Forward flying one-and-a-half somersault in closed-pike position from one-meter height.

BACKWARD AND REVERSE SOMERSAULTING DIVES IN TUCK AND PIKE POSITIONS

As with the forward and inward somersaulting dives, the backward and reverse somersaulting dives have many similarities in how rotation is initiated. The differences lie in how balance is maintained and how movement away from the board to a safe distance is accomplished.

In backward somersaulting dives, as the diver drops from the top of the backward press into the squat position, the shoulders should be aligned over the middle of the thighs to create the proper starting balance for the takeoff. This alignment should be maintained until the arms begin to pass head level. At this point, the diver shifts the balance backward by moving the trunk backward as the arms pass overhead and backward.

As the body nears full extension and the arms are directly overhead, somersault rotation is initiated by a combination of two motions—the hips moving upward and the trunk hyperextending backward—as the arms continue to swing upward and backward over the head. While these movements occur, the legs, ankles, and toes continue to extend. The diver should keep the arms as straight as possible and parallel, and should initiate the arching motion from the hip joint, not allowing the rib cage to move to an open position. The head remains in a neutral position throughout the press and is located between the arms at the point of takeoff. The eyes should remain centered but not focused on any particular point. As in forward and inward somersaulting initiation, these movements are performed in a sequential pattern from the top to the bottom of the body. The arms swing upward and backward, and then the head moves from a horizontal position until it is angled backward between the arms; the chest lifts, the hips hyperextend, and the knees, ankles, and finally the toes extend. As stated in the forward and inward somersaulting section, these movements do not occur one after the other but rather in a flow of movement.

The body shape created by these movements simulates a shallow C position. This description gives the diver a visual picture of the correct takeoff position. Figure 5.15 shows this position. The amount of arch and force created depends on the amount of rotation desired, with more arch and force creating more rotation. The angle of the upper body on takeoff should not exceed approximately 45 degrees for an effective combination of lift and rotation.

Figure 5.15 Backward takeoff in C position.

In reverse somersaulting dives, the diver develops rotation and moves to a tuck or pike position exactly the same way as for backward somersaulting dives. The major consideration for reverse somersaulting dives is to create adequate rotation while achieving safe and proper distance from the springboard. This is accomplished by maintaining correct balance in the press and by moving to the C body position for takeoff using the proper sequence of body movements.

When dropping from the hurdle and squatting down on the board, the diver should align the shoulders over the middle of the thighs. This balance is maintained during the press until the arms pass above head level in the upswing. Because the forces generated in creating rotation push the diver away from the board (review figure 2.16 on page 36), no forward lean is needed to achieve good distance.

After the arms swing overhead to the preliminary takeoff position, the body should move into the C position in the same sequential movement pattern as described for backward somersaulting takeoffs. Because the direction of takeoff for reverse somersaults is opposite that for backward somersaults, the body is in a reverse C position, as shown in figure 5.16. While moving to this position, the diver must move forward away from the board and intiate reverse rotation by keeping the shoulders fixed while the arms continue to swing overhead and the legs drive the hips upward and forward. If the hips are kept fixed while the upper body and shoulders are moved backward, the center of balance will move backward and the diver will strike the board.

Figure 5.16 Reverse takeoff in C position.

Closure

In tuck and pike somersaulting dives, as soon as the feet leave the board, rotation accelerates by closing the body from the extended position to the somersaulting position in one of two ways: direct closure and circular closure.

Direct closure is executed by bringing the arms down in front of the body while lifting the legs either to the tuck or pike position. The arms are kept straight during the beginning of this motion. As the arms approach the legs, the elbows are bent and the hands grasp the legs at the midpoint of the shins for a tuck, or the arms wrap around the legs at knee level for a pike. As these movements take place, the head and upper body move forward toward the legs to assist in speeding up the closing time and thus accelerate the rotation quickly. It is very important that the head does not tilt backward during closure, regardless of which method is used. A visual cue to help prevent the head from tilting backward is to keep the line of sight directed so the knees can be seen coming into the tuck position (see figure 5.17, a-f), or the legs and feet can be seen moving into the pike position (see figure 5.18, a-e). This visual contact should occur as early during closure as possible.

Figure 5.17   Backward somersault in tuck position with direct closure.

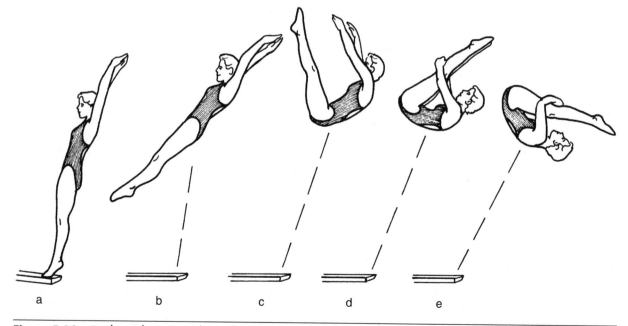

Figure 5.18   Backward somersault in pike position with direct closure.

Circular closure starts from the same takeoff position as that used in the direct closure. Instead of moving in front of the body, the arms follow a downward, lateral path while the legs are lifted to the tuck or pike position and the head and upper body push toward the legs to assist the rapid closure movement.

In tuck and pike dives, the hands and arms move down to shoulder level before moving forward to grab the legs. The arms should be kept straight during this phase. To assume a tuck position, the diver bends the elbows, reaches the hands around the front of the legs, and grasps the shins. To assume a pike position, the diver keeps the arms straight as they reach past the legs, then bends the elbows and wraps the arms around the back of the knees. An aid to making the circle motion easier and faster is to turn the hands and arms as the movement begins so the little finger points in the direction of the circle (inward rotation of the shoulder joint). This eliminates friction in the shoulder area. Throughout this movement, the arms are kept straight until they must bend to catch the legs. An important concept to understand is that as the arms circle, the legs move into the upper body before any contact between arms and legs occurs. In other words, the tuck or pike position is as tight as possible before the arms pull the position even tighter (see figure 5.19, a-d, and figure 5.20, a-e).

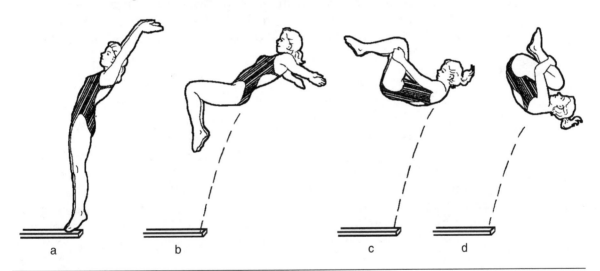

a   b   c   d

Figure 5.19 Circular closure for backward optional dives in tuck position.

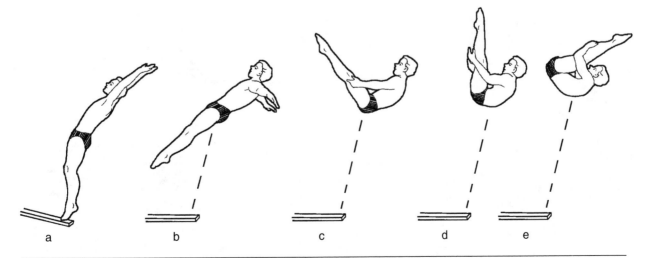

a   b   c   d   e

Figure 5.20 Circular closure for backward optional dives in pike position.

The direct closure method should be learned first. Practice should continue with this technique until the takeoff can be done with a straight and parallel overhead reach of the arms, combined with full body extension and control of balance. Establishing these fundamentals is essential before learning the circular closure technique.

For most divers, circular closure is more effective than direct closure. When the circular closure technique is used, the downward, lateral action of the arms shortens the radius of rotation more quickly, and the forward movement of the arms to grab the legs assists in assuming a tight tuck or pike position, resulting in an earlier acceleration of rotation.

Head Position

As with the forward somersaulting dives, head position in the backward and reverse somersaulting dives is crucial. In tuck dives, the chin is drawn in tightly to the chest, and the line of sight is directed over the top of the knees. The knees may be spread slightly to aid vision and increase the speed of rotation, but they should be kept inside shoulder width, and the feet should be together. If the line of sight is down too far through the legs, disorientation and a tendency to overrotate the entry may result. In pike dives, the head is positioned so the line of sight is over the toes to provide the best opportunity for clear visual orientation.

Coming Out

Coming out of backward and reverse tuck and pike somersaulting rotations can be done by using one of the two methods described in chapter 4: the straight-line come-out or kick-and-stretch actions. If there is little time to complete the dive, the straight-line come-out should be used. If there is time to perform the kick-and-stretch technique, this is preferred. Through repetition and experience, the diver must learn when to begin the kick-out based on the speed of rotation and distance from the water. As a general rule, the come-out for tuck dives starts when the dive is approximately at three-quarters to seven-eighths somersault for one-and-a-half-rotation dives (see figure 5.21d), one-and-three-quarters to

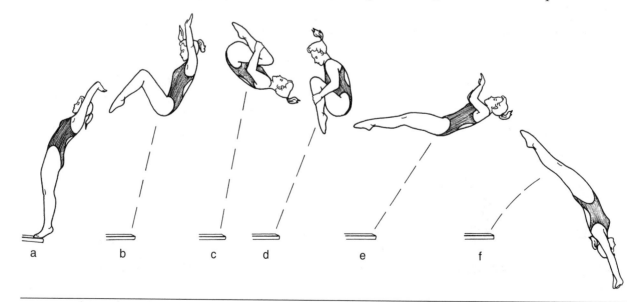

a   b   c   d   e   f

Figure 5.21 Backward one-and-a-half somersault in tuck position with direct closure and straight-line come-out from one-meter height.

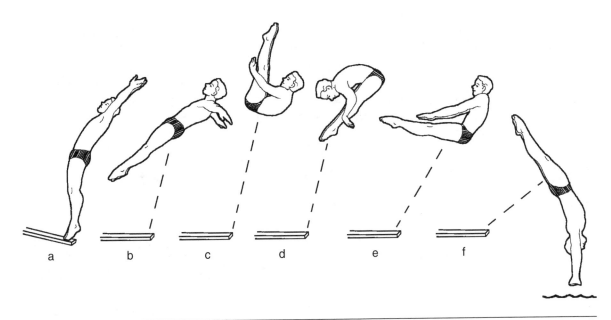

Figure 5.22 Backward one-and-a-half somersault in pike position with circular closure and kick-and-stretch come-out from one-meter height.

one-and-seven-eighths somersault for two-and-a-half-rotation dives, and two-and-three-quarters to two-and-seven-eighths somersault for three-and-a-half-rotation dives. In pike dives, the come-out begins at the one-and-one-eighth- to one-and-a-quarter- (see figure 5.22d), two-and-one-eighth- to two-and-a-quarter-, and three-and-one-eighth- to three-and-a-quarter-somersault positions for one-and-a-half-, two-and-a-half-, and three-and-a-half-rotation dives, respectively.

The backward and reverse one-and-a-half somersault in straight position can be completed with the same arm and hand grab technique described in the kick-and-stretch come-out (see figure 5.23e), or by straightening the arms and moving them in a lateral path (see figure 5.27e) to the overhead entry stretch position.

No matter which body position the diver uses, the kick-and-stretch come-out method affords greater control of rotation in dives that are completed easily and thus create a tendency to overrotate. The more control or "checking" of the rotation the diver needs, the farther he or she should extend the arms away from the

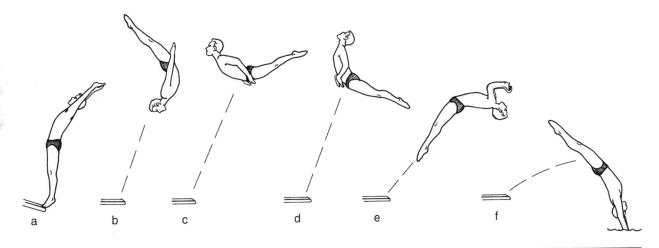

Figure 5.23 Backward one-and-a-half somersault in straight position from one-meter height.

body as they move overhead for the entry. The outward and backward movement of the arms causes a temporary reaction movement of the legs in the opposite direction of rotation. In dives that spin very fast, the arms may move from the grab position to the entry while remaining completely straight. Acute awareness of rotational speed and of time remaining before the entry will determine how much to straighten the arms during the movement to the entry stretch position. Experimentation and experience are the keys.

BACKWARD AND REVERSE ONE-AND-A-HALF SOMERSAULTS STRAIGHT

Backward and reverse somersaulting dives in the straight position involve the same balance and initiation of rotation techniques as are used in the tuck and pike positions. The difference occurs in the movements after leaving the board. As soon as possible after takeoff, the arms (kept straight and parallel) are brought down in front of the body while the head tilts back, the eyes look back, and the upper body continues to pull in the rotating direction. When the arms approach the body, one of the following positions is used:

1. The hands come together, the elbows bend, and the palms are placed on the abdominal area somewhere between the chest and the hips, depending on the diver's preference.

2. The arms are straight, and the hands are placed on the front of the thighs.

Regardless of the arm position, the arms remain still until the stretch for the entry. Analyze the illustrations in figures 5.21 through 5.27 to get a visual picture of how the backward and reverse somersaulting dives are performed.

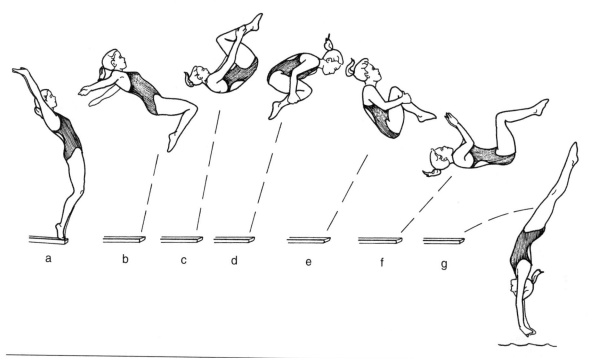

a   b   c   d   e   f   g

Figure 5.24   Reverse one-and-a-half somersault in tuck position with circular closure and straight come-out from one-meter height.

Figure 5.25 Reverse one-and-a-half somersault in pike position with straight come-out from one-meter height.

Figure 5.26 Reverse one-and-a-half somersault in pike position with circle closure and kick-and-stretch come-out from one-meter height.

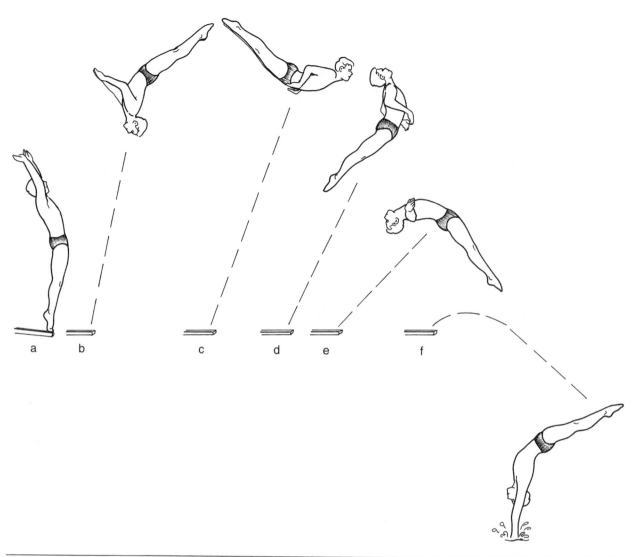

Figure 5.27   Reverse one-and-a-half somersault in straight position with lateral come-out from three-meter height.

VISUAL SPOTTING

For many years, divers have used a technique called *spotting* to assist in spatial orientation and knowing when to come out of the somersaulting dives. Spotting entails visually sighting a particular point on each somersault rotation and on the final rotation; the diver comes out of the dive when he or she sees the spot. It is similar to the way ballet dancers fix their vision on one point and quickly return to look at the point during each rotation in a series. Dancers, however, perform rotations on a different axis than divers do and have the luxury of greater head movement to accomplish this feat. Visual spotting can and should be used on forward and inward as well as backward and reverse somersaulting dives. The information provided by spotting, as well as that provided by kinesthetic sense, allows the diver to be more accurate and consistent in the performance of all somersaulting dives.

Although visual spotting helps tremendously in performance, it is not a panacea and does not guarantee that the dive will finish correctly. Spotting is a visual cue that keeps the diver from coming out of the spin in a totally incorrect place. When the diver sees the spot and performs the kick-out, he or she must still be aware of how fast the somersault is rotating and how much time is available to complete the dive in order to kick the legs at the appropriate angle.

It is extremely important that beginning divers be aware of visual spotting and keep their eyes open at all times. Many beginners close their eyes upon leaving the board for somersaulting dives and open them when coming out of the spin. This creates an uncertain situation as the diver rotates in complete darkness in the air. Not only does this make performance of the dives more difficult and the likelihood of getting hurt greater, but it creates a lot of fearful divers.

When a beginner is learning the first somersault in each rotating direction, he or she should be working on keeping the eyes open. The coach can help by giving the diver visual targets and asking what he or she saw during the dive.

Forward and Inward Spotting

The spotting method used for forward and inward dives differs somewhat from that for backward and reverse dives. Forward and inward dives are spotted between the vertical head position at the completion of each rotation and the quarter somersault position. The visual spot for forward and inward rotating dives begins with the area at approximately a 45-degree angle in front of the diver. The bigger the area the diver can see clearly, the better the opportunity to make correct come-out decisions.

In tuck dives, the eyes should be looking over the tops of the knees to see the spots. Pike dives can be spotted with one of two lines of sight, either over the toes or through the lower legs, depending on which works best for the diver.

Because the forward and inward dives are facing in opposite directions, the spots, although occurring at the same point in rotation, will be different. Forward somersaulting dives spot anywhere from the pool wall ahead to the entry point depending on the skill of the diver. Inward somersaulting dives spot the board (or platform) and the water below on the first rotation, and the pool wall (or platform below) and the water below on the second and third rotations.

In one-and-a-half somersault dives, when the diver sees the spot, the come-out may have already begun if the dive has a lot of time to be completed. Normally, the come-out begins as the diver sees the spot. For two-and-a-half and three-and-a-half somersault dives, the come-out begins as the diver sees the final spot.

Backward and Reverse Spotting

During backward and reverse spinning dives with headfirst entries, visual spotting occurs between the one-half and seven-eighths somersault point for each rotation to be completed in tuck spins, and at the one to one-and-one-eighth somersault point for pike dives. Thus, a diver will spot once at this point for a one-and-a-half somersault dive, twice for a two-and-a-half somersault dive, and three times for a three-and-a-half somersault dive. The diver should look over the knees in tuck dives and over the toes in pike dives to see the spot point. In one-and-a-half somersault dives, the board or water may be the spot point. In two-and-a-half and three-and-a-half somersault dives, the water directly below the diver is used because the spot remains in the same location from somersault to somersault. If the board is used as the spot in these dives, it changes location in each somersault as the diver drops toward the water. Some divers see both the water and the board when spotting. The larger the spotting area and the more focused the spot is, the more accurate the diver can be at determining the angle to kick out of the dive.

Training for Visual Spotting

The best way to learn the spotting techniques just discussed is on a trampoline or dryland diving board with overhead safety equipment. In this situation, the diver can totally concentrate on seeing the spots while being held up and let down safely. In addition, a colorful target can be placed in the location of the spot to help the diver see this area on each rotation.

Keeping the head position neutral and level, and ensuring that the eyes *look straight out of the eye socket* are necessary for good spotting. If the head tilts back through the spin or drops very low, the diver will see the spot either early or late, respectively (or may not see the spot at all). If the eyes look up through the eyebrows or down through the lower eyelid, spotting is very difficult, as this greatly reduces the field of vision and decreases the time for recognition.

On backward and reverse somersault dives, some divers can look at and pass the first spot and then lift the head back to see the next spot earlier and watch this spot longer as the chin comes back in to a neutral position. The same head movement is used on each rotation. This allows great visual and spatial orientation; however, since the motion does tend to slow the spin when the head tilts back in each revolution, there must be plenty of time to complete the dive in order to use this technique.

Techniques for Visual Spotting

1. **When to begin.** Divers should learn visual spotting shortly after learning to do forward and backward single somersaults. The diver should be aware of visual spotting and incorporate it into the somersault as part of the skill. In so doing, he or she will learn to rely on spotting and keep the eyes open at all times.

2. **Targets.** The progression of types of targets to use, from easiest to hardest, is colors, shapes, and numbers. At first, large targets of bright yellow are best. Bright red is also good, but yellow is best if available. A large bath towel works well as a starting point. After the diver learns to see this general target, he or she can move on to a pole with a two-sided placard. Each side of the placard should have a different bright yellow or red shape such as a triangle or square. Once the diver begins the somersault, a coach or helper can hold up one side of the placard and ask the diver to identify the shape. If the diver is doing more than one rotation, the coach can randomly change the shapes for each somersault. When the diver is adept at shapes, the coach should begin to use bright yellow or red numbers. These can be placed on a pole, on an electronic number board under the trampoline, or on a banner hung from overhead in front of the trampoline and draped onto the tramp bed. When using these various targets, the diver's ultimate challenge in the dryland setting is to call out the color or number when passing through the spotting area. When using shapes and numbers, the diver

needs to be tested for accuracy of spotting. Some divers think they see the spot well, but when tested cannot give the correct information.

3. Speed of rotation. When learning to spot on the trampoline and dryboard in the spotting belt, the spotter should control the speed of the diver's somersaults with the ropes. At first, the spotter should hold the diver up strongly to slow the speed of the somersault. As spotting becomes more efficient, the spotter should tip the diver faster and faster while doing the drills and progressions until the diver can spot effectively while rotating faster than actual performance speed. When the diver does the dive at actual speed, spotting will be much easier.

4. Mat work. Before moving to the trampoline, there are some drills on a mat that can help the diver prepare for the more difficult visual spotting while in the air. While the diver does a forward roll followed by a headstand, a coach or helper should note where at the end of the forward roll the diver would be looking at 45 degrees in front (preliminary spot), and where the entry point would be for a one-and-a-half somersault (final spot). The coach or helper should place bright spotting objects (folded towels, paper, etc.) at these locations, then have the diver repeat the drill and look at the objects. This drill can be expanded to a double roll into a headstand and double spots. The same drill can be done backward with a back roll into a backward come-out while the diver lies on his or her back on the mat. The spots should be placed where the diver would be looking at the entry point at the half to three-quarter somersault position (preliminary spot) and at the end of the backward come-out (come-out spot). The come-out spot will have to be placed high enough to simulate the angle of come-out for a backward or reverse one-and-a-half somersault. The next drill is to do a back roll into a backward extension, with assistance in the extension phase. The partner grabs the ankles as the extension begins and lifts the diver at an angle short of vertical while the diver looks over the toes (come-out spot); then the partner moves the diver to vertical as the diver looks at the entry spot on the mat. This drill can also be extended to a double back roll and double spot. After many repetitions of these drills, the diver should develop a sense of awareness of the general spotting area. Next the spotting training should move to the trampoline, with an overhead spotting apparatus. If this equipment is not available, move to the pool progressions described later.

5. Verbal cues. When beginning the spotting progressions, it is helpful for the coach to verbally assist the diver by calling "Look" as the diver approaches the preliminary spot in each rotation. This call should take place slightly before the diver rotates to the spot so that he or she has time to process the call and react to it.

Forward Spotting Progressions

1. The diver starts with a forward somersault on the trampoline, in the safety belt. The bright towel is on the frame of the trampoline in front of the diver (preliminary spot). The diver looks at the towel when coming out of the somersault.

2. After the preceding step becomes routine, the diver does the same except that he or she is rotated to a one-and-a-half somersault, using rope spotting technique, when coming out of the somersault. The diver should be getting a very good, long look at the spot.

3. The coach places a brightly colored towel or paints a spot on the trampoline bed where the entry point is (final spot). The diver looks at the preliminary spot in front and then the final spot while doing a forward one-and-a-half somersault.

4. If a dryboard with overhead spotting equipment is available, the diver can perfom the same progressions at this station.

5. Move to the pool and construct a floating device to place out in front of the one-meter board. For example, a shepherd's crook and a ring buoy (standard equipment at all pools) can be tied together, and the brightly colored towel can be placed on top. Float the spotting equipment out in front of the board about 15 feet. The diver must do a forward somersault and look at the towel (preliminary spot) when coming out of the dive. The diver then does a one-and-a-half somersault, looks at the preliminary spot at the somersault position, and opens to a one-and-a-half somersault. A helper can take the pole used on the trampoline with a shape on it and place it at the entry point (final spot). The diver does a forward one-and-a-half somersault and looks at the preliminary spot out in front at the somersault position, and the final spot as the opening begins. Obviously, the pole should be pulled out of the way before the entry occurs. Most divers have a chamois, and this can be used instead of the pole to mark the entry point. The diver can throw the chamois where the entry point is and sight it during the opening and stretch.

6. On the trampoline, the diver does a forward somersault tuck, and when opening to the straight position, tips over to a double somersault. The result is a double somersault done with the first rotation in tuck position and the second in straight position. The visual spots should be placed out in front and at the entry point. By rotating the second somersault in straight position, the diver can easily see the two spots.

7. When proficient at seeing the spots in the previous step, the diver does a double somersault in tuck position, sighting the preliminary spot at one somersault and the final spot at the one-and-a-quarter somersault and continuing over to a double. When coming out of the double, the diver should see the preliminary spot a second time.

8. Move this progression to the dryland board, if available.

9. At the one-meter board, the diver does the progression of single somersault, one-and-a-half somersault, then double somersault while looking at the preliminary and final spots as described in the previous steps.

10. The same series of progressions can now be done for the forward pike somersaults. In this case, as mentioned previously, the diver can sight over the toes or through the legs. Experimentation with both of these techniques should be done to determine which method best suits the diver.

11. The same progressions can be extended to the two-and-a-half, triple, and three-and-a-half somersaults. As the diver becomes proficient at spotting on the one-meter level, using the same spotting skills at the three-meter and platform levels can be accomplished relatively easily.

12. As forward spotting is learned, inward spotting can be accomplished using the same progressions on the trampoline, dryboard, and one-meter board. In this group, the spotting areas remain the same on the trampoline, but, on the dryboard and one-meter board, the preliminary spot becomes the springboard

while the final spot remains the entry point. To accommodate this change, a brightly colored towel should be draped over the springboard a couple of feet from the front end to serve as the preliminary spot. When doing two and a half or more somersaults from the three-meter and platform levels, a towel on the board or platform as well as a brightly colored spot on the water under the board or platform can serve as the preliminary spots.

Backward Spotting Progressions

1. Prior to beginning these progressions, the diver should know how to do a backward dive in tuck position and sight the toes during the come-out. This is key to learning the proper come-out and spotting techniques employed in the one-and-a-half backward somersaulting dives and beyond.

2. After doing the preliminary mat work described earlier, the diver can move to the trampoline and begin with a backward somersault tuck in the safety belt. A brightly colored towel or a painted spot is on the center of the trampoline bed. The diver takes off from this area and uses this as the preliminary spot in the progressions. The diver looks at this spot while opening from the somersault.

3. Move to the dryboard, if available, and place a brightly colored towel at the entry point and on the springboard. The diver looks at both spots when opening from the somersault.

4. Go to the one-meter board and place the spots in the same locations. The entry point can be the shepherd's crook setup used in forward spotting, the pole with shapes on two sides, or a chamois.

5. If the diver is strong enough and capable, he or she can perform a backward somersault in the straight position on the trampoline in the safety belt. At the half somersault position, the diver should look at the preliminary spot in the center of the tramp bed.

6. After being tipped into a backward double somersault in straight position, the diver looks at the preliminary spot at the half and one-and-a-half somersault positions. This drill teaches the diver to look ahead to see the spot and allows the head to stop rotating for a short period and the eyes to track the spot more effectively.

7. On the trampoline, the diver does a tuck somersault; after the opening, the spotter tips the diver to a double somersault. The result is one somersault in tuck position and one somersault in straight position. This allows a slower rotation through the preliminary spotting area. The diver should spot the preliminary spot when coming out of the tuck and at the one-and-a-half somersault position.

8. When the diver can accomplish step 7 effectively, he or she is tipped into a double somersault tuck and looks at the preliminary spot when passing the half and one-and-a-half somersault positions.

9. Repeat the same progressions on the dryboard. In addition to the bright towel or painted area on the pit (preliminary spot), place a bright towel on the board to enlarge the spotting area.

10. On the one-meter board, the diver repeats the backward somersault progression, then does a backward double somersault and sees the preliminary spot and the towel on the board when passing the half to seven-eighths and the one and one-half to one and seven-eighths somersault positions.

11. On the trampoline, hang a banner with numbers on it in front of the diver's takeoff area and high enough for the diver to see it when coming out of a back one-and-a-half somersault at the correct angle. If a banner is not possible, then find some object or area for the diver to spot in the come-out. The diver first performs a backward dive in tuck position and kicks at the designated area, seeing the spot over the toes before stretching backward for the trampoline. The rope spotter must lower the diver to the trampoline very slowly. Next the diver starts as if doing a backward double somersault, seeing the preliminary spot when passing from the half to three-quarters somersault position; on the coach's call, the diver kicks out of the rotation and maintains a hollow body shape, with the arms down by the thighs and the eyes sighting over the toes to the designated number or area (come-out spot). The rope spotter should hold the diver suspended in this position and slowly lower the diver to the bed onto his or her back.

12. When the diver is proficient at the come-out and spotting skills in the previous step, he or she should come out to the same suspended position and, after seeing the come-out spot, complete the come-out movements while being lowered to the trampoline. The finish should be in a handstand position, just short of a vertical line, with the eyes sighting the trampoline bed and the ears and shoulders aligned.

13. Repeat the same progressions on the dryboard, if available.

14. On the one-meter board, the diver does the single and double somersault progressions.

15. The diver does some backward dives in tuck position to practice the come-out movements.

16. The diver starts as if doing a backward double somersault, looking for the preliminary spot as before, and, on the coach's call, kicks out and does the backward dive tuck movements to complete a backward one-and-a-half somersault in tuck position.

17. When the diver is comfortable doing the backward one-and-a-half somersault, he or she should begin emphasizing seeing the come-out spotting area clearly. The diver can also try to see a chamois placed in the water a little farther out than the entry point when finishing the come-out. This helps ensure that the head is in a slightly up-tilted position for the entry.

18. The same concepts and progressions can now be done in the pike position and extended to the two-and-a-half, triple, and three-and-a-half somersaults in tuck and pike. Continued work on spotting while doing back one-and-a-half and two-and-a-half somersaults in straight position is very valuable. As the diver becomes proficient at the spotting techniques on the one-meter board, the techniques can be transferred to dives on the three-meter board and platform.

19. After learning backward spotting, the diver can accomplish reverse spotting using the same progressions on the trampoline and dryboard with a hurdle. When transferring the skills to the one-meter board, the preliminary spot is targeted using the shepherd's crook or spotting pole. For safety, these should be located out in front of the board a few feet so the diver will not land on them during entry. As the diver becomes proficient at the dive and spotting, a chamois can be placed in the preliminary spot position (entry spot) for further practice.

CALLING DIVERS OUT

Many divers who are learning a new somersault dive or practicing one they haven't performed for a long time like to have a coach's verbal command to cue them when to kick out. This method is termed "calling the diver out." This is a big responsibility for the coach. Obviously, the call needs to be given at the correct time, so here are some guidelines to follow in these situations.

First, the visual spotting section just presented must be thoroughly understood. For any particular dive, the call is given as the diver's head enters the spotting area. It doesn't matter if the diver is actually spotting or not. It *is* important that the coach can see where this area is in the last somersault and can react with a "hup" or "hut" command—and it must be *loud!*

The best way for coaches to practice calling is to watch divers in training and mentally call them out of dives. They can determine if the call is correct by observing whether the diver kicks when they call and whether the dive finishes at or near vertical. For example, if the kick-out occurs before the mental call, and the dive finishes vertical, the call is too late.

When the coach is proficient at calling when the diver's head is in the spotting area, he or she should be prepared to adjust the call a little early or late if the speed of rotation is extremely fast or slow.

PRACTICE FOR SOMERSAULTING DIVES

The most effective way to practice the fundamentals of somersaulting forward and backward is on a trampoline. This practice should be done with the aid of the overhead safety equipment. If the diver is advanced enough, and the coach has adequate spotting skill with the safety equipment, the diver can practice training with double somersaults in the forward and backward directions.

Divers can also practice somersaults from the deck of the pool into the water, depending on the distance from the water to the deck and on the strength and skill of the diver. If the deck-to-water distance is not sufficient for completion of the somersaults, a low bench can be used to make this training possible.

For more advanced divers, practicing somersaults on a mat or from a low platform to a mat is very productive. Such practice not only helps groove the motions of the skill, but also works on speed of execution and leg development due to the landing impact.

The circular closure method of performing backward and reverse somersaults can best be practiced from the side of the pool and from the one-meter board by performing open-tuck and open-pike somersault skills with circular closure as shown in figures 5.28, a through f, and 5.29, a through f, on page 102.

SUMMARY

Throughout a diver's career, consistent work on somersault technique needs be done to ensure a pattern of execution that can be repeated dive after dive. Even for the highly skilled world-class diver, this training should take place daily on the trampoline, dryland diving board, tumbling mat, springboard, platform, and from the side of the pool. When and how this practice occurs can vary to relieve the boredom that comes from repetition.

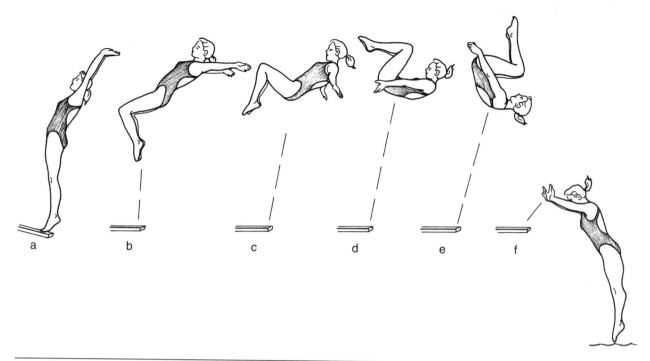

Figure 5.28 Circular closure in open-tuck position.

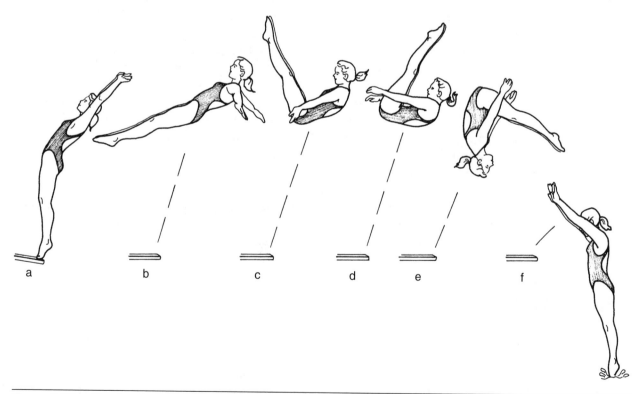

Figure 5.29 Circular closure in open-pike position.

© Rob Tringali/SportsChrome East/West

Twisting Dives

Twisting dives are the most complicated type of dives because they involve two axes of rotation. When combining somersaulting and twisting, more things can go wrong than when just somersaulting.

To successfully coach and perform twisting dives, several things need to be understood. These include the correct basic somersault skill for the type of twist performed, how and when the twist should be initiated, the relationship between the speed of the somersault and the speed of the twist for the various dives, the correct twisting position, and how to stop the twist in preparation for the entry.

When these factors are properly understood, twisting dives are not only easy but also the most enjoyable dives to perform. Divers with good basic twisting fundamentals rarely miss even the most difficult dives in this group.

The two basic types of twisting dives are forward and backward. Forward twisting technique is used in forward and inward somersaulting dives, whereas backward twisting technique is used in backward and reverse somersaulting dives.

The major difference between the forward and inward twisting dives, and between the backward and reverse twisting dives, lies in the takeoff mechanics. For each group of dives (i.e., forward/inward and backward/reverse), the diver must follow the same principles of correct takeoff as described in the sections concerning somersaulting optional dives in chapter 5. Because inward twisting dives are rarely used, they are not included in this discussion.

The best and easiest place to learn all twisting skills is on a trampoline, with the aid of overhead spotting equipment. This situation gives the coach aerial control of the diver and thus gives the diver complete freedom to concentrate on the movements. Using the trampoline and spotting equipment eliminates overriding concerns about how the dive will finish. If the principles and progressions presented here are followed, learning should be safe and successful whether occurring on the trampoline or in the pool.

ESTABLISHING SOMERSAULT MOMENTUM

The most important fundamental to all twisting dives is establishing somersault momentum on a straight axis of rotation and in line with the board. If the somersault is off line to one side or the other, it will be very difficult, if not impossible, to complete the twist correctly and perform a good finish of the dive. A dive that takes off to the side or off axis from the board on the basic somersault must be corrected before attempting to add any twists. Even when the basic somersault skills can be performed correctly, an off-axis somersault can occur when learning the twisting part of the dive. This is usually caused by starting the twist too early. To avoid this, the coach should do two things during the teaching process:

1. Constantly emphasize that the diver must develop the somersault momentum before beginning the twist.

2. Periodically check the straightness of the somersault axis from the front and rear views, even for the most advanced diver.

FORWARD TWISTING DIVES

There are two different methods of learning the forward twisting dives. One method begins from an open-pike somersault and the other from a flying somersault. The open-pike forward somersault action should be learned first; if this action is not satisfactory, the second method should be introduced.

Open-Pike Twisting Method

Twisting from the forward open-pike somersault position is the most widely used technique for forward twisting dives. For most beginners it is also the easiest twisting method to learn. The diver should understand the following three basic concepts of the open-pike forward twisting technique:

1. For the beginner, it is easiest to initiate the twisting movement in the second half of the somersault.

2. The twist begins simultaneously with the opening of the body from the pike to the straight position.

3. The diver generates the twist by turning the upper body and moving the arms around the body.

Let's examine these three points in detail.

Timing the Twist

Initiating the twist in the second half of the open-pike somersault, rather than in the middle or in the first half of the somersault, has several advantages.

- It ensures that the somersault is on the proper somersault axis before starting the twist.
- By somersaulting before twisting, the probability of landing safely on the feet is greatly increased.
- If somersault momentum is established first, twisting momentum can be developed more easily.
- Starting the twist at the point where the come-out of the open-pike somersault would normally take place, to land feetfirst, eliminates the need to think about moving from a pike to a straight position. This will happen naturally because the opening takes place at this point and the force of gravity and the somersault momentum aid in the opening.
- Twisting is done while the head is in an upright position, allowing much better orientation than if upside down.

Simultaneous Twist and Opening

The twist and opening of the body from a pike to a straight position should occur simultaneously. Many coaches and divers emphasize opening to a straight bodyline first and then initiating the twist. Emphasizing this snap-out movement as a lead-up skill to twisting does three things:

1. It causes the focus to be first on opening sharply from the pike and then on twisting. This allows less time to concentrate on the twisting movements to be made. When somersaulting in an upside-down position and trying to twist for the first time, the diver's focus needs to be on twisting.
2. It encourages the opening movement to occur before the twist is initiated rather than at the same time.
3. The snapping motion the diver uses to go from pike to straight can cause an arched body shape to develop, making twisting slower and much less efficient.

Learning to twist in the second half of the somersault, initially, eliminates the need for concern about the opening of the body because it will occur naturally. Once the diver has the feeling of opening and twisting simultaneously, this technique will be retained when he or she performs the twist earlier in the somersault.

Initiating the Twist

A common misunderstanding about starting a twist is that moving the arms into a twisting placement position, tight to the body, develops the twist. Actually, moving the arms into the body accelerates the twist, but a turning motion of the upper body combined with a circular movement of the arms in the direction of the twist starts the twisting momentum by causing the body to tilt off axis.

Forward Somersault With One Twist

Before attempting this dive, the direction in which the twist will take place must be determined. This can be done by performing a front jump with one twist from the side of the pool, first in one direction and then in the other. Usually one direction feels better than the other, and the twist stays on a more vertical line in that direction. In the majority (70 percent) of cases, the twist works best in the opposite direction of the dominant arm: right-handed people twist to the left, and vice versa.

With the direction of twist determined, a good forward somersault in the open-pike position must be learned (see figure 6.1, a-e). This skill should be performed so the rotation is completed easily and there is some drop from the end of the dive to the water. If this is not the case, there will not be enough time to complete the dive when the twist is introduced.

When the diver can do a good forward open-pike somersault, he or she can attempt one twist in the second half of the somersault. The diver should first do an open-pike somersault and concentrate on what is visually prominent in the dive.

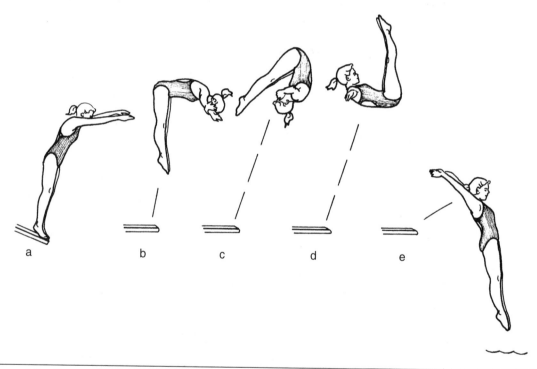

Figure 6.1   Forward somersault in open-pike position.

Generally, the diver sees two things: the lower legs while in the pike position, and the water and the other side of the pool when coming out (or the area in front of the trampoline). The diver should then do an open-pike somersault, making sure to watch the lower legs until it's time to open for the entry or landing. Simultaneously with the opening of the body, the diver turns the upper body in the direction of the twist while moving the arms in the same direction in a circular motion around chest level. It may help for the diver to imagine turning a steering wheel counterclockwise if twisting to the right and clockwise if twisting to the left. This movement must be limited in scope to allow a quick and compact move in the twisting direction. The diver must keep the arms away from the body until the twist starts, then bring them into the body. Figure 6.2, a through d, shows the beginning of the twisting action from the open-pike position.

There are two accepted arm positions for twisting, whether performing forward or backward twisting dives. The first and easiest position to learn is the split-arm method. One arm is placed across the chest (the right arm when twisting left and vice versa); the other arm is overhead, bent at a 90-degree angle so the upper arm is against the ear and the forearm is on top of the head. The second arm position is the arms-together technique. The hands are close together under the chin, the arms are bent, and the elbows are drawn close to the midline of the body. In either case, the elbows must be kept close to the body for a smooth and fast twist action. See figure 6.3, a and b, for an illustration of these arm positions. After the body opens from a pike to a straight position, no arch or pike should be present; the head should be in a neutral position with the chin drawn in.

When initiating a twist with the split-arm position, the arms flow into position from the circular pattern described earlier. However, with the arms-together

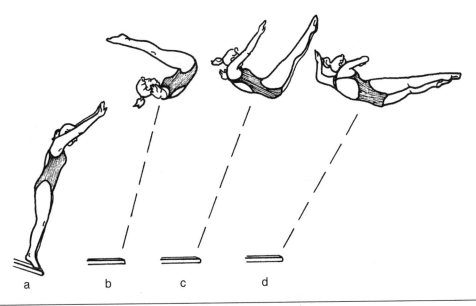

Figure 6.2 Forward somersault with one twist—late initiation of twist.

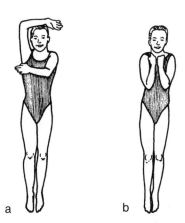

Figure 6.3 Arm positions for twisting: (*a*) the split-arm position and (*b*) the arms-together position.

position, the circular movement is more restricted with the arm on the twisting side as it must be brought into the chest rather than placed overhead.

During the last three-eighths to one-quarter of the twist, the arms begin to "square out" by moving away from the body in preparation for the entry or landing. The arm movement is a reversal of the movements used to initiate the twist—that is, a compact, circular motion in the opposite direction around chest level (clockwise if twisting right and counterclockwise if twisting left). In the split-arm position, this movement can de done directly from the twisting position, but in the arms-together position, the arm on the twisting side must move up the midline of the body to an overhead location before the circular motion can be started. Both arms should reach a lateral position at the same time. The square-out technique is illustrated in figure 6.4, a through c. While the arms unwind from the twist position, the body must remain in a straight line with the head neutral; any movement in these areas will cause a wobbly finish.

Figure 6.4 Square-out technique.

Once this skill is performed successfully on the trampoline and the one-meter springboard, the next step is to learn to twist earlier in the somersault. This is done by starting the open-pike somersault, getting a clear look at the lower legs, and then initiating the twist immediately. Because the diver is already accustomed to opening the body as the twist starts, from the "late" twist technique practiced previously, a reflex straightening of the body will occur. The twist is timed so it takes place at the half somersault position. Study figure 6.5, a through f, to see the sequence of movements.

If the inverted twist technique is done effectively, the dive can be used in competition by bringing the arms down from their lateral location prior to the entry and placing them straight at the sides.

Forward One-and-a-Half Somersault With One Twist

This dive is most easily learned from the three-meter board because it allows plenty of time to complete all the movements correctly without rushing or forcing the dive, which divers often do when they first attempt this dive at the one-meter level. There is no difference between the twisting technique for this dive and the technique for the forward somersault with one twist. However, the diver

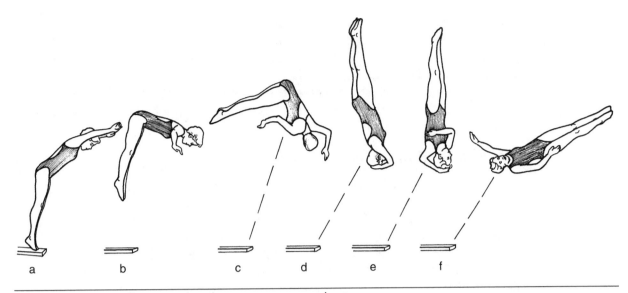

Figure 6.5 Forward somersault with one twist—inverted twist.

must learn to square out with the arms and move back to an open-pike somersault position to complete the required rotation before stretching for the entry.

The square-out motions are the same as described for the forward somersault. As the arms unwind from the twist and the seven-eighths twist point is reached, a pike action at the hips begins. This movement is timed so the pike position is assumed as the arms reach their lateral location. The diver must keep the head neutral, resisting the temptation to look for the entry before completing the square-out. If the dive is performed correctly, the diver should see the toes and the water directly in front when assuming the open-pike position. Analyze this dive, and especially the square-out sequence, carefully in figure 6.6, a through g. The same

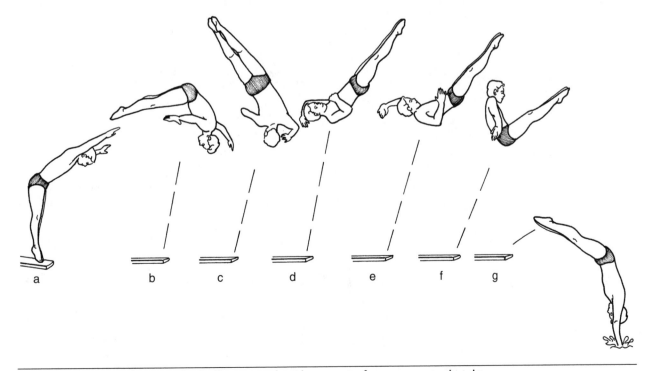

Figure 6.6 Forward one-and-a-half somersault with one twist from one-meter height.

technique is used to finish all headfirst twisting dives, regardless of the direction of the somersault (forward, backward, reverse, or inward). The diver should not move on to other headfirst entry twisting dives until he or she has mastered the square-out on this dive.

Once this dive is performed well at the three-meter level, it can be done from the one-meter board if the diver has enough time to complete the dive with good technique.

Performing Multiple Twists

The square-out in the forward somersault twisting dives and the forward one-and-a-half somersault twisting dives should occur no later than the completion of the first somersault. If the number of twists is increased, then the twist must be initiated earlier and with greater speed in order for the square-out to take place at the correct time. Also, because the straight position is held longer while executing additional twists, more somersault momentum will be needed to complete the necessary rotation. This means that to move from a full twisting somersault or a one-and-a-half somersault to a double or triple twist, the diver must do several things as the number of twists increases:

1. Create more somersault rotation from the board.
2. Don't go as deeply into the open-pike position.
3. Open the pike to initiate the twist earlier and develop more twisting force.

Because the pike is not as deep or long in the multiple twisting dives, it's not possible for the diver to look at the legs before twisting. Look at figure 6.7, a through h, and compare the starting position and the point in the somersault where the twist is initiated with the starting position and twist initiation for the forward one-and-a-half somersault dive with one twist in figure 6.6.

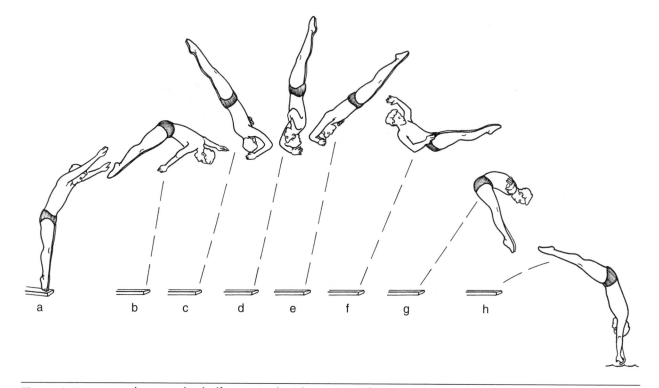

Figure 6.7 Forward one-and-a-half somersault with two twists from one-meter height.

The recommended progression of skills for the forward somersault with two, three, or even four twists is to learn these skills first on a trampoline in a spotting belt and then transfer them to a one-meter springboard. For the forward one-and-a-half somersault dive with multiple twists, the diver should again learn the basic somersault with twists on a trampoline, then move to the lead-up skill of a somersault with two, three, or four twists on the one-meter board. When execution there is good, the diver can then take the dive to the three-meter board. When the diver has developed sufficient strength and elevation to perform the forward one-and-a-half somersault dive with two or three twists well from the three-meter board, he or she can try them on the one-meter board.

Flying Somersault Method

Learning to do a good flying forward somersault is necessary before adding the twist. This can be done on the trampoline with spotting equipment or on the one-meter springboard. Figure 6.8, a through f, illustrates this dive.

The takeoff is done with the arms overhead and some pike at the hips, which is needed to create somersault rotation. However, the amount of pike in the throwing movement should be as little as possible so the upper body, head, and arms can be kept at a high angle of takeoff. As soon as possible after leaving the board, the body straightens, the arms move laterally down to shoulder level, and the head remains neutral with the eyes fixed on the far side of the pool. As the dive rotates to an inverted half somersault position, no movement should occur, but the eyes should shift their focus to the entry point. At the half somersault point, an open-pike position is performed to complete the somersault.

When this skill can be done easily and effectively, the twist can be added. After takeoff, as the body straightens from the pike position and the arms begin to move down laterally, the circular movement pattern of the arms described in the open-pike method of twisting occurs. As the arms move, the trunk turns in the

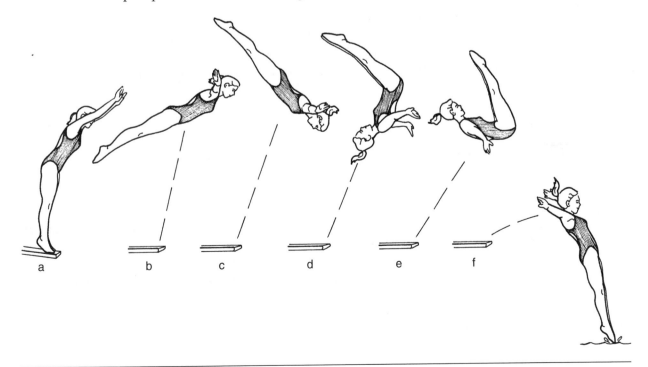

Figure 6.8 Forward flying somersault pike.

direction of the twist. As you can see in figure 6.9, a through g, the square-out and open-pike finish occur much earlier in the somersault with this technique; however, the motions of squaring out of the twist are the same.

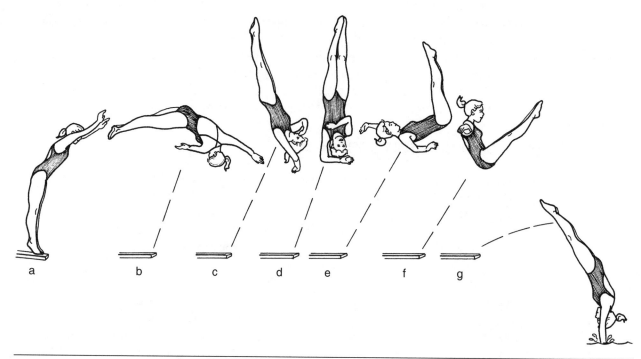

Figure 6.9 Forward one-and-a-half somersault with one twist, flying somersault start, from one-meter height.

Performing Multiple Twists

As with the open-pike twisting method, when adding twists to the dive, more somersault momentum should be created at takeoff since the straight position is held longer to complete the twists.

Obviously, as the number of twists performed increases, additional twisting force and a resultant increased speed of twist are important. However, unlike in the open-pike method, the twist does not have to be initiated earlier in the somersault because it already is early. Adding twists means the diver will square out later in the somersault.

MULTIPLE SOMERSAULT DIVES WITH TWISTS

Two and a half somersaults are performed and combined with one or two twists in several dives. There are two methods of executing these dives, depending on whether the twist is performed in the first or second somersault. I will explain these techniques in the description of each dive.

Forward Two-and-a-Half Somersault With One Twist

This dive can be executed using two distinctly different techniques. In the first, called the "full twist-in" forward two-and-a-half somersault, the twist is done at the beginning of the somersaulting action. In the second technique, termed the "full twist-out" forward two-and-a-half somersault, the twist is performed in the second somersault while the diver is coming out of the spin.

Full Twist-In

This dive is essentially a forward one-and-a-half somersault with one twist and another somersault added at the end. The additional somersault can be performed either tuck or pike. Regardless of the position chosen, the twist must be finished early in the forward one-and-a-half somersault with one twist portion of the dive, and the square-out action must occur with the legs at the horizontal position or above. This makes assuming either the tuck or pike position easier because the hands and arms can get a better grasp on the legs, resulting in a tighter position.

The critical part of this dive is the movement from the twist to the last somersault. It is here that an off-axis or unsquare direction of rotation to complete the dive occurs. Because there is not as much time to finish the square-out action as there is in the forward one-and-a-half somersault with one twist, an abbreviated or half-squaring motion is used.

The arm on the side toward which the twist is done is brought over the head and moved along the square-out path until it is in line with the shoulder or slightly beyond. The other arm moves laterally so the hand is in line with the shoulder and at chest level, with the elbow bent and close to the body. As this opening occurs, the body completes the last quarter twist, and the legs are quickly grabbed to assume the tuck or pike position.

For the tuck position, the knees must be bent and the legs drawn to the body as the hands move down to grasp the shins; for the pike position, the legs are kept straight and lifted.

During this transition from twisting to somersaulting, two major mistakes can result in a lopsided spin.

1. The lead arm in the square-out movement does not move overhead and out to the shoulder line on the normal square-out path, but moves down and across the front of the body to grab the legs. This movement causes an action–reaction situation. As the arm moves down and across in front of the body, the legs react and shift in the opposite direction, making a square final somersault impossible.

2. The legs are drawn up toward the body to assume the tuck or pike position before the hips rotate to the full-twist position during the abbreviated squaring action of the arms. This causes the legs to be out of line—in the opposite direction of the twist.

The full twist-in two-and-a-half somersault technique is shown in figure 6.10, a through j.

If spotting apparatus is available, the diver should learn a forward double somersault with one twist on the trampoline first, followed by a forward two-and-a-half somersault with one twist. The diver can then move to the one-meter board and perform a forward double somersault with one twist. When the diver can perform this well, he or she can perform the forward two-and-a-half somersault with one twist on the three-meter board.

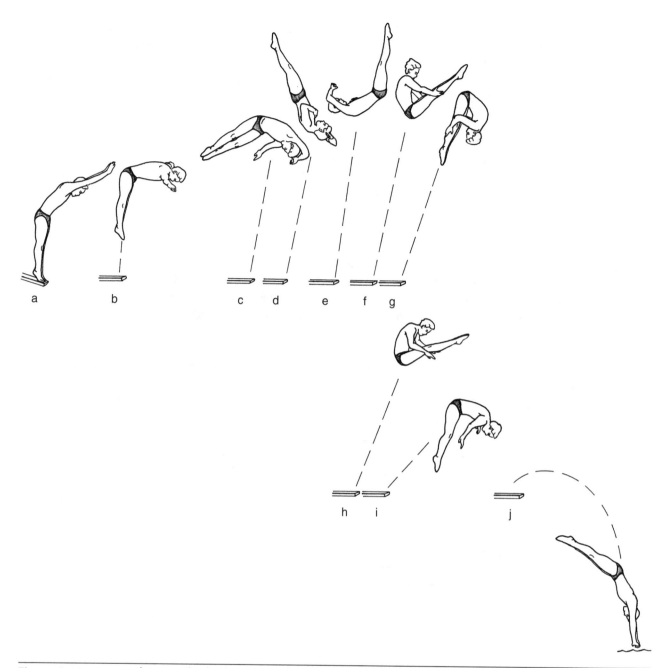

Figure 6.10   Forward two-and-a-half somersault with one twist, twist-in method, from three-meter height.

Full Twist-Out

To perform the full twist-out, the twist is executed during the second somersault and finishes with a square-out action to an open-pike position to finish the dive, just as in the forward one-and-a-half somersault with one twist. The dive can be done in either tuck or pike position, and both positions have advantages and disadvantages. The tuck spin moves faster, making it easier to complete the dive; however, the tuck position is a more difficult one from which to initiate the twisting action. The pike position is more difficult to rotate but is an easier position from which to start the twisting action. If a trampoline with overhead spotting equipment is available, I recommend that the diver first learn to twist from a pike position, then transfer the twisting action to the tuck position.

Regardless of the somersault position, a kick-out to a straight bodyline at approximately the one-and-a-half somersault point occurs, and the twist is done in an inverted position. When initiating the twist, the diver should follow the same principle of opening the body and twisting simultaneously that was presented earlier. As the legs come out of the tuck or pike, the diver turns the upper body and arms in the twisting direction and then into one of the two arm placement positions. If the kick-out takes place first, the twist will finish late and generally will be slow because the somersaulting momentum throws the body into an arched position.

The square-out method to finish this dive is the same as for a forward one-and-a-half somersault dive with one twist. The complete sequence of movements for the full twist-out two-and-a-half somersault is shown in figure 6.11, a through j.

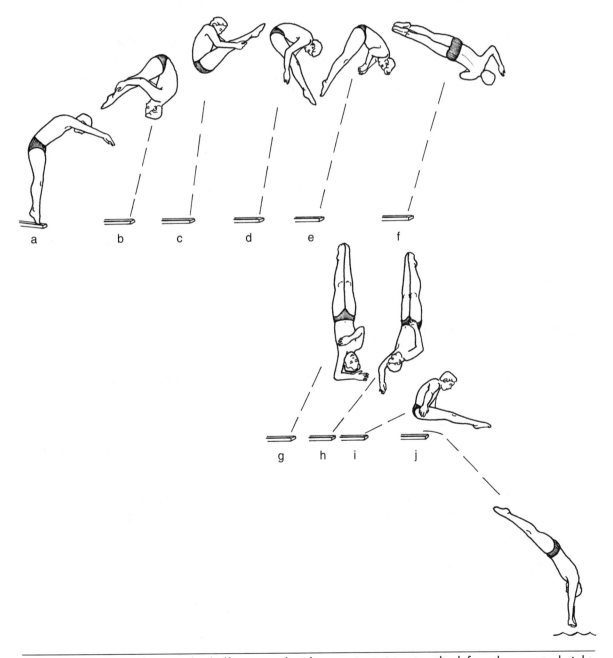

Figure 6.11 Forward two-and-a-half somersault with one twist, twist-out method, from three-meter height.

Forward Two-and-a-Half Somersault With Two Twists

Like the forward two-and-a-half somersault with one twist, this dive can be done with a double twist-in or double twist-out technique. In either case, this is an extremely difficult dive that requires great strength, speed, and lift from the springboard.

Double Twist-In

When broken down into parts, this dive is a forward one-and-a-half somersault with two twists followed by another somersault. It is performed in the same way as the full twist-in forward two-and-a-half somersault, with the exception of the added twist. In order to make the transition from twisting to somersaulting, the double twist must be completed at the same point in the somersault as it is in the single-twist dive. To accomplish this, the diver must have more somersault rotation from the springboard and perform an earlier, faster twist. These requirements make this dive extremely difficult.

Double Twist-Out

The double twist-out is performed in the same way as the full twist-out with regard to moving from the somersault to the twisting action and then squaring out to finish the dive. The addition of the second twist requires that the diver create a stronger somersault rotation at the beginning of the dive. Also, in order to do two twists in time to perform a good square-out finish, the diver must perform the kick-out from the somersault earlier (at approximately the one-and-three-eighths somersault position). The diver follows the same progression of lead-up skills when learning these dives as presented for the forward two-and-a-half somersault with one twist.

BACKWARD TWISTING DIVES

The twisting techniques for backward twisting dives are the same as those for the backward and reverse somersaulting dives. Only the takeoff mechanics differ, as described in chapter 5. For this reason, the techniques discussed in this section will apply to both types of dives.

The diver should first master the backward twisting dives before attempting the reverse twisters because it is easier to rotate the somersault in the backward twisting dives, and achieving safe distance from the board is not a factor. When the diver can perform the backward twisting dives well and complete them easily, he or she can perform the reverse twisting dives, provided that he or she has good balance and control of distance on the reverse optional dives.

Backward/Reverse Hollow Somersault

The backward/reverse somersault in straight position is the basic skill leading to the twisting dives. However, after the diver learns these dives, he or she should be introduced to an additional movement in order to better relate to the body shape used in the twisting dives.

When a backward/reverse somersault in the straight position is performed, the normal sequence of movements is to swing the arms overhead during the takeoff and arch the body while keeping the head in a neutral position. This arched body shape is then maintained throughout the dive. However, when doing a twisting dive, the diver should not arch the body, as this can result in a wobbly, slow twist. Instead, the diver should start the somersault in the straight position, with the arms overhead and the body arched, until leaving the board. At this point, as the twist begins, the body should change to a straight-line shape.

In order to simulate these movements, the diver should learn a hollow back/reverse somersault. To perform this skill, the diver initiates a back/reverse somersault in straight position and then assumes a hollow shape on the front side of the body. As the feet leave the board, the upper body stops pulling backward and curls forward into a concave shape as the rest of the body rotates into the somersault (see figure 6.12, a and b). If the diver performs the dive correctly, he or she should see the feet as they rotate through the one-quarter to three-eighths somersault positions.

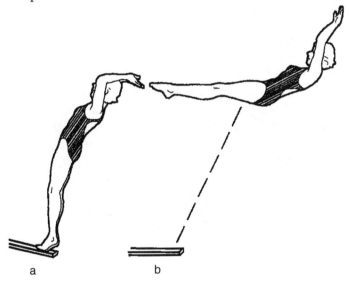

Figure 6.12   Beginning of hollow backward somersault.

When performing twisting dives, divers cannot use this hollow somersault position in the actual form described earlier because the lack of a straight bodyline will result in a wobbly twist. However, the feeling this type of somersault creates, moving from the arched position, can be transferred to twisting dives. This will be discussed in the explanation of each dive.

Before beginning the discussion of the complex multiple backward twisting dives, a more basic type of twisting dive needs to be addressed.

Backward/Reverse Somersault or One-and-a-Half Somersault With Half Twist

These dives can be performed with one of two methods: the single-arm turn or the double-arm turn. Regardless of which technique is selected, the hollow backward/reverse somersault should be learned first, to help in establishing the correct body position when starting the twist.

Single-Arm Turn

To perform the backward/reverse somersault or backward/reverse one-and-a-half somersault with half twist using the single-arm turn action, the diver executes the following sequence of movements:

1. The diver establishes the takeoff position as the feet are ready to leave the board, with the body arched, the arms extended straight and parallel overhead, and the head neutral between the arms.
2. Just as the feet leave the board, the upper body becomes fixed in its position and the beginning of the hollow somersault feeling occurs (the body flattens).
3. Simultaneously with the flattening of the body, the diver bends the arm on the twisting side and brings it down in front of the body to a position in front of the chest with the elbow flexed approximately 90 degrees. The other arm remains stretched overhead.
4. As the arm on the twisting side is brought down, the head and trunk turn in the twist direction.

Due to the movement toward a hollow somersault position, the body should move from an arched to a straight shape, and the head should be in a neutral position as the twist starts. These two factors contribute to a twisting action that is smooth and flat, rather than arched and wobbly.

When the twist nears the half twist point, the arm located across the chest straightens and moves horizontally to a lateral shoulder-high position. At the same time, the arm overhead moves down in line with the body to the same place on the opposite side. As the end of the arm movement to the lateral position occurs, the body can move to a tuck or pike position by drawing the legs into the body. The dive is finished by grabbing the shins in a tuck, grabbing the back of the legs in a closed pike, or simply remaining with the arms to the side in an open-pike position (the easiest and most popular method). Depending on the dive being performed, the come-out can then be either to a feetfirst or headfirst entry.

Figure 6.13, a through e, shows the single-arm turn technique. Regardless of the direction of rotation or number of somersaults, the key requirements for good execution are the same:

- Establish a square line of somersault from the board, with both arms overhead at takeoff.
- Maintain a slightly hollow position as the arm on the twisting side moves down in front of the chest.
- Move to a tuck or pike finish at the end of the arm action. Moving from the straight body shape to the tuck or pike too early will cause an off-axis dive on entry.

Double-Arm Turn

The takeoff position for this technique is the same as for the single-arm turn. As the feet leave the board, the diver keeps the arms straight and parallel overhead as the shoulders and upper body turn in the direction of the twist and the body moves from an arched position to a straight line with the head in a neutral position. This position is held until a half twist is completed. The dive is then finished by moving directly to a tuck, pike, or open-pike position for the remainder of the somersault, or the arms can be spread to a lateral position and a flying

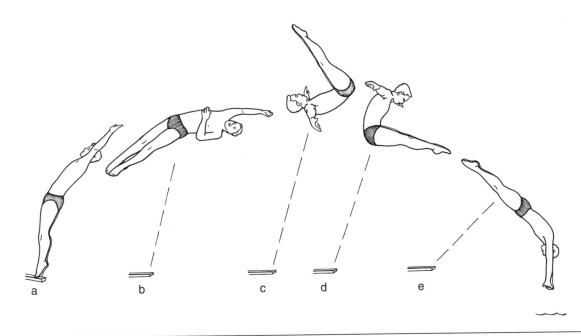

Figure 6.13   Backward one-and-a-half somersault with half twist, single-arm turn technique, from one-meter height.

somersault action performed before assuming a body position for the completion of the dive.

If moving directly to the somersault position (no flying action), the diver moves the arms and legs in a direct line to the desired tuck or closed pike, or spreads the arms laterally while moving the legs to the open-pike position.

When performing the flying somersault action in the middle of the transition from twist to somersault, the diver keeps the body straight as the arms move to their lateral position. The line of sight is fixed momentarily on the entry point below until the movement to the tuck, pike, or open pike is made. Figure 6.14, a through g, shows the double-arm turn technique.

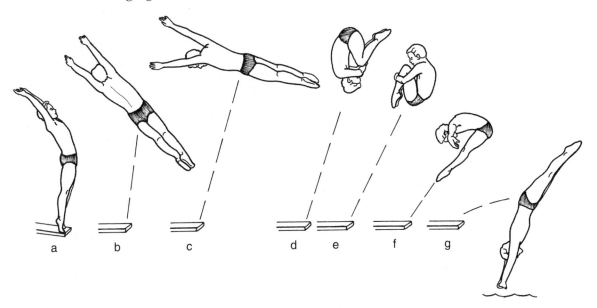

Figure 6.14   Reverse one-and-a-half somersault with half twist in tuck position, double-arm turn technique, from one-meter height.

Any of these techniques are acceptable and can score equally well when executed properly. Which method is used depends on the level of the springboard or platform used, how much time is available for making the movements, and which technique the diver can perform best. Obviously, the flying somersault action takes the most time to perform, and this must be taken into account when making a choice.

Backward Somersault With One and a Half Twists

The sequence of movements used to execute this dive is the same for all the multiple twisting dives. Once the skills are learned correctly for the one-and-a-half twist, the door is opened to effectively adding more twists, when sufficient strength, quickness, and elevation from the board are present.

As with forward twisting, the best way to learn the movements for a one-and-a-half twist is by using the trampoline with overhead spotting equipment. Once the skills are mastered in this situation, transferring the dive to the one-meter board is an easy task. If a trampoline and spotting equipment are not available, then the same learning sequence should take place on the board.

The hollow somersault is the foundation for the start of this dive. Whether doing backward or reverse twisting dives, the corresponding hollow somersault must be performed correctly and completed relatively easily before attempting twisting actions. If the diver is struggling to execute the basic somersault, he or she should delay working on the twist because correct technique will be compromised to complete the dive.

Following are the four steps a diver should follow in learning the backward somersault with one and a half twists:

STEP 1   Do a hollow back somersault.

STEP 2   Start a hollow somersault and, after the arms reach the overhead takeoff position and the feet leave the trampoline or springboard, begin the twisting movement by dropping the arm on the twisting side (left arm if twisting left and vice versa). Keep the arm straight and move it down and back so it points to the trampoline bed or the water directly behind and a few feet from the takeoff point. The upper body follows the arm with a turning motion in the same direction and the head remains neutral while the other arm remains extended overhead. As the twist begins, the action of the hollow somersault is used to change from an arched to a straight bodyline.

After several attempts, a somersault with a half twist should be accomplished. Work on this phase of starting the twist should continue until refinement of the movements allows three-quarters to one full twist to be completed without making any added movements of the arms. One arm should be up and one arm down throughout the twist.

The coach can assist with verbal commands, which help the diver concentrate on the right move at the right time. Just prior to extension for the takeoff into the somersault, the coach can give the command "hollow," and just as the takeoff occurs, he or she can use the cue "drop." The coach should give these commands right before the action being targeted is to occur so the diver can focus on that skill and still have adequate time to react at the correct moment. Figure 6.15, a through g, shows the backward somersault with one twist.

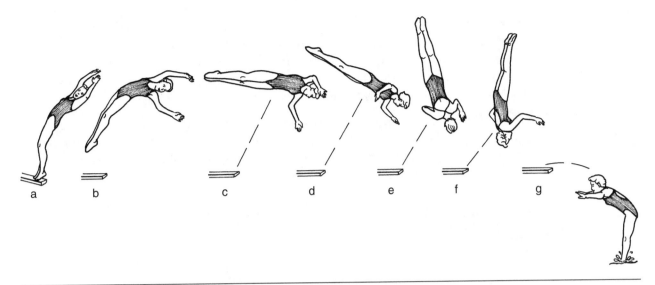

Figure 6.15 Backward somersault with one twist.

STEP 3 Perform the same movements as in step 2 and, at approximately the half twist position, move the arms into the twisting position by making a circular pattern as described in forward twisting. If twisting to the left, the circle will be in the clockwise direction; vice versa if twisting to the right. Bring the top (overhead) arm down and across the chest so the hand rests just below the opposite armpit. Simultaneously, move the bottom arm directly upward and over the head so the upper arm is against the side of the head and the forearm rests on top of the head. The bottom arm should move in an upward and slightly backward direction to guard against it coming in front of the face to reach its destination. Throughout this arm movement, the head should remain still and the body straight. Again, verbal commands can be helpful. The coach can give the same "hollow" and "drop" cues as in step 2 and add a third command, "wrap," to signal the time to move the arms into the twist position.

Practice this step until one and a half twists can be performed (see figure 6.16, a-g).

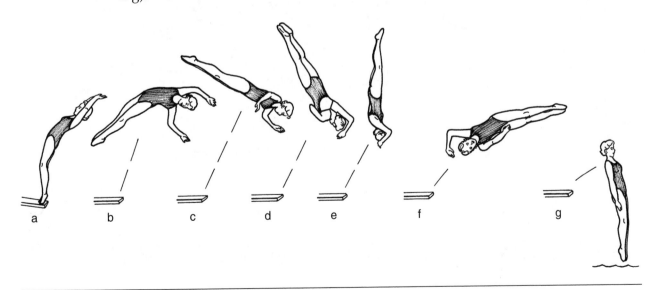

Figure 6.16 Backward somersault with one and a half twists.

STEP 4   Stop the twist by using the same square-out action as described for the forward twisting dives. Move the arm over the head in an upward and lateral path out and down to shoulder level, with the arm straight. Move the arm across the chest in a direct line to a straight position at shoulder level. The head should remain in a neutral position throughout the squaring action.

If the diver chooses the other arm-twisting position (arms together), steps 1 and 2 are performed in the same way; the difference occurs in step 3, when the arms are "wrapped" into the body. For the beginner, the split-arm twisting position is better for accelerating the twist and easier for squaring out.

Backward One-and-a-Half Somersault With One and a Half Twists

The next dive progression is a backward one-and-a-half somersault with one and a half twists. This is best done from the three-meter board first so there is adequate time to execute all the movements without rushing. When the diver can perform this dive effectively from the three-meter level, he or she can then move to the one-meter board, if physically capable.

Moving from the somersault to the one-and-a-half somersault requires the same technique as described for the forward one-and-a-half somersault with one twist. The entire backward one-and-a-half somersault with one and a half twists is shown in figure 6.17, a through g.

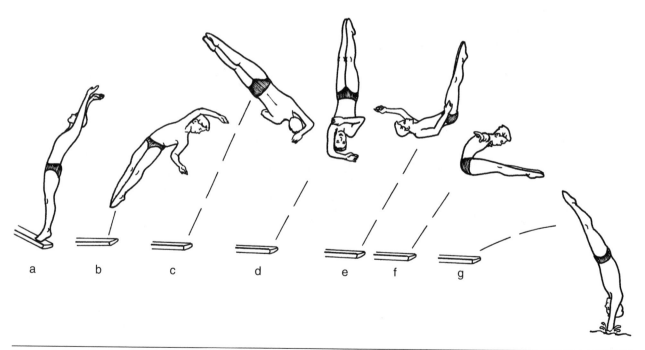

a   b   c   d   e   f   g

Figure 6.17   Backward one-and-a-half somersault with one and a half twists from one-meter height.

Reverse Somersault or One-and-a-Half Somersault With One and a Half Twists

If a diver can do the backward one-and-a-half somersault with one and a half twists from the three-meter level and a good, safe hollow reverse somersault from the one-meter board, it is time to do the reverse somersault with one and a half twists. The diver executes this dive by performing the hollow somersault first, as a lead-up skill and to set the speed of somersault rotation, and then moving on to the reverse somersault with one and a half twists from the one-meter board. When the diver can perform this skill well, he or she can do the reverse one-and-a-half somersault with one and a half twists at the three-meter height. The entire reverse one-and-a-half somersault with one and a half twists is shown in figure 6.18, a through h.

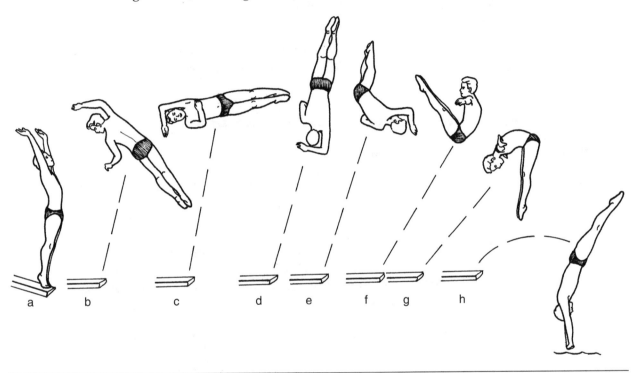

Figure 6.18 Reverse one-and-a-half somersault with one and a half twists from one-meter height.

Performing Multiple Twists

As with the forward twisting dives, the square-out action is extremely difficult to perform with backward and reverse twisting dives if the somersault rotation passes the single somersault position before the required number of twists is completed. Actually, it is best if the twist can be finished earlier than the first somersault position so that squaring out becomes easier. Usually, this timing is not a problem for dives with one and a half twists. However, when executing two and a half or three and a half twists, timing twists and somersaults is a key factor in successful performance.

When performing additional twists, several things must be done in order to complete the required number of twists before passing the square-out point in the somersault:

1. The diver must create more somersault rotation at takeoff because the body will be in the straight position longer in order to complete the greater number of twists.

2. The diver must start as early as possible without affecting the axis of somersault rotation. Twisting too early causes the somersault to leave the board sideways. The diver should concentrate on getting the arms to a complete overhead takeoff position before dropping the arm on the twisting side to start the twist.

3. The diver must develop a faster twist by performing a more forceful circular motion of the arms and keeping the arms in as tight to the body as possible during the twist.

Because twisting dives involve so many factors that can negatively affect performance, the following checklist of common mistakes may help locate problems.

Common Problems and Causes in Twisting Dives

Problem	Possible Causes
The twist is too slow.	1. Adequate somersault rotation is not established first.
	2. The arms are brought directly into the body.
	3. Excessive body arch or pike occurs in the twist.
	4. The elbows are significantly away from the body in the twist.
	5. The arms, head, and upper body turn weakly to initiate the twist.
The twist is wobbly.	1. The body position is arched, piked, or tilted laterally in the upper body.
	2. Head position is forward, backward, or tilted laterally toward a shoulder.
	3. The elbows stick out too far.
The finish is not square.	1. The somersault is off axis or jumps to one side or the other on takeoff.
	2. The diver has the head down and forward in the square-out; thus, he or she sees the water below before finishing the square-out motion.

3. The top or lead arm in the square-out moves down and forward in front of the body.

4. The arm across the chest moves toward the entry before finishing the square-out, or the arm sets behind the body rather than in a lateral placement.

5. A pike at the hips occurs in the square-out before completing the last eighth of the twist.

6. The twist is finished beyond the single somersault point of rotation.

7. The square-out is too late. It should begin in the last quarter portion of the desired number of twists.

CALLING TWISTERS

Most divers like the security of verbal cues during their first attempts at new dives. Because the squaring-out action for twisting dives begins during the last three-eighths to one-quarter twist of the dive, the verbal call to come out of the twist should be given just as the diver enters the last half twist of the dive. This allows time to react to the command and begin the square-out at the appropriate point.

SUMMARY

Patience in teaching and learning the twisting dives is extremely important to successful execution of the complicated maneuvers required. Each prerequisite skill must be learned correctly before moving to the next step. Basic flaws in execution or twist position may become permanent if not corrected early. Diligence in the beginning stages of learning will be rewarded with beautiful, flowing, spectacular twisting dives.

Platform Dives

Platform diving is easier than springboard diving because the takeoff surface is stationary. This eliminates many of the balance and timing problems that make springboard diving so complicated. However, the platform diver needs the courage to perform dives at the higher heights, and the physical strength and durability to absorb the impact with the water, especially from the seven-and-a-half- and ten-meter platforms.

If good springboard skills are learned first, platform diving is much simpler. The balance and control needed for the takeoff, correct mechanics of execution, spatial orientation, and entry techniques of springboard diving all transfer to platform diving. A good springboard background is a valuable foundation for the platform event.

Because the techniques of executing the dives are the same for springboard and platform diving, it is not necessary to discuss the mechanics of the dives in this chapter (with the exception of the armstand group). The focus here will be on the skills every diver should learn at the one-meter, three-meter, and five-meter levels before moving up to seven-and-a-half- and ten-meter heights.

CONTROL OF TAKEOFFS

When divers move to higher and higher platform levels, they frequently become somewhat afraid and tentative in initiating dives. This can result in increased lean from the platform and a delayed push-off with the legs, both of which cause a loss of control. The greater the lean, the greater the somersault rotation.

To avoid this situation, the beginning diver should jump strongly and boldly from the platform, regardless of its height. A strong jump in the takeoff is key to controlled dives, whether basic or optional. If this concept is followed from the start of platform training, it will become ingrained. This is a good reason to start training from deck level, or from a low-level (half-, one-, or three-meter) platform with the basic takeoffs, jumps, and dives before moving to the five-meter height and beyond.

TAKEOFFS

Seven basic takeoffs can be done from the platform: standing forward, inward, backward, standing reverse, running forward, walking reverse, and armstand. These will be discussed in the order in which they should be learned. All the takeoffs should be practiced from the one-, three-, and five-meter heights. If a one-meter platform is not available, the takeoffs can be practiced from the pool deck if it has a safe, nonskid surface.

Standing Forward Takeoff

The diver stands on the front edge of the platform with the arms straight and parallel directly overhead, the palms facing either forward or inward, and the shoulders in a natural, relaxed position. To start the takeoff, the diver rises high on the toes and stretches the arms, shoulders, and body upward. The head must be level and the eyes focused on the water in front. The diver lowers the body into a shallow squat by dropping the heels and flexing the knees and hips. As this squatting movement takes place, the shoulders move downward, the elbows bend over the top of the head, and the weight shifts forward over the toes in preparation for the takeoff. In a sequential pattern, the hands and arms throw upward, the shoulders lift up to the ears, and the body extends from the hips, knees, ankles, and toes into a jump, with the arms held overhead (see figure 7.1, a-f).

The squat and extension movements are performed as quickly and powerfully as possible to generate maximum lift from the platform in the jump. The amount of knee and hip bend in the downward portion of the takeoff depends on leg strength and quickness; however, a moderate amount of downward sitting movement is necessary. If the squat is too deep, movement speed will be lost, and if the squat is too shallow, a weak jump will result. Experimentation will allow the diver to determine how much leg flexion results in the best takeoff.

A variation of the starting position for this takeoff is to stand with the arms at the sides. The arms lift laterally to the overhead position, and as they pass head level, the shoulders lift and the diver rises up on the toes as described earlier. The rest of the takeoff is performed in the same manner as for a jump.

Figure 7.1   Standing forward takeoff with jump.

Inward Takeoff

The inward takeoff movements are performed in the same way as those for the standing forward takeoff, except that the diver stands backward on the end of the platform. One-third to one-half the foot surface should be on the platform. The starting position can be with the arms overhead or at the sides. The difference in the inward takeoff lies in the balance during the squatting phase and in the direction of push during the final extension phase. When the squat begins, the balance is maintained over the balls of the feet until the body stops moving downward. It is important during the downward movement that the ankles drop to a fully stretched position (dorsiflexion) so a powerful ankle extension can occur in the final phase of the takeoff. In the extension phase, the hands and arms are thrown in an upward and forward direction while the legs extend, pushing upward and backward off the toes to move the body up and away from the platform into a jump.

The movement of the body in this press is an up-down-up action done very quickly to achieve a good bouncing motion and corresponding strong jump from the platform (see figures 7.2, a-e, and 7.3, a-g).

Backward Takeoff

The diver stands backward on the edge of the platform with one-third to one-half of the feet on the platform and the heels level. The arms can be located at the sides or lateral at shoulder height. The head is kept level and the eyes sight down the runway. From either starting position, the arms lift laterally to an overhead Y position. As the arms pass head level, the ankles extend as the diver rises up on the toes and the body stretches upward. The squat phase then begins as the diver

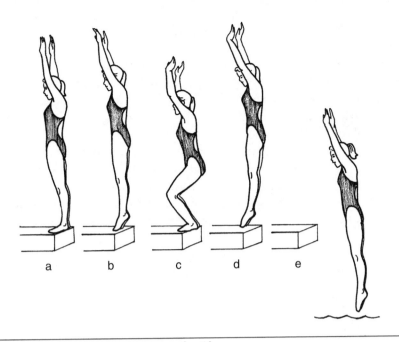

Figure 7.2 Inward takeoff with jump, arms overhead.

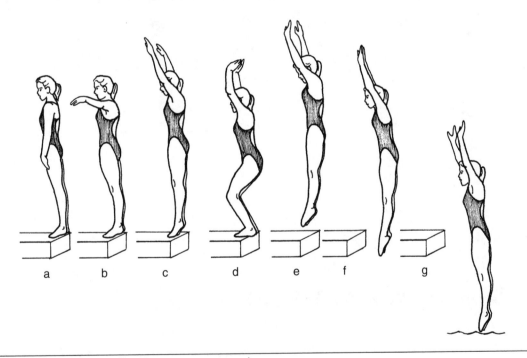

Figure 7.3 Inward takeoff with jump, arms at sides.

drops the ankles, flexes at the knees and hips, and aligns the shoulders over the thighs. The depth of the squat is much greater than that in the forward/inward takeoffs, as the angle at the knee joint should be 90 degrees or greater, if leg strength allows.

As the body moves downward, the arms move back behind the body. At the bottom of the squat, the arms are stretched behind the body at or slightly below shoulder level, and the heels are level. The head is kept level throughout this phase. Keeping the arms straight and parallel, the diver swings them downward, forward, and then upward. During this period of armswing, there is some extension of the hips and knees. When the arms pass head level in the upswing, major extension of the hips and knees occurs, with maximum velocity. As the arms pass overhead, the trunk moves backward to begin movement away from the platform as the hips, knees, ankles, and toes complete extension into a backward jump, with the body straight and the arms straight and parallel overhead (see figure 7.4, a-h).

When beginning the squat phase, the diver can think of the sequence of movements as legs-arms-legs. As the legs squat, the arms are getting into position to swing (legs). As the arms swing from their position behind the body to head level in front, the legs are relatively inactive (arms). Finally, as the arms pass head level and move overhead, the legs are extending vigorously (legs).

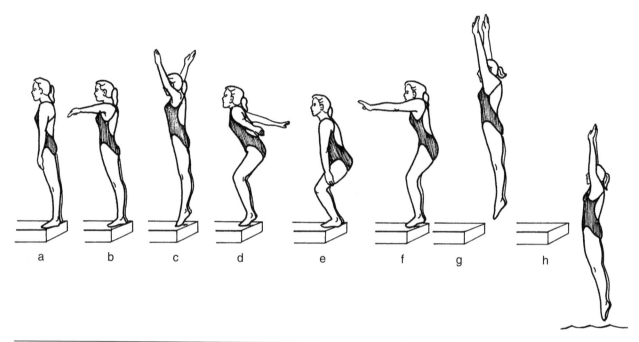

Figure 7.4   Backward takeoff with jump.

Standing Reverse Takeoff

The diver stands at the end of the platform facing forward with the head erect, eyes sighting outward to the water, body aligned, arms at the sides or lateral at shoulder level, and the feet together with the toes even with the edge of the platform. Some divers curl the toes over the edge to get a good grip; however, this technique contributes to jumping too far away from the platform on takeoff because the diver can lean forward and push off the forward edge. When the toes are even with the edge, the diver must push up off the top of the platform surface.

The standing reverse takeoff is performed with the same motions as those of the backward takeoff. The difference is in the balance and direction of extension. During the squat phase, the shoulders should align over the knees and toes, with the heels in contact with the platform. A line connecting the shoulders, knees, and toes should be straight. The balance is over the balls of the feet. As the arms pass above head level in the upswing, the hips are driven upward and forward causing the body to arch as final extension occurs and the diver moves away from the platform (see figure 7.5, a-h).

At a more advanced stage, the diver can perform a reverse jump from the pool deck or one-meter level as a lead-up skill. Just before the feet leave the platform, the hips are driven forward and upward more forcefully than in a jump, causing some reverse rotation so entry is feetfirst at a 45-degree angle backward toward the platform (see figure 7.6, a-h).

Figure 7.5   Standing reverse takeoff with jump.

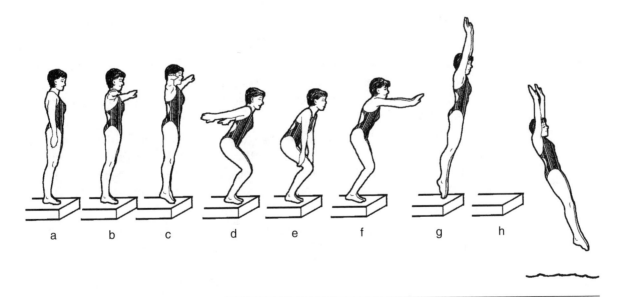

Figure 7.6   Standing reverse takeoff with reverse jump.

Practice should take place on the forward, backward, reverse, and inward take-offs with jumps at all platform levels up to five meters until control, balance, and proper distance are achieved. Actually, the standing forward and backward jumps can also be done at the seven-and-a-half- and ten-meter heights as preparatory skills for dives to be done later. These jumps acclimate the diver to the higher levels and the timing of the drop to the water. The jumps also teach the balance and strong jump action needed for control in the other dives. Divers can do many repetitions of these skills because there is no problem with the force of impact with the water causing fatigue, as is the case in headfirst entries from these heights.

Running Forward Takeoff

The forward running approach is a short, dancelike skill that must be shaped to suit the diver's taste and ability. The steps can be done either walking or running. Many variations of the armswing, as well as various rhythms and timings, can be used. Regardless of the type of approach he or she develops, the diver should follow certain basic fundamentals in order to accomplish a good takeoff with balance, control, and good distance.

Number of Steps

The number of steps should correspond to the springboard approach so there is no confusion regarding which foot to begin with and which foot to hurdle from. Using a similar approach simplifies the learning process.

Head and Eyes

The head is kept level throughout the approach, and the eyes focus on the end of the platform where the landing and takeoff will occur. During the hurdle, just before landing on the end of the platform, the diver shifts his or her vision to the water out in front while keeping the head level.

Arms

No matter which swing pattern or timing is used, three factors are most important as the arms are preparing for the takeoff:

1. The arms reach a position directly over the head in a straight and parallel alignment *before* the feet land for the takeoff. This is necessary because the takeoff occurs so quickly that effective use of the arms is not possible unless they are in position first.

2. The path of the arms to their overhead position is lateral. If the arms are brought up in a lateral-forward path, the trunk will tend to bend over too much on the takeoff. If the arms are brought directly up the front, or if the arms move up laterally behind the bodyline, a backward lean on takeoff can occur.

3. The arms are kept straight throughout the approach and the hurdle until just before the feet make contact with the platform, when the elbows bend and the hands drop close to the head. The wrists may even cross as the arms bend. This position prepares the hands and arms for a strong upward, forward throwing motion during the takeoff.

Upper Body

The diver should maintain the torso in a vertical or slightly forward of vertical position throughout the approach and the landing on the end of the platform. As the landing and takeoff take place, the center of balance shifts forward, depending on the dive being performed.

Legs

As the hurdle to the end takes place, the legs flex at the hip and knee joints in preparation for the landing. The legs are positioned in front of the upper body so they can act as brakes to control the strong horizontal momentum that is present as a result of the run.

A very quick landing of the body weight onto the legs and a corresponding recoil into the takeoff should occur. The less time the diver spends in contact with the platform, the stronger the jump into the takeoff will be.

Feet

The last step prior to the hurdle is taken with the heel contacting the platform first. The foot then rocks forward until the push-off occurs with the toes at the end of the platform. When performing basic dives such as the forward one-and-a-half somersault or forward one-and-a-half somersault with one twist, the diver should land on the end of the platform on the balls of the feet or the whole foot, with an immediate and explosive extension into the takeoff to control distance and rotation. When doing forward optional dives such as a forward three-and-a-half somersault, the diver should land on the heels with the front of the foot slightly elevated, followed by a rock forward onto the balls of the feet as a strong and quick leg and ankle extension occurs. Landing on the heels first allows the weight to shift forward more easily and aids in achieving proper distance from the platform. The rocking movement, although very short in duration, provides more time to initiate somersault rotation.

Hurdle

Unlike springboard diving, the platform hurdle has a long, low trajectory. When the diver is moving through the air after the push-off into the hurdle, the feet should be only a few inches above the platform surface. The length of the hurdle depends on the speed of the approach. Hurdles taken with the walking approach are three to four feet long, whereas hurdles taken with the running approach are four to six feet long.

Keeping all these fundamentals in mind, let's construct the forward platform approach. Whatever approach is selected, practice should take place with a forward jump, first at the one-, three-, and five-meter levels, and later from the seven-and-a-half- and ten-meter platforms. The running forward approach with a jump is valuable in learning balance and control of distance with the increased horizontal velocity.

Walking Method

This is the simplest and easiest approach for the beginner to learn; divers should learn this before moving to the more difficult running method.

The diver marks off the approach on the deck by taking the appropriate number of steps and a low three- to four-foot hurdle, taking off from one foot and landing on two feet. During practice, the length and speed of the approach can be adjusted so it feels good.

Divers should remember one point when marking off any approach: After taking the hurdle and landing, the place where the tip of the big toe lands is where the heels, not the toes, should be placed when turning around to perform the approach in the direction from which it was measured. Failing to do this is a common mistake that adds a one-foot length to the measured approach.

To combine the arm and leg actions, the diver performs the walking approach by lifting the arms straight and laterally in a gradual movement during the last three steps prior to the hurdle so the arms are directly overhead when pushing off into the hurdle. If only three steps are taken, the arms must begin their lateral and upward movement on the first step. When a four-step approach is used, the arms begin to move on the second step; for the five-step approach, they move on the third step. Study the four-step walking forward approach in figure 7.7, a through i.

a   b   c   d   e   f   g   h

Figure 7.7   Four-step forward approach, walking.

Running Method

There are two basic ways to use the arms in the running approach. The first method is a combination of forward and backward armswing and lateral armlift, whereas the second method involves just forward and backward swings. In both cases, during the final two steps prior to the hurdle the arms are moved laterally to an overhead position prior to landing on the end of the platform. Therefore, even though the various approaches may appear different, the same fundamentals apply in all cases.

Because three, four, or five steps are usually taken in the approach, the next sections describe each type of approach as well as both types of armswing. By using imagination and ingenuity, divers and coaches can use the basic patterns described to create the running takeoff.

Three-Step Run

The diver stands with the body aligned, the head level, and the eyes focused on the end of the platform. He or she lifts the arms laterally halfway to shoulder height, and while taking the first step, swings the arms down to the sides and upward and forward to a horizontal and parallel position in front of the body. The diver takes the next two steps in a slow running fashion; during step 2 the arms swing from their forward position back to the sides, and during step 3 the arms swing in a continuous motion laterally up to shoulder height. The hurdle then begins as the arms continue to move to their straight and parallel alignment overhead; the arms reach this position just before the diver lands back on the platform. The first step is taken at a moderate speed, and the next two steps change to a loping type of running speed (see figure 7.8, a-i).

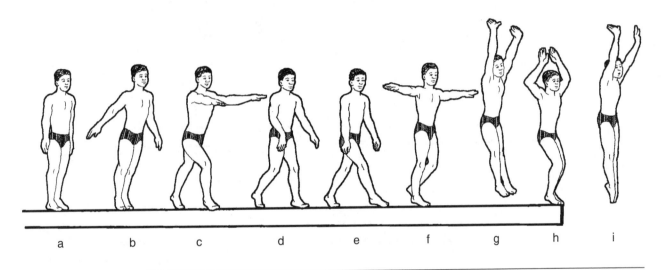

| a | b | c | d | e | f | g | h | i |

Figure 7.8 Forward approach, three-step run.

Four-Step Run

Before taking the first step, the diver swings the arms forward to a parallel position 45 degrees below horizontal in preparation for the arm movement in the first step. As in the three-step run, the first step is taken at a moderate speed. As the step is taken, the arms swing back toward the body and up laterally to shoulder height. In the second step, speed is increased to a slow running tempo for the remainder of the steps. As the second step occurs, the arms swing down to the sides and in a continuous motion up to a parallel alignment in front of the body at shoulder height. In the third and fourth steps, the arms swing down to the sides and laterally up to shoulder height again. As the hurdle begins, the arms continue to move upward to an overhead position prior to landing on the platform. These arm patterns allow the approach to be done in a very rhythmic, aesthetic manner (see figure 7.9, a-k).

Figure 7.9 Forward approach, four-step run.

If this armswing pattern is done with a five-step run, the first two steps are taken at walking speed while the arms move forward in front of the body on step 1 and back to the sides and laterally up to shoulder height in step 2. The rest of the run and movements are the same.

Five-Step Run

The following text describes a forward and backward armswing action for a five-step approach. Although there is some difference in the first three steps, the arm action in the last two steps and the hurdle are the same as for the three- and four-step approaches.

The diver takes the first step at walking speed, keeping the arms parallel and swinging them up in front of the body 45 degrees below horizontal, then breaks into a slow run for the last four steps. When the second step is taken, the arms swing on a straight line back behind the body approximately one foot. During the third step, the arms swing back to the same position as in the first step. In the fourth and fifth steps, the arms swing back to the sides and laterally up to shoulder height. As the hurdle begins, the arms continue to move to an overhead position prior to landing (see figure 7.10, a-j). This run can also be done in a very rhythmic, dancelike way.

Figure 7.10 Forward approach, five-step run.

Whatever approach is chosen, it should be smooth, flowing, and graceful followed by a forceful, bold takeoff. The diver should practice first on dry land, then on the pool deck, and then on the various platform levels. Practicing the running forward takeoff with a jump and an open-pike forward dive from the one-, three, and five-meter levels is the best way to develop control of balance, rotational speed, and distance.

Walking Reverse Takeoff

Although most divers prefer the standing reverse takeoff, some use the walking method. If the standing takeoff is not particularly effective, the walking method may be the answer.

One advantage of the walking technique is that it provides horizontal momentum prior to takeoff. This may alleviate the fear of being too close to the platform for divers who struggle with that problem.

In performing the walking reverse takeoff, the diver should take the same number of steps as in the forward approach. The drive leg of the hurdle should be used as the takeoff leg.

If the diver uses a three-step walk, in the first step the arms stay parallel and swing forward to a position approximately 45 degrees below horizontal. During the second step, the arms swing back behind the body, and in the last step the arms swing forcefully forward and up to an overhead takeoff position. How far up and back overhead the arms move in the takeoff depends on the dive being done.

When using a four- or five-step approach, the arms hang at the sides during the first step of the four-step method and the first two steps of the five-step approach. The diver then performs the same movement pattern as used in the three-step approach for the remaining steps.

The size of the steps should be a natural length for a medium speed walk; however, the last step should be somewhat longer to allow for an increase in speed and force in preparation for the takeoff. Divers and coaches should experiment with various last-step lengths to find what looks good, is comfortable, and affords a strong jump from the platform.

The takeoff is performed from one foot with the foot placed on the end of the platform after the last step. The takeoff foot is placed on the end of the platform with the heel first. Then, as the foot rocks down on the sole of the foot, the hips and knee joints flex and the arms and other leg begin a swinging movement forward with the ankle extended. The arms remain straight, but the swinging leg bends so as not to drag across the surface of the platform. As the arms and leg pass the drive leg, the diver rises up on the toes and extends the drive leg forcefully while the arms and swinging leg continue upward to create lift and whatever rotation is needed.

There are two methods of completing the lifting action of the swinging leg; the method used depends on the type of dive to be done. If the dive performed is in the straight or pike position, or is a reverse twisting dive, as the foot passes the edge of the platform, the knee straightens and the leg is lifted to a position as high as possible before the other foot leaves the platform. When the pushing leg does leave the platform, it is kept straight and lifted to bring the legs together as quickly as possible. Figure 7.11, a through h, illustrates this type of takeoff.

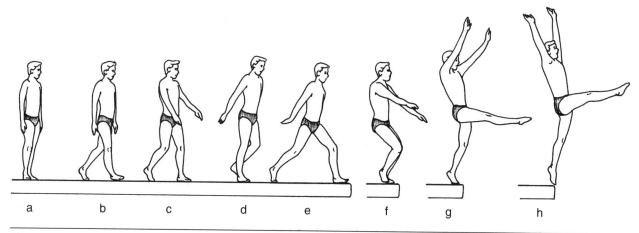

Figure 7.11   Running reverse takeoff with straight leg.

When performing a tuck position dive, the diver keeps the swinging leg bent while lifting it up in front of the body. After the foot passes the edge of the platform, the thigh is lifted to approximately waist height while the knee bends to a 90-degree angle. When the drive leg leaves the platform, it is lifted alongside the other leg and flexed as the arms come down from their overhead position to assume a tuck position. Figure 7.12, a through i, shows this method of takeoff.

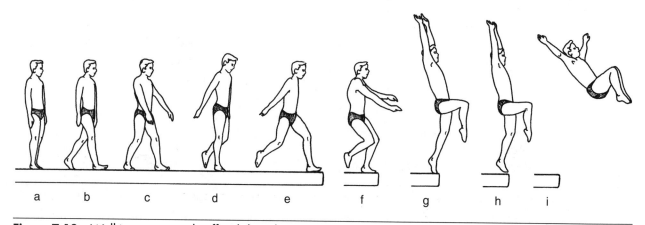

Figure 7.12   Walking reverse takeoff with bent leg.

Armstand (Handstand) Takeoff

Balance and proper alignment must be learned while performing an armstand on dry land. The diver should first practice the armstand against a wall, placing the hands on the floor shoulder-width apart a few inches from the wall, with the back facing the wall. The diver kicks up into the armstand by lifting one leg to the wall and then bringing the other leg up so that both feet are against the wall at the start of the exercise. The diver then moves the feet off the wall to balance the armstand. After repeating this drill until he or she has achieved a feel for balance, the diver can then practice kicking up and holding the armstand without the wall. The coach can help the diver achieve good body alignment by manually manipulating the hips and rib cage until a straight line in the back occurs.

When the diver can hold the armstand reasonably well, he or she can begin practicing from the edge of the pool or a half- or one-meter platform. Following are some basic points in performing this armstand:

- The hands are positioned shoulder-width apart.
- The fingers are spread and overlap the edge of the platform by no more than the first or second joint of the middle three fingers.
- The shoulders are directly over the edge of the takeoff surface before the kick-up starts.
- The eyes focus on the edge of the takeoff surface between the hands.

Ultimately, the diver should learn an armstand "press." A press starts from a tuck or pike position; the feet are lifted from the platform, the balance is shifted to the hands, and the legs are lifted up to the armstand by whatever method is chosen.

Figures 7.13 through 7.15 show the most popular armstand press techniques: the tuck press, pike straddle press, and pike press. When performing backward armstand dives, the diver can use the same three types of press; however, the starting position needs to be adapted. The diver stands backward on the end of the platform with half of the foot on the platform. Instead of placing the hands in front of the legs, as in the forward armstand, the diver places the hands at the side of the feet for the tuck and pike presses and between the legs for the straddle press. In all cases the hands are positioned with the heel of the hand even with the edge of the platform. The rest of the press techniques are the same as those in the forward armstand.

When the diver has learned the armstand by kick-up or press method with good balance and bodyline, it is time to learn the three directions of rotation that can be done from this takeoff. These will be presented in a later section of this chapter.

ENTRY DRILLS, LINEUPS, AND OPTIONAL COME-OUTS

Practice should continue on the takeoffs and various jumps described to improve balance and control. At the same time, training should begin on the entry drills, lineups, and optional come-out techniques described in chapter 4. A review of chapter 4 may be helpful because the following sections will not explain those skills again but will merely refer to them. If a three-meter platform is not

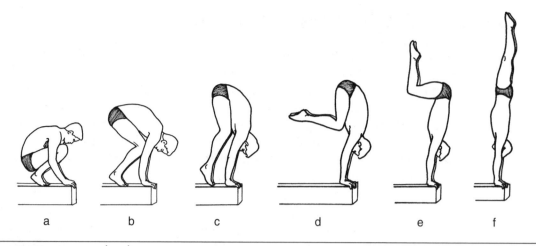

Figure 7.13 Armstand tuck press.

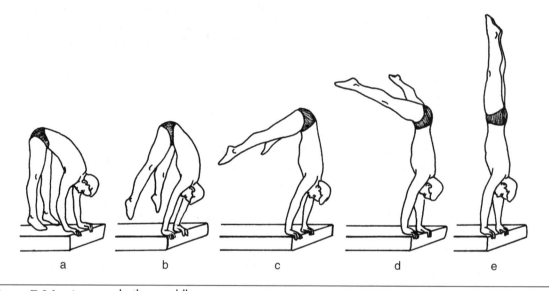

Figure 7.14 Armstand pike straddle press.

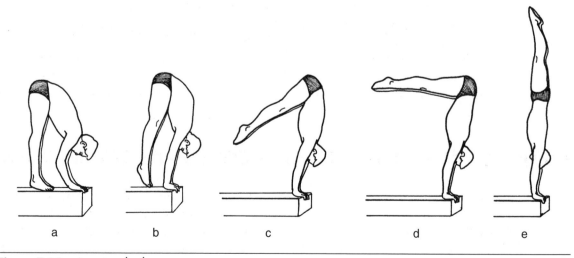

Figure 7.15 Armstand pike press.

available for the following lineup drills, the diver can practice them from a three-meter springboard with the fulcrum in the most forward position.

Entry Drills

These drills consist of the standing forward hollow fall and standing backward fall. The three-meter platform is the best place to practice these drills. The diver should do both the forward and backward falls with the arms first overhead in the entry position and then in a lateral shoulder-high placement at the start and closing to the entry stretch during the fall-in.

When the diver can perform these well at the three-meter height, he or she can move to the five-meter platform and execute the same series of exercises. The eventual result should be entries that finish in a vertical path with proper body alignment, a flat-hand entry technique, the swimming motion of the arms underwater, and the appropriate somersault or backward knee save actions. If all of these occur and the entry path follows the "go with the flow" concept, a rip entry should result.

Basic Dive Lineups

The basic forward, backward, reverse, and inward dive lineups are done with a lateral path of stretch for the entry. The diver should practice these lineups first and then add the optional come-out lineup.

Forward Lineup

This skill can be performed using five different starting positions: sitting roll-off, supported roll-off, standing fall, standing with spring, and running. Since the sitting roll-off, standing open-pike fall, and standing-with-spring technique were covered in the springboard lineup section, and because the running (forward approach) takeoff is self-explanatory, only the supported roll-off needs to be described.

The supported roll-off can only be done in the pike position. The diver sits with the legs straight and extended over the end of the platform from the knees down. He or she places the hands palm down on the edge of the platform next to the legs, with the first two joints of the fingers curled around the edge. By straightening the arms, the diver lifts and supports the body on the hands while maintaining a pike position. The diver then shifts the weight forward with the upper body and *rolls* off the platform into an open-pike position with the arms moving to a straight and lateral placement at shoulder height as soon as the hands leave the platform. See figure 7.16, a through e.

The following list describes lineups that should be practiced, the order in which they should be practiced, and the various platform levels from which each can be performed. Keep in mind that all of these lineups are done with a lateral path of stretch for the entry.

Lineup	Platform level
Standing open-pike fall	1, 3, 5, 7 1/2
Sitting open-pike roll-off	3, 5, 7 1/2
Sitting tuck roll-off	3, 5
Supported pike roll-off	3, 5, 7 1/2, 10

Figure 7.16   Supported forward pike roll-off from five-meter height.

Standing open pike with spring	1, 3, 5
Standing tuck dive with spring	1, 3, 5
Running open pike	1, 3, 5

The running open-pike lineup exercise is particularly valuable because it not only affords lineup practice with a dive having more movement but also teaches the diver to jump strongly from the platform while maintaining control of rotation and distance. This is an absolutely essential skill in platform diving, especially when moving to the seven-and-a-half- and ten-meter heights.

Inward Lineup

Because the inward and forward dive movements are so similar, the inward lineup should be learned next. Unlike the forward lineup, the inward lineup has only one starting position: the basic inward takeoff described previously. Also, only two dives can be done with the inward lineup: the inward dive in open-pike position and the inward dive tuck. The open-pike dive should be learned first because it is easier to control. Both of these dives can be practiced from the one-, three-, and five-meter heights.

Backward Lineup

There are five starting methods for this lineup: sitting roll-off, squatting roll-off, pop-up, standing fall, and standing with spring. All of these, except the pop-up technique, are described in the springboard presentation.

The pop-up is done with a small spring from a backward squatting position. The heels are kept above the platform level, and the takeoff is initiated by dropping the heels to platform level and quickly extending the ankles while pulling upward on the legs, whether in a tuck or pike position. These movements, when coordinated, result in a hop-up or pop-up from the platform into the dive. This method provides more of the feeling of an actual dive because of the spring involved and because the rotation of the dive occurs while moving upward instead of while falling (as in the other takeoff methods).

The backward squat tuck roll-off and backward pike pop-up techniques are not illustrated in the springboard presentation, so they are shown in figure 7.17, a through g, and figure 7.18, a through g.

Consult the following list to determine the skills to practice, the learning progression, and the platform heights from which each skill should be performed. Again, use a lateral arm path to stretch for the entry.

a   b   c   d   e   f   g

Figure 7.17 Backward squat tuck roll-off with lateral come-out from five-meter height.

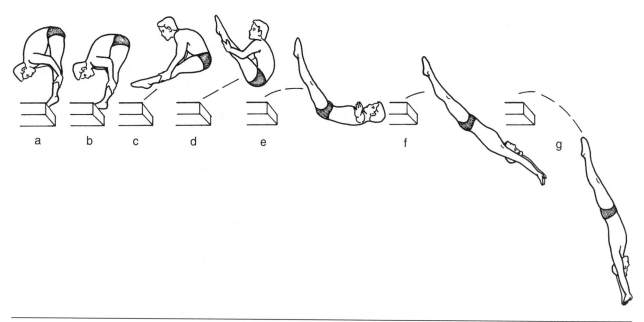

Figure 7.18 Backward pike pop-up with lateral come-out from three-meter height.

Lineup	Platform level
Squat tuck roll-off	3, 5
Tuck pop-up	3, 5
Sitting tuck roll-off	3
Closed-pike pop-up	3
Standing closed-pike fall	5, 7 1/2
Closed-pike pop-up	5, 7 1/2
Sitting closed-pike roll-off	3
Standing backward dive tuck with spring	3, 5

Reverse Lineup

The reverse lineup is performed from the standing reverse takeoff position by doing a reverse dive tuck with a lateral come-out. Even though the methods for practicing the reverse lineup are severely limited, practicing the various backward lineup exercises will have a strong carryover effect because the skills are very similar. Divers who develop good back entry technique and good reverse takeoff action will perform the reverse lineup very well.

Before doing the reverse dive tuck, the diver should practice reverse jumps from the pool deck or one-meter platform in order to develop balance and proper distance. When this is accomplished, he or she can practice the reverse dive tuck, first from the three-meter height and then from the five-meter height.

Optional Come-Outs

The choices for coming out of optional somersaulting dives are the same for platform and springboard dives. Forward and inward optional dives are done with the straight-line come-out if not much time is left before the entry, or with the pike-out method if time permits (see figure 7.19, a-e). Backward and reverse optional dives are performed with the straight-line come-out for dives with little time for completion, and with the kick-and-stretch method when there is sufficient time. For a more detailed description of these techniques, refer to chapter 4.

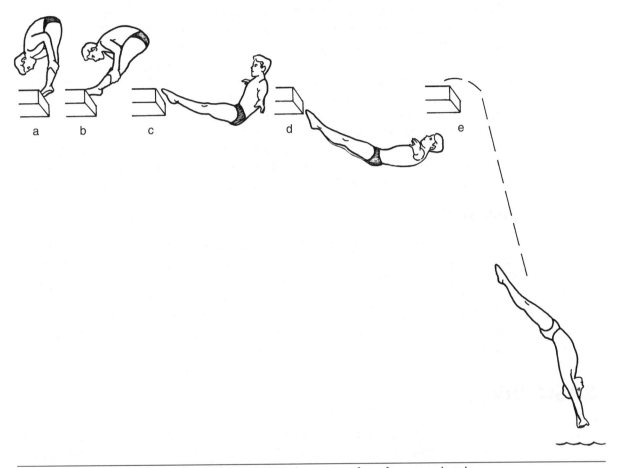

Figure 7.19 Backward closed-pike fall with lateral come-out from five-meter height.

Forward Come-Outs

These drills are done from the sitting roll-off starting position. They can be practiced, using the two types of come-outs, while doing the tuck roll-off and closed-pike roll-off drills. The straight-line come-out in tuck and pike positions is best done at the three-meter height. Because this come-out is used in dives that allow little time to prepare for the entry, the lower takeoff height more closely simulates actual dive situations. Because the pike-out technique is used in dives with much more time before the entry, it is best practiced at the five- and seven-and-a-half-meter levels.

Inward Come-Outs

The inward dive tuck is used to practice tuck come-outs. It is best to practice the straight-line technique at deck level and from one- and three-meter heights and the pike-out technique from three- and five-meter heights.

Pike position come-outs can be practiced using a closed-pike inward dive for the straight-line come-outs, at the recommended lower heights. The inward dive in open-pike position is done to practice the pike-out technique.

Backward Come-Outs

All five starting methods described under basic backward dive lineups can be used to practice these come-out skills: sitting roll-off, squatting roll-off, pop-up, standing fall pike, and standing with spring (backward dive tuck). Experiment with all of these to determine which provides the best results. These lineups are usually confined to the five-meter level and lower, although the closed-pike fall and pop-up takeoffs are sometimes done at the seven-and-a-half-meter level, combined with the kick-and-stretch come-out action.

Here again, follow the guideline of doing the straight-line come-out at the lower levels and the kick-and-stretch movements at the higher levels. A good drill for learning how to get into the straight-line stretch quickly is the sitting tuck roll-off from a two- to two-and-a-half-foot-high bench placed on the one-meter platform.

Reverse Come-Outs

Like the inward come-outs, reverse come-outs offer limited choices for practice. The reverse dive tuck with standing reverse takeoff is the only skill available for this type of lineup. Performing the reverse dive tuck from the three-meter platform with the straight-line come-out, and from the five-meter level with the kick-and-stretch action, is the best training method. However, both the straight-line and kick-and-stretch come-outs can be done at either the three- or five-meter height.

BASIC DIVES

After developing the fundamentals of the takeoffs, jumps, and lineups that are the keys to effective platform diving, the diver is ready to learn the basic forward, backward, reverse, and inward dives in certain selected positions. Even though all of these dives may not be used in the actual program of competitive dives, they are essential to the continued development of good takeoff control, good balance, and proper distance. The mechanics of execution are the same as those explained for springboard diving in chapter 3.

Forward Dive

The forward dive should be done in the tuck or pike position because the takeoff can be done with a strong jump and in good distance. These dives are done from a standing takeoff and should be performed first from the three-meter platform and then from the five-meter platform. If no three-meter platform is available, the dive can be from the five-meter platform first.

Inward Dive

The inward dive can be performed in the tuck, pike, and straight positions. However, the tuck and pike positions should be learned first and done from the three-meter platform, if that option is available, and then from the five-meter platform. The inward dive straight should be done from the five-meter platform.

If the inward dive straight is not needed in the diver's program of competitive dives, then practicing the inward dives tuck and pike is sufficient.

Backward Dive

This dive is learned in the tuck or pike position. The backward dive in straight position forces the diver to jump away from the platform at takeoff to allow a safe clear distance with the feet as they pass platform level. This is not conducive to good takeoff technique, especially for the beginning diver. At a later stage of development, when takeoff mechanics are well established, the diver can perform the backward dive in straight position.

Before doing the backward dive tuck or pike, the diver can learn to develop good control of the takeoff by practicing a lead-up skill from the pool deck. After the basic backward dive takeoff, the diver jumps up and back from the pool deck, and then either tucks or touches the toes and lands on the seat in a pike position (see figure 7.20, a-d).

a   b   c   d

Figure 7.20   Backward dive pike lead-up skill.

Notice that the arms do not reach quite to a vertical line on takeoff (as they do with a springboard dive), and the hands touch the feet at approximately a 45-degree angle short of vertical. This angle of touch is done to control the amount of rotation. Use the same technique in the actual backward dive tuck or pike from the platform. When the diver can perform this lead-up drill with control, it is time to move to the platform.

If possible, execute this dive from the three-meter level and perform it with an angle of entry short of vertical. When the diver can do this well, he or she can move to the five-meter platform.

Reverse Dive

Learn the reverse dive in the tuck or pike position first, which will better develop the proper jump and distance from the platform. When this dive in either of these positions is done with good balance and distance, the reverse dive straight can be introduced.

Before performing the reverse dive tuck or pike, the diver can practice the same type of lead-up skill that was used for the backward dive tuck or pike (see figure 7.21, a-d). When the diver is able to perform this drill with reasonable skill, he or she can move on to the reverse dive tuck or pike from the five-meter platform. Because controlling rotation is much easier in this dive than in the backward dive pike, it is not usually necessary to do this dive at the three-meter level first.

Practicing a reverse jump from the pool deck or one-meter platform serves as a good lead-up drill to the reverse dive straight (review figure 7.6). When the diver can perform this skill with good balance and distance, he or she can do the reverse dive straight from the five-meter platform.

| a | b | c | d |

Figure 7.21 Reverse dive pike lead-up skill.

OPTIONAL DIVES

With the exception of the armstand dives, which are covered in this section, the mechanics of execution for the optional dives are explained in the springboard presentation in chapters 5 and 6. Because the techniques used for optional springboard dives are the same as those used in platform diving, I will not reiterate this material here. The important things to know about optional platform dives are which dives to do at which level and in which order to learn the dives.

Information on core skills and lead-up skills from the various platform heights is presented after the discussion of armstand dives. The order in which these dives should be learned is covered in chapter 8.

Armstand Dives

Armstand dives can rotate in three directions on takeoff from the platform: forward, backward, and reverse. From the armstand position, the forward dives begin with the body falling toward the water and rotating in the same direction as forward dives. Backward dives start with a backward armstand (front of body facing the water on the end of the platform) and a fall away from the platform. The reverse dives begin with the forward armstand as forward rotating dives. As the body moves away from the platform, the diver initiates a rotatation toward the platform, bringing the legs through the space created between the front of the body and the edge of the platform.

Initiating Armstand Dives

Fall, *set*, *snap*, and *push* are the key words to describe the common sequence of movement pattern for all armstand dives, except the armstand forward somersault, in which only a falling motion is used to initiate rotation. This sequence makes the initiation of armstand dives simple and clear for the coach and diver. Of course, the degree and force of movement performed will vary with the difficulty of the dive, but knowing what to do and when to do it should make the armstand dives easier.

Fall

Regardless of the direction of rotation, the body begins a fall away from the platform as the first movement of the takeoff. This fall is a one-piece action with no arch, pike, or knee bend initially. The amount of fall is less in the reverse dives than in the forward and backward dives.

Set

This phase of the takeoff refers to getting the body in a position to create more somersault rotation. One or two movements, depending on the difficulty of the dive, comprise this phase of the takeoff. The first movement is setting the body in a shape to snap into the somersault rotation. This shape is described here for the different directions of rotation.

- Forward—After the fall begins, the body moves to a pike position. The degree of pike depends on the amount of rotation needed.
- Backward and Reverse—After the fall begins, the body moves to an arched position. In addition, to create greater force into the next phase, the knees may be bent. The major emphasis is on body arch so the larger body parts can be used to create rotation. Although knee bend and a kicking movement add to the rotational force, the amount of knee bend used should be kept to a minimum for aesthetic reasons. Excessive knee bend is unattractive and should be scored accordingly by the judges.

The second movement in the set phase is done with the arms and shoulders when extra force is needed to develop rotation. Simultaneous with the change in body shape, the shoulders drop and the elbows may flex some to make a stronger pushing movement possible when the snap takes place. Care should be exercised in the backward armstand dives that the shoulder joint angle does not change too much (toward a push-up position). This results in lack of lift during takeoff and makes closing quickly and tightly to a tuck or pike position difficult.

Snap

This is the movement out of the set position. In the forward rotating dives, the snap is a whip of the legs from the pike set position to a straight or slightly arched shape. As last contact with the platform occurs, it is important that the leg snap stop quickly. This will allow a rapid transfer of momentum from the legs to the upper body and aid in assuming a fast and tight tuck or pike position.

In the backward and reverse spinning dives, the snap occurs from the arched position in a top to bottom sequence. This means that if the knees are flexed, extension of the knees begins the snap, followed by the legs, hips, chest, and shoulders moving from the arch to the tuck or pike position. If the knees are not bent, the snap would start with the legs, hips, and so on. In either case, the desired effect is a body whip.

Push

The final movement, prior to last contact with the platform, is a push-off through the shoulders and arms if the drop-down movement in these areas has been incorporated into the set phase. After the snap has been initiated, a strong elevation of the shoulders, followed by extension of the elbows and finally the wrists, adds lift and rotation to the takeoff. When last contact with the platform occurs, it is important that the head and trunk hold a fixed position. This allows the diver to transfer momentum to the legs and assume a quick and tight tuck or pike position.

Flow

The movements described earlier are executed with a flow from one to the other (domino effect), not in isolation. If the diver remembers to fall-set-snap-push, the armstand dive takeoffs will be more balanced and rotate more easily.

After executing the movements described earlier for the appropriate direction of rotation, the armstand dives are performed the same as described in springboard diving, relative to assuming the somersault position, visual spotting, and come-out technique. Study figures 7.22 through 7.30 to get a visual picture of the basic takeoff actions and dives for the three directions of rotation.

Figure 7.22   Armstand forward fall to feet in tuck position from three-meter height.

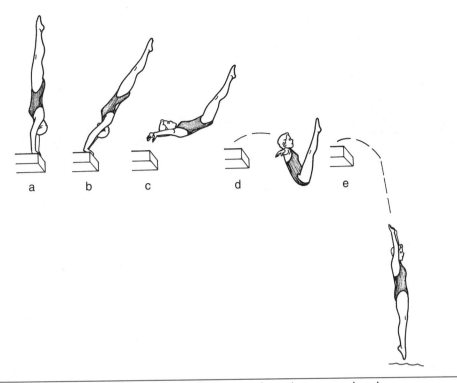

Figure 7.23 Armstand forward fall to feet in pike position from three-meter height.

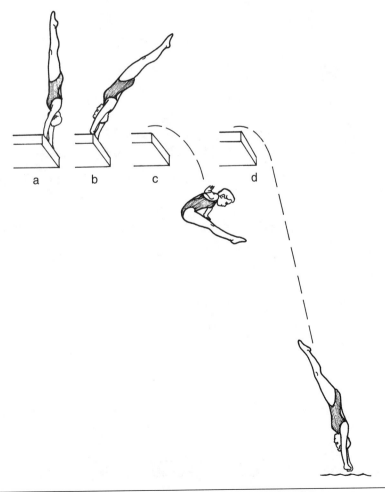

Figure 7.24 Armstand somersault in pike position from five-meter height.

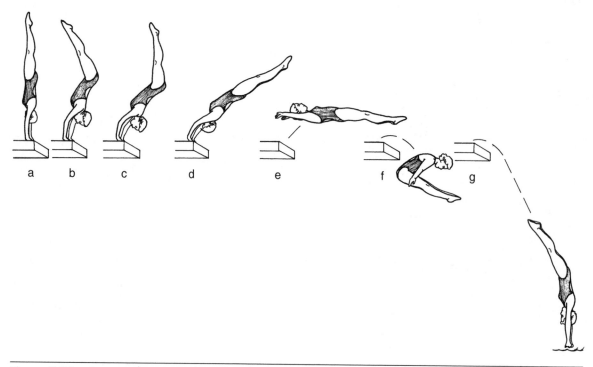

Figure 7.25 Armstand somersault in closed-pike position from three-meter height.

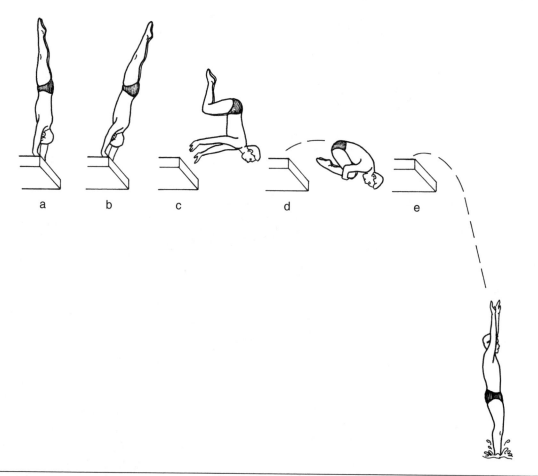

Figure 7.26 Armstand reverse half somersault in tuck position from five-meter height.

Figure 7.27 Armstand reverse somersault in tuck position from five-meter height.

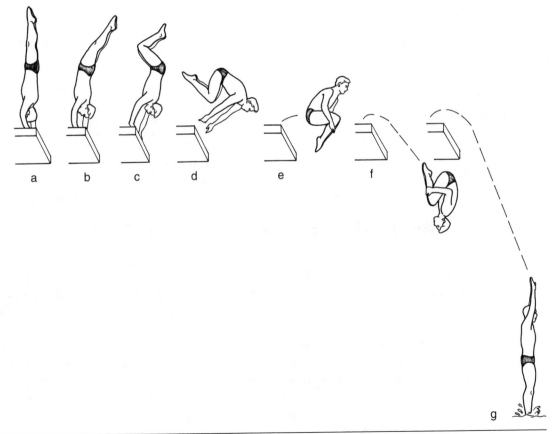

Figure 7.28 Armstand reverse one-and-a-half somersault in tuck position from five-meter height.

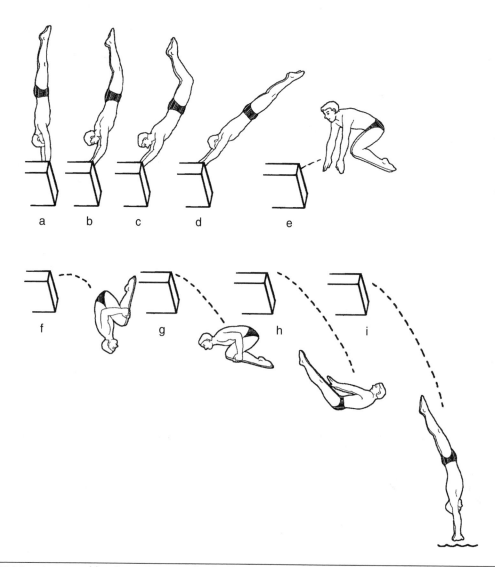

Figure 7.29 Armstand backward one-and-a-half somersault in tuck position from five-meter height.

Once the diver has achieved basic takeoff technique for a direction of rotation, he or she can follow the skill progression tables in chapter 8 to determine which dive should be done next and at what platform level it should be performed.

Armstand Backward Somersault With Half Twist

The takeoff for this dive is different from that in the other armstand dives because a twist is introduced. The same sequence of fall-set-snap-push takes place as in the other backward armstand takeoffs. As the snap and push phases take place, a turn of the hips in the twist direction will initiate twist from the platform surface. As the half twist is performed, the arms are kept straight and parallel overhead. When the twist is completed, the arms move in a direct line to the legs to assume a tuck or closed-pike position. Another option is to move the arms laterally from the overhead position into an open-pike position (see figure 7.30). Once the diver can perform the armstand backward somersault with half twist well from the three- or five-meter platform, he or she can add somersaults at the higher-level platforms.

Figure 7.30 Armstand backward somersault half twist in open-pike position from three-meter height.

WHICH DIVE ON WHICH PLATFORM?

Knowing which optional dives and lead-up skills a diver can do from the one-, three-, and five-meter platforms is important to ensure that he or she does not attempt skills that are either unsafe or impossible. If a good springboard background has been established first and sufficient work has been done on the take-offs, basic dives, and entries from the platform, performing most of the optional dives in the following list should be easy. Some of the more advanced optional dives will require more time and training to master.

Core Skills

The following optional dives, combined with the takeoffs, jumps, lineups, and basic dives, form a group of core skills that every platform diver should learn at some time in the training process. In the early stages of platform diving, the diver should practice these skills repeatedly to establish the correct pattern of movements, balance, and spatial orientation. When the diver is more advanced, his or her program of competition dives will determine whether to maintain all of these skills in training.

The lists of dives presented here for the one-, three-, and five-meter platform levels show the skills that should be practiced at these levels. The order in which they should be performed is discussed in chapter 8.

One Meter

- Standing forward somersault tuck and pike
- Running forward somersault tuck and pike
- Running forward one-and-a-half somersault tuck and pike
- Backward somersault tuck and pike
- Reverse somersault tuck
- Inward somersault tuck
- Armstand backward half somersault straight

Three Meter

- Standing forward somersault tuck and pike
- Running forward somersault tuck and pike
- Running forward one-and-a-half somersault tuck and pike
- Backward somersault tuck, pike, and straight (hollow)
- Reverse somersault tuck and pike
- Inward somersault tuck and pike
- Inward one-and-a-half somersault tuck
- Forward somersault with one twist
- Backward somersault with half twist
- Backward somersault with one and a half twists
- Armstand reverse half somersault tuck
- Armstand half somersault (feetfirst) tuck and pike
- Armstand backward somersault tuck

Five Meter

- Standing forward one-and-a-half-somersault tuck and pike
- Running forward one-and-a-half somersault tuck and pike
- Running forward two-and-a-half somersault tuck
- Backward somersault straight (hollow)
- Backward somersault tuck and pike
- Backward one-and-a-half somersault tuck and pike
- Reverse somersault tuck and pike

- Reverse one-and-a-half somersault tuck
- Inward one-and-a-half somersault tuck and pike
- Forward one-and-a-half somersault with one twist
- Backward one-and-a-half somersault with half twist
- Backward somersault with one and a half twists
- Armstand reverse half somersault tuck
- Armstand forward somersault tuck and pike
- Armstand backward somersault with half twist

Lead-Up Skills

Although many of the core skills also serve as optional dives and lead-up skills, additional dives done from the one-, three-, and five-meter platforms are specific lead-up steps for the more difficult optional dives at the ten-meter level. Some of these dives may also be used as optional dives in competition from the five-meter platform.

One Meter
- Standing reverse somersault pike
- Inward one-and-a-half somersault tuck
- Armstand reverse half somersault tuck
- Armstand somersault tuck

Three Meter
- Backward one-and-a-half somersault tuck
- Backward double somersault tuck
- Reverse one-and-a-half somersault tuck
- Reverse double somersault tuck
- Inward one-and-a-half somersault pike
- Forward somersault with two twists
- Backward somersault with two and a half twists
- Armstand forward somersault tuck or pike
- Armstand forward double somersault tuck
- Armstand backward somersault with half twist

Five Meter
- Running forward two-and-a-half somersault pike
- Running forward three-and-a-half somersault tuck
- Backward double somersault tuck and pike
- Backward two-and-a-half somersault tuck
- Reverse one-and-a-half somersault pike
- Reverse double somersault tuck and pike
- Reverse two-and-a-half somersault tuck
- Inward two-and-a-half somersault tuck

- Forward somersault with three twists
- Backward somersault with two and a half twists
- Backward somersault with three and a half twists
- Reverse somersault straight (hollow)
- Reverse somersault with one and a half twists
- Reverse somersault with two and a half twists
- Reverse somersault with three and a half twists
- Armstand reverse somersault tuck
- Armstand reverse one-and-a-half somersault tuck
- Armstand forward double somersault tuck
- Armstand backward somersault pike
- Armstand backward one-and-a-half somersault tuck

SUMMARY

Having covered the basic fundamentals of platform diving and the dives that can be done from the one-, three-, and five-meter levels, the next chapter discusses how to use these skills to develop a list of dives from the seven-and-a-half- and ten-meter platforms. Performing dives from these higher platforms will be safe and successful if the diver has devoted a sufficient amount of time and practice to developing good control, balance, and spatial orientation in executing the fundamental skills covered in this chapter.

CHAPTER 8

Skill and Dive Progressions

In order to organize all the dives and skills discussed in the preceding chapters, a plan of diving progressions must be developed. This plan entails two distinct areas: the order in which the dives should be learned, or dive progressions, and the component skills within each dive, or skill progressions. When the coach and diver know what dive to work on next, and the diver practices the essential parts of that dive before attempting it, a safe, logical, and successful transition from dive to dive is ensured.

GENERAL GUIDELINES

Before specifically discussing dive and skill progressions, some basic general guidelines need to be covered. The following guidelines will help the coach and diver make sound decisions when moving through the dive or skill progression process.

1. Have a plan to follow for both dive and skill progressions. Don't guess what comes next!

2. Evaluate the following three areas before attempting a new dive or skill.

    a. Technique—The diver should possess good balance in the required take-off, consistently demonstrate safe distance from the board or platform, show sufficient spatial awareness in the lead-up skills, and possess proper mechanics of execution.

    b. Physical readiness—The diver should possess sufficient strength and quickness to perform the dive or skill correctly and easily. Learning dives before being physically ready results in incorrect technique, uncorrectable bad habits, and repeated failure in the performance. It is better to learn a dive too late than too soon.

    c. Mental readiness—The diver should demonstrate a level of confidence that reflects the ability to handle the stress of performing the dive or skill without panic and a willingness to attempt the dive.

3. Ensure that the evaluation of the diver as presented in step 2 takes precedence over all other extraneous factors, such as the parent's wishes, the diver's wishes, or the requirements of an upcoming event.

4. Insist on correct performance of the preceding dive or skill before moving to the next step. Most coaches and divers move too quickly through the dive and skill progressions for the diver to achieve high levels of execution along the way.

5. At the first sign that the dive or skill being done is too difficult or that technique is breaking down, return to the dive or skill level that the diver can perform successfully. Then return to the new dive when the diver is ready. Many times, regressing is a way of progressing.

By following these guidelines and making wise decisions, the diver will develop confidence in his or her ability to do what is expected. When the coach says it is time to do a new dive or skill, the diver will know that he or she is well prepared and will perform it successfully and safely. Patience and repetition of correct technique are the keys to smooth, safe, and successful progress!

SKILL PROGRESSIONS

For any dive, several skills are combined to produce the overall result. When a diver segments a particular dive, learns and practices the component skills individually in a planned sequence, and then links those skills together in the execution of the dive, performance is optimized. The adage "a chain is only as strong as its weakest link" indicates the value of each skill or link to the ultimate execution of a dive. When a skill in any area of the dive is weak, that is the point where performance breaks down. A well-executed backward three-and-a-half somersault dive is merely an extension of a fundamentally sound single backward somersault with other skills added to it. If the diver doesn't have a good backward somersault technique, he or she either will not be able to perform a backward three-and-a-half somersault or will perform it poorly, no matter how much practice takes place.

To develop a logical and productive "skill chain," the diver must know the skills that are involved in each dive, how to practice those skills, and the sequence in which to practice them. The general skill areas that comprise dives are as follows:

- Springboard or platform technique prior to the takeoff
- Balance and angle of takeoff
- Initiation of somersault rotation
- Initiation of twist rotation
- Spatial orientation
- Come-out technique
- Lineup and entry

Isolate each of these components and gradually combine them as each part is executed correctly through work on specific skills. Before discussing each of these skills, the tremendous importance of correct body alignment to the success of each phase of the dive must be pointed out. If the diver does not constantly emphasize this foundation, the degree of expertise developed in the skill chain is significantly reduced. Pay attention to body alignment as each part of the dive is practiced.

Springboard or Platform Technique

This phase of the dive can best be practiced by performing the appropriate board or platform work with a jump or tuck dive. These simpler skills allow a high degree of concentration on the forward approach and backward takeoff. The ability to do a controlled, balanced jump or tuck dive with correct distance requires excellent skill in this area.

Balance and Angle of Takeoff

Performing the basic tuck dives in the various takeoff directions from the springboard and platform hones the skill required here. The forward and inward dives in open-pike position are also helpful. These dives in the tuck and pike position require a high degree of accuracy, and mastering them will help the diver perform the basic and optional dives with good elevation and distance on takeoff.

Initiation of Somersault Rotation

Performing an easy somersaulting dive in the desired direction of rotation affords practice of the correct movements needed to develop rotation while eliminating the pressure that accompanies a more difficult dive. Doing a forward one-and-a-half or double somersault in tuck position leads to a more relaxed and successful forward two-and-a-half somersault if the harder two-and-a-half-rotation dive can be started with the same general pattern of movement as the easier dives. When practicing platform diving, executing a single standing somersault in the direction of rotation from the edge of the pool is also beneficial.

Initiation of Twist Rotation

Twisting can also be practiced most effectively by doing an easy twisting dive that is similar to a more difficult one. This can be done in two steps. First, the diver performs a dive with the same number of somersaults but fewer twists to practice the skills of somersaulting, twisting, and squaring out along with the completion of the dive. Next, the diver performs a lead-up skill with the same number of twists, but with a half less somersault or a feetfirst entry.

▶ **Example: Backward one-and-a-half somersault with two and a half twists**
Lead-up skill: Backward one-and-a-half somersault with one and a half twists
Lead-up skill: Backward somersault with two and a half twists

Spatial Orientation

Orientation for the whole dive can best be developed by practicing the dive repeatedly on a trampoline or dryland springboard with safety spotting equipment and a coach who is trained in advanced spotting techniques. Regardless of whether this type of equipment and training are available, when attempting a new dive, a diver can enhance his or her concentration on the proper angle of come-out by practicing a dive with one somersault less rotation than the dive he or she is attempting.

Let's use a backward two-and-a-half somersault as an example. The diver can develop spatial orientation for a backward two-and-a-half somersault from the springboard or platform by doing a backward one-and-a-half somersault from a lower level and concentrating on kicking out at the same approximate spot as desired when doing the two-and-a-half somersault. Another example would be doing the inward one-and-a-half somersault from the one-meter board as preparation for the inward two-and-a-half somersault from the three-meter board.

Come-Out Technique

Three different skills can be used to practice for a come-out: a lineup, a tuck or open-pike dive, and an easier dive in the same direction of rotation. The less refined a diver's ability level, the more important it becomes to perform all three of these skills in preparation for the more difficult dive.

Lineup and Entry

The diver can practice lineups and entries with the same three lead-up skills used for the come-out technique. It should be apparent that jumps, tuck dives, lineups, and easy optional dives are paramount to a skill-chain plan of preparation for a dive. As the diver becomes more proficient at the various skills in the chain, the amount of time he or she devotes to training for such skills may diminish. However, even the most skilled world-class divers should use this type of practice in the early stages of the training program and at any time a particular dive, type of takeoff, or somersaulting or twisting skill deteriorates.

Training Guidelines

Using the categories and ranking system illustrated in the FINA Table of Degree of Difficulty (see table 8.1 on page 169), springboard and platform skill progressions (see tables 8.2 and 8.3 on pages 176 and 179, respectively) were developed as road maps to follow in the complicated development of skill chains for each particular dive. The skill progression tables list the dives, the lead-up skills at the various heights of springboard and platform, and their order of performance. Locate the dive and height for which the diver is preparing; the links of the chain leading to it are listed below, in the numerical order of execution. In the case of platform dives, if your training facility does not have the recommended platform height for the skill indicated, eliminate that skill from the preparation and training process or practice the skill on the springboard.

Hopefully, these skill progression tables will help the diver train more effectively for better performance. Use these progressions in two distinct ways within the training program, as described in the next two sections.

Individual Skill Training Program

Divers should begin with the individual skill training program. With this type of program, work on each of the skills leading to the ultimate dive, performing a high number of repetitions of each skill before progressing to the next. If one particular skill is the weakest link in the chain, it would be very appropriate to devote an entire pratice or several practices to that skill. Individual skills may have to be broken down further into component parts. Training may then take place for each part first, either in the dryland or pool setting, before combining the parts into the whole performance.

Progressive Skill Training Program

After the individual skill training process has been used to practice and master each of the skills in the chain leading toward a particular dive, the parts can be put together more rapidly. This is done by performing each skill in order, doing only the minimum number of repetitions necessary to achieve a good execution, and then moving to the next skill.

▶ Example: Forward two-and-a-half somersault tuck from the one-meter springboard

Skill 1: Forward approach and front jump from one-meter level

Skill 2: Forward dive tuck with straight-line come-out from one-meter level

Skill 3: Forward one-and-a-half somersault tuck from one-meter level

Skill 4: Forward tuck roll-off with straight-line come-out from three-meter level

The diver then performs the forward two-and-a-half somersault tuck a few times. If the results are good, the diver may move to another dive, but if not, he or she must repeat the progressive skill process. The coach and diver must decide how many times this skill chain is done.

Using the Tables

The dives on the skill progression tables are listed by dive number and body position in the official diving table for competition (see table 8.1). The skill progressions begin with the assumption that the diver has learned the basic dives and single somersault dives in all four directions, so progressions for these skills are not included. Also, dives that are rarely performed and dives that are not recommended because they do not lead to a suitable competitive dive have been omitted from the tables.

The dives to be done at the highest height possible—three meters for springboard and ten meters for platform—are listed horizontally across the top of the table (see tables 8.2 and 8.3). The skill progression for the particular dive selected is shown vertically under the dive number, with the recommended numerical order in which the skills should be performed. To determine the skill progression for a dive at any other height, locate the dive number at the appropriate level (1, 3, 5, or 7.5 meters) on the left side of the table for that group. Follow across the table horizontally to the first column with a number in it. All of the progressions leading to that dive are listed numerically below that point. The springboard table contains a separate progression for the three-meter and one-meter heights.

Additionally, following are some clarifications on the performance of specific skills and unusual situations that may occur:

- Before the diver performs each skill progression, an evaluation of his or her ability to perform it needs to be done. The 107C, which is listed at the seven-and-a-half-meter platform level as a progression toward that dive on the ten-meter level, is to be done by divers who spin unusually fast and may have control problems in the first few attempts at the ten-meter height. Most divers will not somersault fast enough to do the three-and-a-half somersault at seven and a half meters and should move from the 105C at five meters to the 107C at ten meters. The opposite situation may also occur. The diver may not spin fast enough to do a recommended progression. For example, many divers may not be able to make the 305C at the seven-and-a-half-meter level. In this case, the diver should progress from the 304C at five meters to 305C at ten meters.

- When the same skill progression number occurs at two different platform levels, a decision needs to made, based on the diver's skills, whether to do the progression from both heights or only one. These dual numbers also account for facilities in which all levels of platform are not available.

- Whenever a platform height is not available for a skill progression, and also as a complement to the progression process, use the one- and three-meter springboard to learn and practice platform dives. Where a lineup is indicated on the chart, select the lineup and come-out method that best fit the dive being done.

- When performing the 104B progression listed for the 5152 and 5154 dives from the springboard, the diver should move from the pike position to the straight position at the one-and-a-half somersault point and remain straight for the completion of the dive. This lead-up skill will help orient him or her as to when to come out of the somersault into the twist in the actual dives.

- Where 202A or 302A dives are shown, the diver should perform these in the hollow straight position, as described in chapter 6.
- There are two abbreviations on the charts: S = standing takeoff; OP = open-pike position

DIVE PROGRESSIONS

By following the guidelines presented here and referring to the skill progression tables found in this chapter, the diver and coach can construct an appropriate plan of action for dive progressions. Keep in mind that the most important factors to consider are a logical progression of skills and the diver's safety and readiness for each skill.

Springboard Dive Progressions

As a general rule, in springboard diving the basic dives and somersaults are learned in this sequence: forward, backward, inward, reverse. These dives should be learned first in the tuck position, then in the pike position, and finally in the straight position. Straight position somersaults are only done in the backward and reverse directions. The backward somersault straight can be learned in the early stages, but the reverse somersault straight is a more advanced dive and it should not be learned until the diver is preparing to do reverse twisting dives or a reverse one-and-a-half somersault straight.

When doing the more difficult optional somersault and twisting dives, the diver should learn the dive in the forward direction before attempting it in the inward direction, and in the backward direction before attempting it in the reverse direction. The exact learning sequence of forward/inward versus backward/reverse dives depends on the difficulty of the dive and the diver's technique and readiness to successfully execute it. For instance, most divers learn an inward two-and-a-half somersault tuck before doing a reverse two-and-a-half somersault tuck. However, this sequence may not be the best if the inward technique is poor and the reverse takeoff action and spatial awareness on backward and reverse spinning dives is good. Carefully assess each diver's abilities in determining which dive he or she should do next.

In most situations, when progressing through the somersault dives the diver should practice the dives in the given direction (group) with one somersault rotation less and with a half somersault rotation less than the dive to be attempted. For example, if preparing for a forward two-and-a-half somersault pike from the three-meter springboard, the lead-up skills practiced from the one-meter board are a forward one-and-a-half somersault pike to practice the come-out and a forward double somersault pike to practice takeoff and speed of somersault preparation.

The same general pattern applies to moving ahead on twisting dives. As lead-up skills, the diver should perform the same number of somersaults with one less twist, then with a half less somersault rotation but the same number of twists as the new dive. For example, if the new dive to be performed is a forward one-and-a-half somersault with two twists from the three-meter board, the lead-up skills are a forward one-and-a-half somersault with one twist from the one- and three-meter levels and a forward somersault with two twists from the one-meter board.

One final guideline to follow when developing a dive progression plan is that more difficult dives should be learned first on the three-meter springboard before being performed on the one-meter springboard. The reason for this recommendation is that the added time available at the three-meter height allows the diver to execute this harder dive with correct technique. If the dive is done first at the one-meter level, the difficulty of completing the dive pressures the diver to force the dive and thereby use poor mechanics. Once the new dive is learned with incorrect actions and practiced repeatedly, it is extremely difficult for the diver to correct those bad habits.

Therefore, a three-meter springboard must be used. Unfortunately, many coaches and divers do not see the importance of using the three-meter board because high school divers usually compete at the one-meter level. The chance of learning the more difficult dives correctly on the one-meter board is improved when they are done at the three-meter height first.

Platform Dive Progressions

Because most divers and coaches are less experienced in teaching platform diving and less familiar with the order in which dives and skills are learned, a list of dive progressions for the dives covered in chapter 7 is presented here.

Lineup	Platform level
Standing reverse takeoff with jump	1, 3, 5
Backward takeoff with jump	1, 3, 5
Standing forward takeoff with jump	1, 3, 5
Inward takeoff with jump	1, 3, 5
Running forward takeoff with jump	1, 3, 5
Running reverse takeoff with jump	1
Standing forward hollow fall	3, 5
Backward fall (arms overhead)	3
Standing forward fall (arms lateral)	3, 5
Backward fall (arms lateral)	3
Forward lineup series	1, 3, 5
Inward lineup open pike	1, 3, 5
Inward lineup tuck	1, 3, 5
Backward fall (arms overhead)	5
Backward fall (arms lateral)	5
Backward lineup series	3, 5
Reverse dive tuck	3, 5
Forward come-out lineups	3, 5
Inward come-out lineups	3, 5
Backward come-out lineups	3, 5
Reverse come-out lineups	3, 5
Standing forward dive pike	3, 5

Inward dive pike	3, 5
Backward dive pike	3, 5
Reverse dive pike	3, 5
Inward dive straight	5
Reverse dive straight	5
Armstand dive	1, 3
Armstand half somersault tuck and pike	3
Armstand reverse half somersault	3, 5
Standing forward somersault tuck	1, 3
Standing forward somersault pike	3
Backward somersault tuck	1, 3, 5
Backward somersault pike	3, 5
Running forward somersault tuck	1, 3
Running forward somersault pike	1, 3
Running forward one-and-a-half somersault tuck	3
Running forward one-and-a-half somersault pike	3
Standing forward one-and-a-half somersault tuck	5
Standing forward one-and-a-half somersault pike	5
Running forward one-and-a-half somersault tuck	5
Running forward one-and-a-half somersault pike	5
Armstand somersault tuck and/or pike	5
Inward somersault tuck	1, 3
Inward one-and-a-half somersault tuck	5
Reverse somersault tuck	3, 5, 1
Running forward somersault open pike	3
Backward somersault straight (hollow)	3, 5
Running forward somersault with one twist	3
Running forward one-and-a-half somersault with one twist	5
Inward somersault pike	3
Inward one-and-a-half somersault pike	5
Backward one-and-a-half somersault tuck or pike	5
Running forward one-and-a-half somersault tuck	1
Running forward two-and-a-half somersault tuck	5
Reverse one-and-a-half somersault tuck	5
Backward somersault with one and a half twists	3, 5
Armstand backward half somersault straight	1, 3
Armstand backward somersault with half twist	3, 5

Using the chart on platform skill progressions in table 8.3, study how these dives and skills fit into a plan for specific dives at all platform levels.

WHICH DIVE TO USE?

As new dives are learned in each of the groups, the question of which dive to use in competition always arises. Should the diver perform the higher degree of difficulty dive, which will probably result in lower judges' scores, or the lower degree of difficulty dive, which may net higher judges' scores? To solve this dilemma, determine what the average expected judges' scores would be for each of these dives if they were performed in competition several times. Next, apply the formula: ±.2 degree of difficulty is equal to ±.5 point in judges' scores.

> ▶ **Example:**
> 2.2 degree of difficulty × 7-point judges' scores =
> 2.6 degree of difficulty × 6-point judges' scores =
> 3.0 degree of difficulty × 5-point judges' scores =

This simple calculation can help you decide what dive to use. Because total point score, not degree of difficulty, is the determining factor in place finish, the dive to use should be obvious. If the net result for the two dives is similar, use the higher degree of difficulty dive, providing the diver's technique is fundamentally sound.

One other point to keep in mind is that in high-pressure meets (championships), the stress involved brings out flaws in the mechanics of dives and can result in poor execution. In these circumstances, select the dive that is most technically correct.

SUMMARY

Hopefully, this chapter will help you take all the technical information from the other chapters and put it together into a well-planned and well-thought-out training program. With precise direction, correct step-by-step practice, and some wise decision making along the way, remarkable progress is sure to occur.

The principles and guidelines presented here provide only a framework. It is important to continually use imagination and inventiveness to improve on and add to the learning process. Experimentation and trial and error are the cornerstones of progress. Without the willingness of coach and diver to use these tools of training, teaching and learning skills will stagnate, so be creative in your approach to diving.

Table 8.1 FINA Table of Degree of Difficulty

SPRINGBOARD		1 meter				3 meter			
		Strt	Pike	Tuck	Free	Strt	Pike	Tuck	Free
	Forward Group	A	B	C	D	A	B	C	D
101	Forward Dive	1.4	1.3	1.2	-	1.6	1.5	1.4	-
102	Forward Somersault	1.6	1.5	1.4	-	1.7	1.6	1.5	-
103	Forward 1-1/2 Somersault	2.0	1.7	1.6	-	1.9	1.6	1.5	-
104	Forward Double Somersault	2.6	2.3	2.2	-	2.4	2.1	2.0	-
105	Forward 2-1/2 Somersault		2.6	2.4	-	2.8	2.4	2.2	-
106	Forward Triple Somersault		3.2	2.9	-		2.8	2.5	-
107	Forward 3-1/2 Somersault		3.3	3.0	-		3.1	2.8	-
109	Forward 4-1/2 Somersault				-			3.5	-
112	Forward Flying Somersault	-	1.7	1.6	-	-	1.8	1.7	-
113	Forward Flying 1-1/2 Somersault	-	1.9	1.8	-	-	1.8	1.7	-
115	Forward Flying 2-1/2 Somersault	-			-	-	2.7	2.5	-
	Back Group	A	B	C	D	A	B	C	D
201	Back Dive	1.7	1.6	1.5	-	1.9	1.8	1.7	-
202	Back Somersault	1.7	1.6	1.5	-	1.8	1.7	1.6	-
203	Back 1-1/2 Somersault	2.5	2.3	2.0	-	2.4	2.2	1.9	-
204	Back Double Somersault		2.5	2.2	-	2.5	2.3	2.0	-
205	Back 2-1/2 Somersault		3.2	3.0	-		3.0	2.8	-
206	Back Triple Somersault		3.2	2.9	-		2.8	2.5	-
207	Back 3-1/2 Somersault				-		3.7	3.4	-
212	Back Flying Somersault	-	1.7	1.6	-	-	1.8	1.7	-
213	Back Flying 1-1/2 Somersault	-			-	-		2.1	-
215	Back Flying 2-1/2 Somersault	-			-	-	3.3	3.1	-
	Reverse Group	A	B	C	D	A	B	C	D
301	Reverse Dive	1.8	1.7	1.6	-	2.0	1.9	1.8	-
302	Reverse Somersault	1.8	1.7	1.6	-	1.9	1.8	1.7	-
303	Reverse 1-1/2 Somersault	2.7	2.4	2.1	-	2.6	2.3	2.0	-
304	Reverse Double Somersault	2.9	2.6	2.3	-	2.7	2.4	2.1	-
305	Reverse 2-1/2 Somersault		3.2	3.0	-	3.4	3.0	2.8	-
306	Reverse Triple Somersault		3.3	3.0	-		2.9	2.6	-

(-) indicates the dive is not possible; empty spaces have not been calculated

(continued)

Table 8.1 (continued)

SPRINGBOARD		1 meter				3 meter			
		Strt	Pike	Tuck	Free	Strt	Pike	Tuck	Free
	Reverse Group	A	B	C	D	A	B	C	D
307	Reverse 3-1/2 Somersault				-		3.8	3.5	-
312	Reverse Flying Somersault	-	1.8	1.7	-	-	1.9	1.8	-
313	Reverse Flying 1-1/2 Somersault	-	2.6	2.3	-	-	2.5	2.2	-
	Inward Group	A	B	C	D	A	B	C	D
401	Inward Dive	1.8	1.5	1.4	-	1.7	1.4	1.3	-
402	Inward Somersault	2.0	1.7	1.6	-	1.8	1.5	1.4	-
403	Inward 1-1/2 Somersault		2.4	2.2	-		2.1	1.9	-
404	Inward Double Somersault		3.0	2.8	-		2.6	2.4	-
405	Inward 2-1/2 Somersault		3.4	3.1	-		3.0	2.7	-
407	Inward 3-1/2 Somersault				-			3.4	-
412	Inward Flying Somersault	-	2.1	2.0	-	-	1.9	1.8	-
413	Inward Flying 1-1/2 Somersault	-	2.9	2.7	-	-	2.6	2.4	-
	Twisting Group	A	B	C	D	A	B	C	D
5111	Forward Dive 1/2 Twist	1.8	1.7	1.6	-	2.0	1.9	1.8	-
5112	Forward Dive 1 Twist	2.0	1.9		-	2.2	2.1		-
5121	Forward Somersault 1/2 Twist	-	-	-	1.7	-	-	-	1.8
5122	Forward Somersault 1 Twist	-	-	-	1.9	-	-	-	2.0
5124	Forward Somersault 2 Twists	-	-	-	2.3	-	-	-	2.4
5126	Forward Somersault 3 Twists	-	-	-	2.7	-	-	-	2.8
5131	Forward 1-1/2 Somersault 1/2 Twist	-	-	-	2.0	-	-	-	1.9
5132	Forward 1-1/2 Somersault 1 Twist	-	-	-	2.2	-	-	-	2.1
5134	Forward 1-1/2 Somersault 2 Twists	-	-	-	2.6	-	-	-	2.5
5136	Forward 1-1/2 Somersault 3 Twists	-	-	-	3.0	-	-	-	2.9
5138	Forward 1-1/2 Somersault 4 Twists	-	-	-	3.4	-	-	-	3.3
5151	Forward 2-1/2 Somersault 1/2 Twist	-	3.0	2.8	-	-	2.8	2.6	-
5152	Forward 2-1/2 Somersault 1 Twist	-	3.2	3.0	-	-	3.0	2.8	-
5154	Forward 2-1/2 Somersault 2 Twists	-	3.6	3.4	-	-	3.4	3.2	-
5172	Forward 3-1/2 Somersault 1 Twist	-			-	-	3.7	3.4	-

SPRINGBOARD		1 meter				3 meter			
		Strt	Pike	Tuck	Free	Strt	Pike	Tuck	Free
	Twisting Group	A	B	C	D	A	B	C	D
5211	Back Dive 1/2 Twist	1.8	1.7	1.6	-	2.0	1.9	1.8	-
5212	Back Dive 1 Twist	2.0			-	2.2			-
5221	Back Somersault 1/2 Twist	-	-	-	1.7	-	-	-	1.8
5222	Back Somersault 1 Twist	-	-	-	1.9	-	-	-	2.0
5223	Back Somersault 1-1/2 Twists	-	-	-	2.3	-	-	-	2.4
5225	Back Somersault 2-1/2 Twists	-	-	-	2.7	-	-	-	2.8
5227	Back Somersault 3-1/2 Twists	-	-	-	3.1	-	-	-	3.2
5231	Back 1-1/2 Somersault 1/2 Twist	-	-	-	2.1	-	-	-	2.0
5233	Back 1-1/2 Somersault 1-1/2 Twists	-	-	-	2.5	-	-	-	2.4
5235	Back 1-1/2 Somersault 2-1/2 Twists	-	-	-	2.9	-	-	-	2.8
5237	Back 1-1/2 Somersault 3-1/2 Twists	-	-	-		-	-	-	3.2
5239	Back 1-1/2 Somersault 4-1/2 Twists	-	-	-		-	-	-	3.6
5251	Back 2-1/2 Somersault 1/2 Twist	-	2.9	2.7	-	-	2.7	2.5	-
5253	Back 2-1/2 Somersault 1-1/2 Twists	-			-	-	3.5	3.3	-
5311	Reverse Dive 1/2 Twist	1.9	1.8	1.7	-	2.1	2.0	1.9	-
5312	Reverse Dive 1 Twist	2.1			-	2.2			-
5321	Reverse Somersault 1/2 Twist	-	-	-	1.8	-	-	-	1.9
5322	Reverse Somersault 1 Twist	-	-	-	2.0	-	-	-	2.1
5323	Reverse Somersault 1-1/2 Twists	-	-	-	2.4	-	-	-	2.5
5325	Reverse Somersault 2-1/2 Twists	-	-	-	2.8	-	-	-	2.9
5331	Reverse 1-1/2 Somersault 1/2 Twist	-	-	-	2.2	-	-	-	2.1
5333	Reverse 1-1/2 Somersault 1-1/2 Twists	-	-	-	2.6	-	-	-	2.5
5335	Reverse 1-1/2 Somersault 2-1/2 Twists	-	-	-	3.0	-	-	-	2.9
5337	Reverse 1-1/2 Somersault 3-1/2 Twists	-	-	-	3.4	-	-	-	3.3
5339	Reverse 1-1/2 Somersault 4-1/2 Twists	-	-	-		-	-	-	3.7
5351	Reverse 2-1/2 Somersault 1/2 Twist	-	2.9	2.7	-	-	2.7	2.5	-
5353	Reverse 2-1/2 Somersault 1-1/2 Twists	-		3.5	-	-	3.5	3.3	-
5371	Reverse 3-1/2 Somersault 1/2 Twist	-			-	-	3.4	3.1	-

(continued)

Table 8.1 (continued)

SPRINGBOARD		1 meter				3 meter			
		Strt	Pike	Tuck	Free	Strt	Pike	Tuck	Free
	Reverse Group	A	B	C	D	A	B	C	D
5411	Inward Dive 1/2 Twist	2.0	1.7	1.6	-	1.9	1.6	1.5	-
5412	Inward Dive 1 Twist	2.2	1.9	1.8	-	2.1	1.8	1.7	-
5421	Inward Somersault 1/2 Twist	-	-	-	1.9	-	-	-	1.7
5422	Inward Somersault 1 Twist	-	-	-	2.1	-	-	-	1.9
5432	Inward 1-1/2 Somersault 1 Twist	-	-	-	2.7	-	-	-	2.4
5434	Inward 1-1/2 Somersault 2 Twists	-	-	-	3.1	-	-	-	2.8
5436	Inward 1-1/2 Somersault 3 Twists	-	-	-		-	-	-	3.4

PLATFORM		10 meter				7.5 meter				5 meter			
		Strt	Pike	Tuck	Free	Strt	Pike	Tuck	Free	Strt	Pike	Tuck	Free
	Forward Group	A	B	C	D	A	B	C	D	A	B	C	D
101	Forward Dive	1.6	1.5	1.4	-	1.6	1.5	1.4	-	1.4	1.3	1.2	-
102	Forward Somersault	1.8	1.7	1.6	-	1.7	1.6	1.5	-	1.6	1.5	1.4	-
103	Forward 1-1/2 Somersault	1.9	1.6	1.5	-	1.9	1.6	1.5	-	2.0	1.7	1.6	-
104	Forward Double Somersault	2.5	2.2	2.1	-	2.4	2.1	2.0	-	2.6	2.3	2.2	-
105	Forward 2-1/2 Somersault	2.7	2.3	2.1	-		2.4	2.2	-		2.6	2.4	-
107	Forward 3-1/2 Somersault		3.0	2.7	-		3.1	2.8	-			3.0	-
109	Forward 4-1/2 Somersault			3.5	-				-				-
112	Forward Flying Somersault	-	1.9	1.8	-	-	1.8	1.7	-	-	1.7	1.6	-
113	Forward Flying 1-1/2 Somersault	-	1.8	1.7	-	-	1.8	1.7	-	-	1.9	1.8	-
114	Forward Flying Double Somersault	-	2.4	2.3	-	-	2.3	2.2	-	-	2.5	2.4	-
115	Forward Flying 2-1/2 Somersault	-	2.6	2.4	-	-		2.5	-	-			-
	Back Group	A	B	C	D	A	B	C	D	A	B	C	D
201	Back Dive	1.9	1.8	1.7	-	1.9	1.8	1.7	-	1.7	1.6	1.5	-
202	Back Somersault	1.9	1.8	1.7	-	1.8	1.7	1.6	-	1.7	1.6	1.5	-
203	Back 1-1/2 Somersault	2.4	2.2	1.9	-	2.4	2.2	1.9	-	2.5	2.3	2.0	-
204	Back Double Somersault	2.6	2.4	2.1	-	2.5	2.3	2.0	-		2.5	2.2	-
205	Back 2-1/2 Somersault	3.3	2.9	2.7	-		3.0	2.8	-			3.0	-
206	Back Triple Somersault		3.0	2.7	-		2.8	2.5	-		3.2	2.9	-
207	Back 3-1/2 Somersault		3.6	3.3	-			3.4	-				-
212	Back Flying Somersault	-	1.9	1.8	-	-	1.8	1.7	-	-	1.7	1.6	-
213	Back Flying 1-1/2 Somersault Back	-	2.4	2.1	-	-	2.4	2.1	-	-	2.5	2.2	-

		10 meter				7.5 meter				5 meter			
		Strt	Pike	Tuck	Free	Strt	Pike	Tuck	Free	Strt	Pike	Tuck	Free
	Reverse Group	A	B	C	D	A	B	C	D	A	B	C	D
301	Reverse Dive	2.0	1.9	1.8	-	2.0	1.9	1.8	-	1.8	1.7	1.6	-
302	Reverse Somersault	2.0	1.9	1.8	-	1.9	1.8	1.7	-	1.8	1.7	1.6	-
303	Reverse 1-1/2 Somersault	2.6	2.3	2.0	-	2.6	2.3	2.0	-	2.7	2.4	2.1	-
304	Reverse Double Somersault	2.8	2.5	2.2	-	2.7	2.4	2.1	-	2.9	2.6	2.3	-
305	Reverse 2-1/2 Somersault	3.3	2.9	2.7	-	3.4	3.0	2.8	-		3.2	3.0	-
306	Reverse Triple Somersault		3.1	2.8	-		2.9	2.6	-		3.3	3.0	-
307	Reverse 3-1/2 Somersault			3.4	-				-				-
312	Reverse Flying Somersault	-	2.0	1.9	-	-	1.9	1.8	-	-	1.8	1.7	-
313	Reverse Flying 1-1/2 Somersault	-	2.5	2.2	-	-	2.5	2.2	-	-	2.6	2.3	-
	Inward Group	A	B	C	D	A	B	C	D	A	B	C	D
401	Inward Dive	1.7	1.4	1.3	-	1.7	1.4	1.3	-	1.8	1.5	1.4	-
402	Inward Somersault	1.9	1.6	1.5	-	1.8	1.5	1.4	-	2.0	1.7	1.6	-
403	Inward 1-1/2 Somersault		2.0	1.8	-		2.1	1.9	-		2.4	2.2	-
404	Inward Double Somersault		2.6	2.4	-		2.6	2.4	-		3.0	2.8	-
405	Inward 2-1/2 Somersault		2.8	2.5	-		3.0	2.7	-		3.4	3.1	-
407	Inward 3-1/2 Somersault		3.5	3.2	-			3.4	-				-
412	Inward Flying Somersault	-	2.0	1.9	-	-	1.9	1.8	-	-	2.1	2.0	-
413	Inward Flying 1-1/2 Somersault	-	2.5	2.3	-	-	2.6	2.4	-	-	2.9	2.7	-
	Twisting Group	A	B	C	D	A	B	C	D	A	B	C	D
5111	Forward Dive 1/2 Twist	2.0	1.9	1.8	-	2.0	1.9	1.8	-	1.8	1.7	1.6	-
5112	Forward Dive 1 Twist	2.2	2.1		-	2.2	2.1		-	2.0	1.9		-
5121	Forward Somersault Forward 1/2 Twist	-	-	-	1.9	-	-	-	1.8	-	-	-	1.7
5122	Forward Somersault Forward 1 Twist	-	-	-	2.1	-	-	-	2.0	-	-	-	1.9
5124	Forward Somersault Forward 2 Twists	-	-	-	2.5	-	-	-	2.4	-	-	-	2.3
5131	Forward 1-1/2 Somersault 1/2 Twist	-	-	-	1.9	-	-	-	1.9	-	-	-	2.0
5132	Forward 1-1/2 Somersault 1 Twist	-	-	-	2.1	-	-	-	2.1	-	-	-	2.2
5134	Forward 1-1/2 Somersault 2 Twists	-	-	-	2.5	-	-	-	2.5	-	-	-	2.6
5136	Forward 1-1/2 Somersault 3 Twists	-	-	-	2.9	-	-	-	2.9	-	-	-	3.0
5138	Forward 1-1/2 Somersault 4 Twists	-	-	-	3.3	-	-	-	3.3	-	-	-	3.4
5152	Forward 2-1/2 Somersault 1 Twist	-	2.9	2.7	-	-	3.0	2.8	-	-	3.2	3.0	-
5154	Forward 2-1/2 Somersault 2 Twists	-	3.3	3.1	-	-	3.4	3.2	-	-	3.6	3.4	-
5172	Forward 3-1/2 Somersault 1 Twist	-	3.6	3.3	-	-	3.7	3.4	-	-			-

(continued)

Table 8.1 (continued)

	PLATFORM	10 meter				7.5 meter				5 meter			
		Strt	Pike	Tuck	Free	Strt	Pike	Tuck	Free	Strt	Pike	Tuck	Free
	Twisting Group	A	B	C	D	A	B	C	D	A	B	C	D
5211	Back Dive 1/2 Twist	2.0	1.9	1.8	-	2.0	1.9	1.8	-	1.8	1.7	1.6	-
5212	Back Dive 1 Twist	2.2			-	2.2			-	2.0			-
5221	Back Somersault 1/2 Twist	-	-	-	1.9	-	-	-	1.8	-	-	-	1.7
5222	Back Somersault 1 Twist	-	-	-	2.1	-	-	-	2.0	-	-	-	1.9
5223	Back Somersault 1-1/2 Twists	-	-	-	2.5	-	-	-	2.4	-	-	-	2.3
5225	Back Somersault 2-1/2 Twists	-	-	-	2.9	-	-	-	2.8	-	-	-	2.7
5231	Back 1-1/2 Somersault 1/2 Twist	-	-	-	2.0	-	-	-	2.0	-	-	-	2.1
5233	Back 1-1/2 Somersault 1-1/2 Twists	-	-	-	2.4	-	-	-	2.4	-	-	-	2.5
5235	Back 1-1/2 Somersault 2-1/2 Twists	-	-	-	2.8	-	-	-	2.8	-	-	-	2.9
5237	Back 1-1/2 Somersault 3-1/2 Twists	-	-	-	3.2	-	-	-	3.2	-	-	-	3.3
5239	Back 1-1/2 Somersault 4-1/2 Twists	-	-	-	3.6	-	-	-	3.6	-	-	-	3.7
5251	Back 2-1/2 Somersault 1/2 Twist	-	2.6	2.4	-	-	2.7	2.5	-	-	2.9	2.7	-
5253	Back 2-1/2 Somersault 1-1/2 Twists	-	3.4		-	-	3.5		-	-			-
5255	Back 2-1/2 Somersault 2-1/2 Twists	-	3.8	3.6	-								
5271	Back 3-1/2 Somersault 1/2 Twist	-	3.2	2.9	-	-							
5311	Reverse Dive 1/2 Twist	2.1	2.0	1.9	-	2.1	2.0	1.9	-	1.9	1.8	1.7	-
5312	Reverse Dive 1 Twist	2.3			-	2.3			-	2.1			-
5321	Reverse Somersault 1/2 Twist	-	-	-	2.0	-	-	-	1.9	-	-	-	1.8
5322	Reverse Somersault 1 Twist	-	-	-	2.2	-	-	-	2.1	-	-	-	2.0
5323	Reverse Somersault 1-1/2 Twists	-	-	-	2.6	-	-	-	2.5	-	-	-	2.5
5325	Reverse Somersault 2-1/2 Twists	-	-	-	3.0	-	-	-	2.9	-	-	-	2.8
5331	Reverse 1-1/2 Somersault 1/2 Twist	-	-	-	2.1	-	-	-	2.1	-	-	-	2.2
5333	Reverse 1-1/2 Somersault 1-1/2 Twists	-	-	-	2.5	-	-	-	2.5	-	-	-	2.6
5335	Reverse 1-1/2 Somersault 2-1/2 Twists	-	-	-	2.9	-	-	-	2.9	-	-	-	3.0
5337	Reverse 1-1/2 Somersault 3-1/2 Twists	-	-	-	3.3	-	-	-	3.3	-	-	-	3.4
5339	Reverse 1-1/2 Somersault 4-1/2 Twists	-	-	-	3.7	-	-	-	3.7	-	-	-	
5351	Reverse 2-1/2 Somersault 1/2 Twist	-	2.6	2.4	-	-	2.7	2.5	-	-	2.9	2.7	-
5353	Reverse 2-1/2 Somersault 1-1/2 Twists	-	3.4	3.2	-	-	3.5	3.3	-	-		3.5	-
5371	Reverse 3-1/2 Somersault 1/2 Twist	-	3.3	3.0	-	-				-			-

PLATFORM	10 meter				7.5 meter				5 meter			
	Strt	Pike	Tuck	Free	Strt	Pike	Tuck	Free	Strt	Pike	Tuck	Free
5411 Inward Dive 1/2 Twist	1.9	1.6	1.5	-	1.9	1.6	1.5	-	2.0	1.7	1.6	-
5412 Inward Dive 1 Twist	2.1	1.8	1.7	-	2.1	1.8	1.7	-	2.2	1.9	1.8	-
5421 Inward Somersault 1/2 Twist	-	-	-	1.8	-	-	-	1.7	-	-	-	1.9
5422 Inward Somersault 1 Twist	-	-	-	2.0	-	-	-	1.9	-	-	-	2.1
5432 Inward 1-1/2 Somersault 1 Twist	-	-	-	2.3	-	-	-	2.4	-	-	-	2.7
5434 Inward 1-1/2 Somersault 2 Twists	-	-	-	2.7	-	-	-	2.8	-	-	-	3.1
5436 Inward 1-1/2 Somersault 3 Twists	-	-	-	3.3	-	-	-		-	-	-	
Armstand Group	A	B	C	D	A	B	C	D	A	B	C	D
600 Armstand Dive	1.6	-	-	-	1.6	-	-	-	1.5	-	-	-
611 Armstand Forward 1/2 Somersault	2.0	1.9	1.7	-	2.0	1.9	1.7	-	1.8	1.7	1.5	-
612 Armstand Forward 1 Somersault	2.0	1.9	1.7	-	1.9	1.8	1.6	-	1.8	1.7	1.5	-
614 Armstand Forward Double Somersault		2.4	2.1	-		2.3	2.0	-		2.5	2.2	-
616 Armstand Forward Triple Somersault		3.3	3.0	-				-				
621 Armstand Backward 1/2 Somersault	1.9	1.8	1.6	-	1.9	1.8	1.6	-	1.7	1.6	1.4	-
622 Armstand Backward Somersault	2.3	2.2	2.0	-	2.2	2.1	1.9	-	2.1	2.0	1.8	-
623 Armstand Backward 1-1/2 Somersault		2.2	1.9	-		2.2	1.9	-		2.3	2.0	-
624 Armstand Backward Double Somersault	3.0	2.8	2.5	-	2.9	2.7	2.4	-	3.1	2.9	2.6	-
626 Armstand Backward Triple Somersault		3.5	3.2	-		3.3	3.0	-			3.4	-
631 Armstand Reverse 1/2 Somersault	2.0	1.9	1.7	-	2.0	1.9	1.7	-	1.8	1.7	1.5	-
632 Armstand Reverse 1 Somersault		2.3	2.1	-		2.2	2.0	-		2.1	1.9	-
633 Armstand Reverse 1-1/2 Somersault		2.3	2.0	-		2.3	2.0	-		2.4	2.1	-
634 Armstand Reverse Double Somersault		2.9	2.6	-		2.8	2.5	-		3.0	2.7	-
636 Armstand Reverse Triple Somersault			3.3	-			3.1	-				-
6122 Armstand Forward Somersault 1 Twist	-	-	-	2.6	-	-	-	2.3	-	-	-	2.2
6124 Armstand Forward Somersault 2 Twists	-	-	-	2.9	-	-	-	2.6	-	-	-	2.5
6142 Armstand Fwd. Double Som. 1 Twist	-	3.4	3.1	-	-	3.1	2.8	-	-	3.3	3.0	-
6144 Armstand Fwd. Double Som. 2 Twists	-	3.7	3.4	-	-	3.4	3.1	-	-	3.6	3.3	-
6162 Armstand Fwd. Triple Som. 1 Twist	-		3.8	-	-			-	-			-
6221 Armstand Back Somersault 1/2 Twist	-	-	-	1.9	-	-	-	1.8	-	-	-	1.7
6241 Armstand Back Double Som. 1/2 Twist	-	2.7	2.4	-	-	2.6	2.3	-	-	2.8	2.5	-
6243 Armstand Back Double Som. 1-1/2 Twists	-	-	-	3.2	-	-	-	3.1	-	-	-	3.3
6245 Armstand Back Double Som. 2-1/2 Twists	-	-	-	3.6	-	-	-	3.5	-	-	-	3.7
6261 Armstand Back Triple Som. 1/2 Twist	-	3.4	3.1	-	-	3.2	2.9	-	-	3.6	3.3	-

Reprinted, by permission, from Colonel Marculescu, La Federation Internationale de Natation, "FINA", Lausanne, Switzerland.

Table 8.2 Springboard Skill Progressions

GROUP I - FORWARD

3M	103C	103B	105C	105B	107C	107C	109C
Line-up	4	4	5	5	4		
1M							
107C							3
105B						3	
105C					3		2
104B				4			
104C			4				
103B				3	2		
103C			3	2			
102B		3					
102C	3						
101C	2	2	2	2	1	1	1
Jump	1	1	1	1			
1M	103c	103B	104C	104B	105C	105B	107C
105C							3
104C				4			
103B				3		3	
103C			3		3		2
102B		3					
102C	3						
101C	2	2	2	2	2	2	1
Jump	1	1	1	1	1	1	
3M							
Line-up	4	4			5	4	

GROUP II - BACKWARD

3M	203C	203B	203A	205C	205B
Line-up	4	4	3	5	5
1M					
204B					4
204C				4	
203B					3
203C				3	
202A		2			
202B		3			
202C	3				
201C	2	2		2	2
Jump	1	1	1	1	1
1M	203C	203B	203A	205C	
204C				2	
202A			3		
202B		3			
202C	3				
201C	2	2	2	1	
Jump	1	1	1		
3M					
Line-up	4	4	4	3	

GROUP III - REVERSE

3M	303C	303B	303A	305C	305B
1M					
304B					3
304C				3	
303B					2
303C				2	
302A			3		
302B		3			
302C	3				
301C	2	2	2	1	1
Jump	1	1	1		
1M	303C	303B	303A	305C	
304C				1	
302A			2		
302B		2			
302C	2				
301C	3	3	3	2	
Jump	1	1	1		

GROUP IV - INWARD

3M	403C	403B	403C	405C	405B
Line-up					1
1M					
403B					4
403C			3	4	
402B		2			
402C	2				
401C	3	3	2	3	3
Jump	1	1	1	2	2
1M	403C	403B	405C		
403C		2			
402B		3			
402C	3				
401C	2	2	1		
Jump	1	1			
3M					
403B		4			

GROUP Va - TWISTING															
3M	5132	5134	5136	5231	5233	5235	5237	5331	5333	5335	5337	5152 in	out	5154 in	out
Line-up	4			4	4										
5132		4													
5134			3												
5233						4									
5235							3								
5333										4					
5335											3				
5152															3
1M															
5126			4												
5124		5	2												
5122	3	3													
102B	2	2	1												
5227							4								
5225						5	2								
5223					3	3									
5221				3											
202A				2	2	2	1								
5327										5	4				
5325											2				
5323									3	3					
5321								3							
302A								2	2	2	1				
5144															4
5142													2		2
5134															
5132												2			
104B													1		1
103B (OP)												1		1	
Jump	1	1		1	1	1		1	1	1					

(continued)

Table 8.2 *(continued)*

GROUP Vb - TWISTING														
1M	5122	5132	5124	5134	5136	5231	5223	5233	5225	5235	5331	5333	5335	5152 (in)
5126					3									
5134					2									
5124														
5132				4										
5122		4	3											2
103B (OP)		6		3	1									
102B (OP)	2	3	2										1	
5225										2				
5233														
5223								4	3					
5221						4								
202A						3	2	3	2	1				
5325													2	
5333														
5323												4		
5321											4			
302A											3	3	1	
Jump	1	2	1	2		2	1	2	1		2	2		
3M														
5136					4									
5134				5										
5132		5												
5235										3				
5233								5						
5335													3	
5333												5		
5152														3
Jump		1		1		1		1			1	1		

Table 8.3 Platform Skill Progressions

	GROUP I - FORWARD								
10M	101B(S)	103C(S)	103C	103B(S)	103B	105B	107C	107B	109C
7.5M									
107C							4		
105B						7			
103B					8				
103B(S)				8					
103C			9						
103C(S)		7							
101B(S)	8								
5M									
107C									3
105B								2	
105C							3		
103B					7	5			
103B(S)				7					
103C			8						
103C(S)		6							
101B(S)	7								
101B (S-OP)	6	5		6					
101B (OP)			7		6				
Line-up	5	4	6	5	5	6			
3M									
105C									2
103B						5			
103B(S)									
103C			5						
103C(S)		3							
102B					4	4			
102B(S)				4					
102C			4						
102C(S)		4							
101B(S)	4								
101B (S-OP)	3			3					
101B (OP)			3		3	3			
101C(S)		3							
1M									
103B								1	
103C							2		1
102B					2	2			
102C			2				1		
102B(S)				2					
102C(S)		2							
101B(S)	2								

(continued)

Table 8.3 (continued)

GROUP I - FORWARD (continued)									
10M	101B(S)	103C(S)	103C	103B(S)	103B	105B	107C	107B	109C
101B (S-OP)	1			1					
101B (OP)					1	1			
101C(S)		1							
101C			1						

GROUP II - BACKWARD							
10M	201A	201B	203A	203B	205C	205B	207C
7.5M							
206C							4
205C					7		
203B				11			
203A			3				
201B		9					
201A	8						
Jump	7	8		10			
5M							
205C							3
204C					5		
204B						5	
203C					9		
203B				9		4	
202B				7			
202A			2				
201B		7					
201A	6						
Jump	4	6	1	6	3	3	
Line-up	5			8	6	6	
3M							
204C							2
203C							1
202B				4			
201B		5					
201C		4					
Jump	2	3		3			
Line-up	3	2		5			
1M							
202B				2		2	
202C					2		
Jump	1	1		1	1	1	

GROUP III - REVERSE							
10M	301A	301B	303C	303B	305C	305B	307C
7.5M							
306C							5
305C					5		
303B				5			
303C			6				
301B		8					
301A	6						
Jump		7					
5M							
305C							4
304C					3		
304B						3	
303C			5		2		
303B						2	
302B				4			
302C			4				
301A	5						
301B		6					
301C					4		
Jump	4	5					
3M							
304C							3
303C							2
302B				3			
302C			3				
301B		4					
301C	3	3					
Jump	2	2	2	2			
1M							
302B						1	
302C					1		1
Jump	1	1	1	1			

GROUP IV - INWARD							
10M	401A	401B	403C	403B	405C	405B	407C
7.5M							
405C					5		
403B				4			
403C			6				
401B		6					
401A	5						
5M							
405C							3
403B				3	3		
403C			5		4		
401B		5					
401A	4						
401B (OP)	3	4	4		1		
3M							
403C				4			
403B						4	
402B			3		2		
402C			3				
401B		3					
401B (OP)	2			2			
401C		2	2		3		
1M							
403C							2
402C					2		
401B (OP)	1			1			
401C		1	1		1		1 ·

(continued)

Table 8.3 (continued)

GROUP V - TWISTING															
10M	5132	5134	5136	5231	5233	5235	5237	5331	5333	5335	5337	5152 in	5152 out	5154 in	5154 out
7.5M															
5152												2	2	2	
5333									3						
5331								3							
5235						6									
5233				4	3										
5231															
5136			4												
5134		6	3												
5132	5	4													
5M															
5327											3				
5325										3	2				
5323									2	2					
5331								2							
302A									1	1	1				
5227							3								
5225						5	2								
5223				3	4	4									
5231															
202A					3	3	1								
5134															1
5132	4	3										1			
103B (OP)	3	2													
3M															
5321								1							
5223					2	2									
5221				2											
202A				1	1	1									
5124		5	2												
5122	2														
102B (OP)	1	1	1												
103C-B															
1M															
103C-B													1		1

GROUP VI- ARMSTAND									
10M	612C-B	614C-B	616C	624B	626C-B	6241B	631C-B	632C-B	634C-B	636C
7.5M										
612C-B	3									
614C-B		3								
623B				3						
6241B						4				
625C-B					6					
631C-B							2			
632C-B								2		
634C-B									4	
635C										4
5M										
612C-B	2	1								
614C			2							
623C-B					2					
623B				2						
624C-B					5					
631C-B							1	1		
632C-B									2	
633C-B									3	
634C										3
3M										
611C-B	1									
612C-B		2								
614C			3							
622C-B					1					
622B				1						
623C-B					3					
6221B						3				
633C										2
1M										
612C			1							
621A						1				
6211A						2				
623C-B					4					
632C										1
631C-B									1	

Training and Peaking for Competition

The technical material covered in the previous chapters is essential to excellent coaching and diving performance. However, competition excellence requires not only technical knowledge but also an effective training program. A great deal of planning must go into creating a training program in which exercise and diving training fit together in a productive manner. The volume and intensity of work done in these areas should vary during different periods of the season. In addition, when preparing for championship competition, a significant amount of time must be spent in meet simulation training to get the diver in the right mind-set for a peak performance.

The information presented here is intended to be a blueprint from which training plans specific to each program can be developed. Keep in mind, should you decide to construct your own plan, that it is a living document and must constantly be adapted from cycle to cycle and from year to year. It may take some time to produce the most effective program. As new information becomes available, the plan must continue to change.

Specific planning and peaking for competition as presented here is not suitable for beginning and intermediate-level divers. These divers should be spending their time developing skills, learning dives, and improving their physical fitness. Once they have attained a more advanced level of skill and are participating in major championship events, the type of training programs described here can be implemented for better results.

GENERAL PRINCIPLES

The following principles have been gathered from several different exercise physiology and training methodology sources. I have supplemented this information with knowledge gained from my own personal experience and applied it specifically to diving. These principles have been incorporated in the year-long training plan blueprint presented in this chapter.

1. Prior to specializing in sport-specific weight training exercises, undertake a six- to eight-week general overall body strengthening program at the beginning of the year. Athletes who are lifting for the first time should undertake overall body strengthening for two years before specializing.

2. Develop strength first, then work on power.

3. When developing strength, use a minimum of 60 percent of the 1-repetition maximum (1RM). This is the amount of weight that can be lifted at one time. Gradually build to using higher percentages of the 1RM. The 1RM should be retested approximately every four weeks and the weight lifted adjusted accordingly. In the extension phase of the exercises, move with as much speed as possible and not slow down at the end of the motion.

4. To develop power, use 30 to 40 percent of 1RM. When doing leg training, move the weight in quickly, hold for one count, and extend quickly. At the end of the extension, let the weight leave the feet and catch. For lunges, jump up at the end of the extension.

5. Use a stair step model of training for the exercise program, in which the intensity of the training load increases 5 to 10 percent each week for three weeks. The intensity is then reduced by 20 percent in the fourth week for recovery purposes. The next cycle starts at the same intensity as the third week in the previous cycle and increases in intensity as before. This model applies to the weight, trunk, and running/jumping programs.

6. The amount of time spent in each phase of the exercise and diving programs will depend on the schedule of events and the priority assigned to each.

7. The longer the preparation period prior to the competition period, the longer the effect of training will last. Postpone detraining to prevent loss of strength and power during the peaking and championship meet periods.

8. The preparation and competitive periods may overlap. If divers train through these early competitions, they should be low-priority events.

9. At the end of the cycle, divers and coaches should evaluate the program and determine the key elements to work on in the next cycle. If this can be done immediately after the major championship, divers' strengths and weaknesses will be clearest.

ORGANIZING THE YEAR

In order to begin organizing a training program, the training year must be divided into significant periods with appropriate time frames designated for each phase. This process is dictated by the diver's competitive schedule and the events that are a high priority for him or her. Most divers training on a year-round basis have two cycles in training and competition. The first cycle begins in the fall and ends in the spring, and the second cycle starts after the last championship event in the spring and ends in mid-August. The plan presented here assumes a two-cycle plan. Coaches and divers with significantly different schedules should adapt the principles of this plan to fit their needs. In all cases, the peaking for competition phase of preparation is the same.

There are four periods to each cycle of the training year:

1. Preparation period
2. Competitive period (includes a six-week peaking program)
3. Championship period
4. Transition period

The preparation period takes place from the first week of training in the cycle until the beginning of the six-week peaking program in the competitive period. The preparation and competitive periods can overlap because the events in the early competitive season are usually not a high priority and the diver can train through them. The championship period occurs at the end of the peaking program and may extend up to six to eight weeks in some cases. The transition period takes place after the last championship event and before the start of the next cycle. Table 9.1 lists the approximate weeks for each of these phases. The dates indicated for the weeks are arbitrary but give a general picture of the unfolding season. These dates would be adapted for different years. The training model presented later in this chapter (see page 195) is based on the cycles and weeks shown here.

The heaviest training takes place in the preparation period and at the beginning of the competitive period. The lightest training occurs in the six-week peaking program and during the championship period. If the championship period extends over several weeks, heavy training should be alternated with competition preparation. The transition period is inactive with regard to diving, but divers should participate in other activities during that time.

EXERCISE PROGRAM

With the training year defined, the coach and diver must determine what training will occur in each period, how frequently it should be done, and on which days of the week. This section describes the exercise program; the section that

Table 9.1 Sample Training Year

Period	Cycle 1	Cycle 2
Preparation	Week 1-26	Week 38-43
	Sept. 7-Mar. 7	May 24-July 4
Competitive	Week 27-31	Week 44-48
	Mar. 8-Apr. 10	July 5-Aug. 8
(Peaking period)	Week 27-32	Week 44-49
	Mar. 8-Apr. 18	July 12-Aug. 15
Championship	Week 32-36	Week 49
	Apr. 12-May 16	Aug. 9-Aug. 15
Transition	Week 37	Week 50-52
	May 17-May 23	Aug. 16-Sept. 5

follows presents a training program model that combines the exercise program and technical training.

Organizing the Week

Determining the days that training will take place and the type of exercise program that will be done is important to the success of training. Diving training needs to be structured so that what is asked of the diver in the pool is not in conflict with the load and intensity of the exercise program. In other words, the program shouldn't include a heavy weight training session on Tuesday and then a heavy training day with a lot of optional dives on Wednesday. This is a setup for failure!

During weeks 1 through 6, only weight and trunk training occurs; the daily organization is as follows:

M	T	W	Th	F	Sa
Trunk	Weights	Trunk	Weights	Trunk	Weights

In the first week or two, this schedule may have to be altered to allow for muscle soreness. After two weeks this should not be a problem, as the diver will adapt to the workload. Based on the position of the weight training days, the heaviest diving days should be Monday, Tuesday, Thursday, and Saturday.

Starting with week 7, the running and jumping program is added two days a week. The daily schedule would reflect this change:

M	T	W	Th	F	Sa
Trunk	Weights	Trunk	Weights	Trunk	Weights
Running				Running	

This training week indicates that the heaviest diving days should be Monday and Thursday. Tuesday and Saturday would be somewhat lighter diving days, and Wednesday and Friday would be the lightest days.

Beginning with week 13, weight training is reduced to twice a week for the rest of the cycle. This is to reduce the load during the time when new optional dives are introduced and more quality in performing all optional dives is desired. The daily schedule is as follows:

M	T	W	Th	F	Sa
Trunk Running	Weights	Trunk	Rest	Trunk Running	Weights

This schedule allows heavy diving days on Monday, Tuesday, Thursday, Friday, and Saturday. Wednesday is a light day or a day spent on less demanding skills.

These schedules would also be used in the preparation period of cycle 2; however, the time allocated to each phase would be considerably shorter due to the fact that the cycle has fewer weeks.

Weight Training for Prepubescent Divers

Junior prepubescent divers can benefit from weight training for all muscle groups and will gain in strength. For safety reasons, much of the first year should be spent learning proper lifting technique for the exercises chosen. Young divers should perform weight training at first with little or no weight. A broomstick or empty barbell is suggested. Once they have learned proper technique, weight can be added. However, the prepubescent diver should not exercise with a weight heavier than can be lifted correctly six times. The diver's 6RM should be determined first, and that weight should be used to determine the starting load. As strength increases, retesting should be done and the 6RM load increased accordingly. The biggest challenges in weight training for these divers are supervision and availability of equipment. In most programs, the coach is not able to oversee the program due to time constraints, and equipment (or time in the weight room) is not available. In this case, body resistance or rubber tubing exercises can be used as a substitute.

For an excellent source of exercise programs for young divers, consult the additional readings section at the end of this chapter.

Weight Training for Postpubescent Divers

Junior postpubescent and senior divers should participate in a weight training program if possible. Training starts in the preparation period of the first cycle. If the diver is in the first two years of weight training, all muscle groups should be included throughout the training program. If the diver has had at least two years of total body weight training, then the first six to eight weeks of training should work all muscle groups. This prepares the ligaments, tendons, and muscles for the more intense exercise and diving training to follow. Training begins with relatively light weight and high repetitions (one set of 15 repetitions) and progresses to heavier weight and lower repetitions (three sets of 8-10 repetitions). At this point, specialization and more intense strength training can begin.

Specialization consists of training for the legs that will contribute to diving performance. Exercises such as the leg press, squat, lunge, ankle extension (plantar flexion), squat jump, hang clean, and power clean will accomplish this. Explanations of these exercises can be found in any weight training manual. Three or four of these exercises should be performed in one training session. Rotating the exercises on a periodic basis can provide better variety in muscle training and prevent boredom.

Some arm and shoulder work should be done to strengthen the muscle groups used when making contact with the water during entries and when pulling into a tuck or pike position. These exercises include the biceps curl and military press, finishing with a shoulder shrug and lat (latissimus) pull-down with a narrow grip. The pull-down machine is a standard piece of equipment in weight training setups. In addition, practicing holding handstands can be of great value.

Strength training should build up over several weeks depending on how much time is available before the peaking phase begins. During the course of the program the number of repetitions per set should decrease and the number of sets and the weight lifted should increase. If failure does not occur in previous sets (i.e., the lifter cannot finish a repetition due to fatigue), failure should be reached in the last set of each exercise, regardless of the number of repetitions needed to accomplish this. Time and experience will show what percentages of 1RM and 6RM sets and repetitions are appropriate for each diver. The 1RM should be retested every four or five weeks and adjustments made in the weight used. At the end of this strength training phase, a typical session for senior divers would be six sets of two repetitions at 90 to 95 percent of 1RM.

Running and Jumping

On non-weight-training days, running, hopping, stair jumping, squat jumps, and drop (depth) jumps are done to develop the legs for power and plyometric movements.

Running, hopping, and bounding are done on level ground or going up stairs. On level ground, these activities include sprinting, hopping on one leg, and bounding on both legs for a distance of 30 yards. When using stairs (stadium steps), the exercises include sprinting two steps at a time, hopping one to two steps at a time on one leg, bounding two steps at a time on both legs, and jumping the maximum number of steps possible on both legs. All junior and senior divers can participate in these exercises.

Squat jumps are done on the ground and consist of squatting down to a 70- to 90-degree angle at the knee joint, with the heels on the ground, and jumping as high as possible into the air. Jumping is done in three directions: upward, upward and forward, and upward and backward. Repetitions range from six to ten, and sets range from one to three. After doing these jumps without resistance, divers can add weight in the form of handheld dumbbells or a weight vest or belt. The running program described earlier should precede squat jump training so the legs are conditioned first. Prepubescent divers should do squat jump programs without added weight.

Only postpubescent divers should perform drop jumps. Prepubescent divers run the risk of growth plate injury while doing drop jumps. All divers should perform squat jump training before attempting drop jumps so that the legs are prepared for the added load.

Drop jumps are performed by stepping off an elevated takeoff area of varying heights onto a landing mat. These jumps are done in two ways: with a deep squat or with minimal squatting after landing on the mat. In the deep-squat drop jump the diver squats to a 70 to 90 degree angle at the knee joint and jumps back up to the maximum height. Alternatively, after contact with the landing mat, the diver can jump upward as quickly as possible with minimal squatting movement. Deep-squat drop jumps are done from heights of 16 and 20 inches for females and 20 and 24 inches for males. These heights correspond to respective hurdle heights in springboard diving. The shallow drop jumps are performed from 30- and 42-inch heights, and no more than two sets of 10 repetitions at each level are done in one training session. The deep-squat drop jump exercise is used in training by springboard and platform divers, while the shallow jump is used only by platform divers. After an initial training period of deep-squat drop jumps, resistance can be added in the form of handheld dumbbells or a weight vest or belt. Resistance should not be used in the shallow jumps.

Who Does What?

There are three categories of divers: springboard specialists, platform specialists, and springboard and platform combination divers. All three should take part in the six- to eight-week total body weight training at the beginning of the initial training period in cycle 1.

Following the preparation phase, all divers should begin strength training. A running, hopping, and bounding program to condition the legs should also take place. After this period, the three types of divers follow somewhat different programs.

The springboard specialist continues a strength weight training program until 10 days before the major championship. On the other days, maximum step jumps, squat jumps, and deep-squat drop jumps are performed.

The platform specialist continues a strength weight training program for 10 to 12 weeks, then changes to a power and speed weight program. This entails reducing the weight lifted and increasing the speed of the movement. Strength is maintained with a once-a-week strength training session. Weight training stops 10 days before the major competition. On the other days, maximum step jumps, step hopping, step bounding, squat jumps, and drop jumps using both techniques are performed.

The combination springboard and platform diver continues the strength weight training program until 10 days before the major competition. On the other days a program of maximum step jumps, step hopping, step bounding, squat jumps, and drop jumps using both techniques is followed.

Abdominal/Trunk Training

All three types of divers—springboard, platform, and combined—should perform abdominal/trunk training. This program consists of three phases: conditioning, strength, and power. A set of core exercises is presented here, but many variations of these can be substituted or rotated through the program. For exercises 1, 2, 3, 4, and 7, the initiation of movement should occur in the abdominal area. As each of the three phases take place, the way the chosen exercises are performed varies. The core exercises are as follows:

1. Pike-ups performed on the ground from a curved surface. The curved surface can be created by folding a mat and placing it under an open mat, or by placing a curved object under an open mat. The starting position is lying stretched out, face up, in an arched shape with the legs and arms straight (see figure 9.1).

Figure 9.1   Pike-up on curved surface.

2. Inverted sit-ups on an inclined board performed with the legs straight and the arms folded on the chest (see figure 9.2).

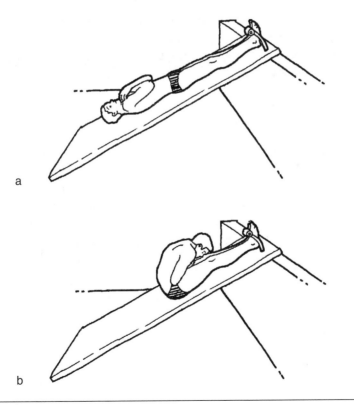

Figure 9.2   Inverted sit-up.

3. Hanging leg lifts on wall bars with a padded surface over the bars so the lifts can be done quickly and without discomfort. The legs are kept straight and lifted to touch the bars overhead, then returned to their original hanging position (see figure 9.3).

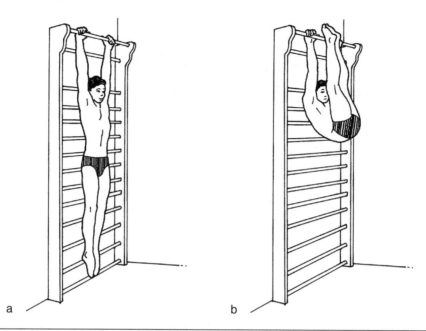

Figure 9.3   Leg lift to bar.

4. Inverted hanging trunk curl and tuck-up. This is done on a chin-up bar with gravity boots on the ankles. The body hangs straight with the arms folded across the chest; then the trunk curls upward as the body pulls into as tight a tuck position as possible (see figure 9.4).

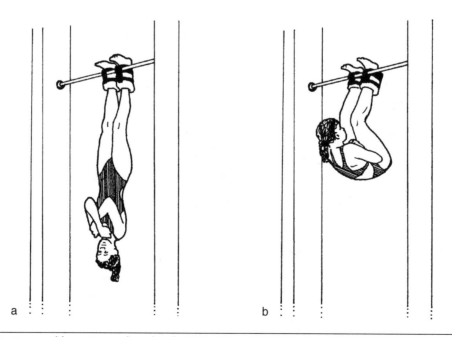

Figure 9.4   Inverted hanging curl and tuck-up.

5. Prone trunk lifts. This is done lying face down on an elevated flat surface with the trunk extended over the edge of the support area and a partner securing the legs. The arms are folded across the chest. Beginning with the trunk horizontal, the diver quickly moves the trunk alternately from approximately one foot below to one foot above horizontal (see figure 9.5).

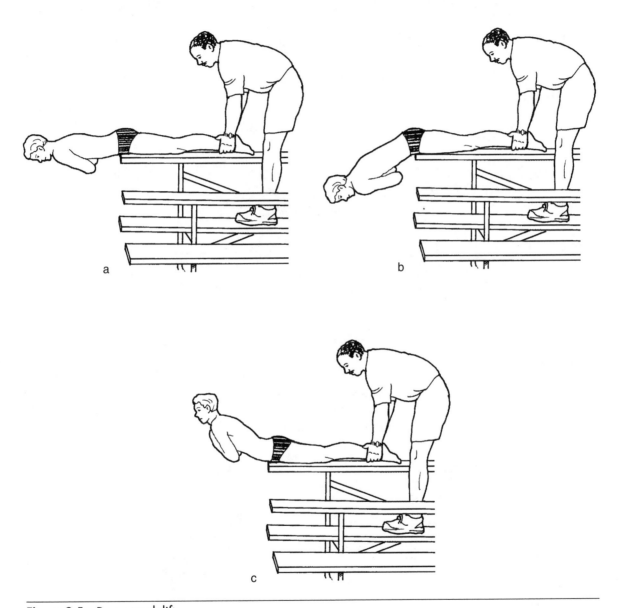

Figure 9.5 Prone trunk lift.

6. Prone leg lifts. These are done in the same way as the trunk lifts, except that the legs are extended beyond the support area. If necessary, the trunk can be secured by a partner (see figure 9.6).

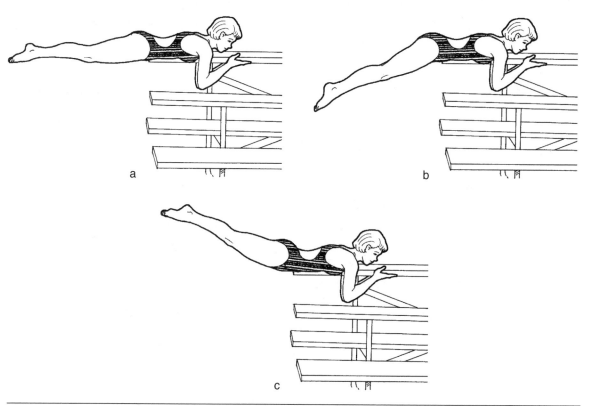

Figure 9.6   Prone leg lift.

7. Tuck-ups on wall bars. From a hanging position the legs are tucked up and brought to a position with each knee beside the head at the top of the lift, then returned to the starting position (see figure 9.7).

Figure 9.7   Hanging tuck-up.

8. Side-ups. Using the same elevated support area as in the prone exercises, the diver lies on one side with the trunk extended beyond the support area and a partner securing the legs. With the hands clasped behind the head, the diver drops the trunk below horizontal, then lifts it above horizontal (see figure 9.8). The exercise is repeated on both sides. These are done as a conditioning exercise with three sets of 10 to 15 repetitions throughout the training cycle. No resistance is added while performing this exercise.

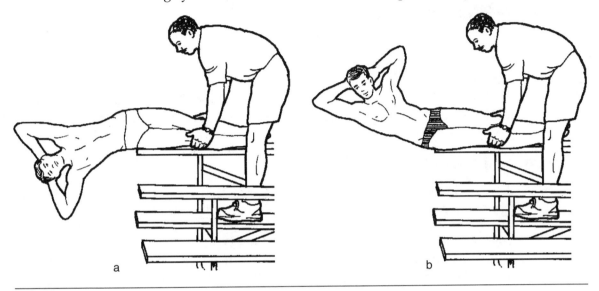

Figure 9.8 Side-up.

The first phase of training, conditioning, consists of many repetitions of each exercise, up to three to four sets of 15 repetitions on a given day. The next training phase should not begin until this level of performance can be accomplished.

In the second phase, strength training, resistance is added in the form of ankle weights for leg movements and either weight plates or a weight vest for trunk movements. The amount of weight used will have to be determined by experimentation for each exercise and for each diver. The key factor is to reach failure in at least the final set of each exercise. In this phase the number of repetitions will decrease from one set of 12 repetitions with light resistance, to three sets of eight repetitions with heavier resistance.

The final phase is power training, which occurs prior to the peaking period and continues into the peaking period, with a gradually decreasing number of repetitions, down to a maintenance level for the championship. During this phase no resistance is used. Each repetition of each exercise is performed as an individual movement and done as quickly as possible. The diver begins with one set of 12 repetitions and builds to three sets of eight repetitions before tapering for the peaking period.

TRAINING PROGRAM MODEL

This training model is broken down into two training cycles, with the first and longer cycle taking place over 37 weeks and the second cycle covering 15 weeks. Since divers are in better physical and diving condition entering the second cycle, cycle 2 training is shorter and starts at a different level. Throughout the program, divers train twice a day (for a minimum total of four hours of training), six days a week. Not everyone's training and competitive year will follow the same schedule, so you may have to adjust the length of time spent in each phase of a cycle. When making these adjustments, keep the general principles presented at the beginning of the chapter in mind.

Cycle 1—Weeks 1-36

This cycle begins with a lengthy period for preparation and a shorter period for the early stages of the competition period. Next comes a more intense competition period, which leads into the championship period. (The peaking program is the same for cycles 1 and 2; it is presented in the section that follows the end of cycle 2—see "Peaking for Competition" on page 201). A brief transition phase completes cycle 1.

Preparation Period: Weeks 1-26

During the preparation period, the diver's goals are to achieve the best physical condition possible and to develop the diving skills and new dives necessary for success in the competitive period. In weeks 18 to 26, the exercise program is designed to continue strength gains but place more emphasis on power. At the same time, the diver begins to dive for score in practice and actual competition, which helps to hone the competitive skills needed for the peaking period and the major championship(s).

Technical Training

Weeks 1-8

Dry land—Comprises 75 percent of the training in weeks 1 through 4 and 65 percent in weeks 4 through 8. Emphasis is mostly on boardwork and platform takeoffs; basic dives on the trampoline; somersaults on the ground, trampoline, and dryland board; one-and-a-half somersaults in all directions with come-out work; and some optional dive work on trampoline and dryland board using the overhead spotting equipment.
Pool—Comprises 25 percent of training in weeks 1 through 4 and 35 percent in weeks 5 through 8. Emphasis is on boardwork, lineups, tuck dives, springboard and platform takeoffs, and voluntary dives with degree of difficulty limit.

Weeks 9-12

Dry land—Comprises 50 percent of training time. The same emphasis applies as in weeks 1 through 8, with a shift to 50 percent work on basic dives and skills and 50 percent work on optional dive lead-ups and the introduction of skills for the new dives that are planned.
Pool—With the added pool time (50 percent), work on the basic skills takes place in the first practice session. In the second session, the diver begins performing optional dives in the present dive lists, at all levels. The diver should gradually phase these optional dives in over the first three weeks. The coach and diver should continue to emphasize transferring the skills and fundamentals worked on in weeks 1 through 8 to these dives. All lead-ups for new dives should be done in this period.

Weeks 13-16

Dry land—Comprises 40 percent of training time. The emphasis is on basic drills and skill work 30 percent of the time and on optional dives 70 percent of the time. More time should be spent on new dive lead-up skills.

Pool—The diver should continue to work on basic skills and optional dive lead-ups in the morning. The second practice is devoted to the current optional dives and new dives. All new dives should be performed during these three weeks.

Week 17

Rest for Christmas break.

Weeks 18-21

Dry land—Comprises 30 percent of training time. Basic dives and skills occupy 25 percent of the time, and optional dive work occupies 75 percent of the time, with emphasis on the new dive skills.

Pool—Comprises 70 percent of training time. The morning practice is devoted to dryland and pool work on basic skills and dives, plus optional dive lead-ups. The second practice focuses on optional dives. The final list of dives to be used in competition must be determined during this four-week period.

Weeks 22-26

Continue the same percentage of time allocation as in weeks 18 through 21, but introduce repetitions of dives for score to prepare for the six-week peaking program to follow. Monday, Tuesday, Friday, and Saturday can be used to conduct this scoring. A springboard or platform specialist would use Monday and Friday as scoring days. A springboard and platform combination diver would do springboard scoring on Monday and Friday and platform scoring on Tuesday and Saturday. These are the days the exercise program affords the best opportunity for quality diving. Each day the springboard diver would do five of each basic dive for score in the morning and the same for the optional dives in the afternoon. This provides 10 repetitions a week for score. The platform diver would do the same on these days, but the number of repetitions performed for score would depend on how much workload he or she can handle. The number of scored repetitions of each dive should not be fewer than three. The combination diver follows the same program but performs scored dives four days a week instead of two. Coaches should keep a record of the scores in order to observe progress and identify weak dives. The results of scoring should provide the direction for training in the nonscoring sessions.

Exercise Program

The exercise program for the preparation period presented on the following page first emphasizes general conditioning. With this as a foundation, the emphasis then shifts to strength gains and finally to developing power.

Competitive Period: Weeks 27-31; Championship Period: Weeks 32-36

During the competitive period and the first week of the championship period (weeks 27 through 32), a six-week peaking program takes place. Training is arranged so that the diver has an opportunity to perform high quality dives by gradually reducing the volume of exercise done but maintaining the strength and power gains of the previous periods. During the remainder of the champi-

TRUNK TRAINING	WEIGHT TRAINING	RUNNING/JUMPING
Weeks 1-8	**Weeks 1-8**	**Weeks 1-6**
Conditioning phase	Total body preparation	None
Weeks 9-17	**Weeks 9-20**	**Weeks 7-12**
Strength phase	Specialized strength	Running/hopping
Weeks 18-26	**Weeks 21-26**	**Weeks 13-19**
Power phase	Specialized strength and power	Squat jumps
		Weeks 20-26
		Drop jumps

onship period, training is adapted to the competition schedule to maintain a peak for each event. This six-week peaking program is discussed in the section titled "Peaking for Competition" on page 201.

Technical Training

Dry land—Comprises 25 percent of the training time. Work focuses on the weak dives and skills to supplement the pool training aimed at improving scoring potential on each dive.

Pool—Comprises 75 percent of training time. The training program throughout this period changes to doing lists of dives for score instead of repetition scoring. A list of dives for score means performing one repetition of each dive in the order in which they will be done in competition. However, several of these lists can be done in one training session. On nonscoring days, the diver repeats the dives and works on weak dives and skills to improve scores achieved on the next scoring day.

The springboard and platform specialists should use Monday, Wednesday, and Thursday for normal training and Tuesday, Friday, and Saturday for list scoring. The number of lists done can vary from three to five each day for springboard divers. Platform divers should do three lists on Tuesday and Friday and two lists on Saturday. Combination divers should do three to five lists on the springboard on Monday and Friday and three lists on the platform on Tuesday and Saturday. The basic dives can be done in the morning and the optional dives in the afternoon.

All scores for dive lists should be recorded and analyzed throughout this period.

Exercise Program

The exercise program entails maintaining strength and power while reducing the volume of work done. This allows the diver to feel more rested and able to perform better in the pool. The specifics of how this is accomplished are described in the "Peaking for Competition" section later in the chapter.

Transition Period: Week 37

Active rest occurs during this time. The diver does not participate in any diving activities, but does participate in other types of cross-training sports such as basketball, volleyball, tennis, and so on.

Cycle 2—Weeks 38-49

Cycle 2 is similar to cycle 1 except that the periods span different lengths of time. The preparation, competitive, and championship periods are considerably shorter, while the transition period is longer. The peaking for competition program remains the same in both cycles. Because the diver is in better physical condition entering cycle 2, the exercise program can begin at a higher level.

There is not enough time to begin with weight training three times a week and then drop to two times a week, as in cycle 1, so the daily training schedule is as follows:

M	T	W	Th	F	Sa
Trunk	Weights	Trunk	Rest	Trunk	Weights

Preparation Period: Weeks 38-43

Because the preparation period in this cycle is only six weeks in length, training must start at a higher level than in cycle 1. Some deterioration of diving and physical skills has most likely occurred in the last period of cycle 1. However, as mentioned before, the diver should be in much better condition than at the beginning of cycle 1.

Technical Training

Weeks 38-40

Dry land—Comprises 50 percent of training time. An evaluation of performance in cycle 1 should provide the direction for training. The two or three weakest dives and skills should be targeted to work on.

Pool—Comprises 50 percent of training time. All dives at all levels should be performed in the first week to get the diver back to full training quickly. Any new dives to be considered should be performed by the second week. Dive repetitions and technique improvement should once again be the emphasis.

Weeks 41-43

Dry land—Comprises 30 percent of training time, with the emphasis remaining the same.

Pool—Comprises 70 percent of training time, with the emphasis remaining the same. All new dives should be finalized by week 43.

Exercise Program

Trunk training: Begin with two sets of eight repetitions at 80 percent of the resistance used in cycle 1. Use 90 percent the second week and 100 percent the third week.

Trunk Training	Weight Training	Running/Jumping
	Weeks 38-40	
Strength phase	Strength phase	Squat jumps

Weight training: Retest the 1RM and begin with 85 percent load, doing three sets to failure. Increase the load to 90 percent and 95 percent, respectively, during the second and third weeks.

Jumping training: The first week, perform three sets of 10 repetitions with no resistance. The second week, use 90 percent of the maximum resistance used in cycle 1. Increase to 100 percent in week 3.

Trunk Training	Weight Training	Running/Jumping
	Weeks 41-43	
Power phase	Strength phase	Drop jumps

Trunk training: The first week, do one set of 12 repetitions with no resistance. The second and third weeks, do two sets of 8 repetitions and three sets of 8 repetitions, respectively, with no resistance.

Weight training: The first week, begin with two sets to failure with 90 percent load. The second and third weeks, do three sets to failure with 95 percent and 100 percent load, respectively.

Jumping training: Do two sets of 10 repetitions from the two heights described in the running/jumping section presented earlier. The types of jumps used would depend on the event(s) for which the diver is training. No resistance is used during any of the three weeks.

Competitive and Championship Periods: Weeks 44-49

The goals here are the same as in cycle 1—to maintain strength and power while doing meet simulation training to prepare for competition. Details on the peaking for competition program are presented on page 201.

Technical Training

Dry land—Comprises 25 percent of training time.
Pool—Comprises 75 percent of training time. Use the same training focus as described for this period in cycle 1 for the competitive and championship period. Follow the peaking for competition program.

Exercise Program

Use the same exercises as in the previous preparation period (weeks 38-43), and follow the guidelines presented in the next section to reduce the volume of exercise performed.

Transition Period: Weeks 50-52

The diver does not dive but does participate in cross-training activities during this period of active rest.

PEAKING FOR COMPETITION

This program is designed for the final six weeks of a training cycle, leading up to the major championship event. The first week of this program is week 1, and the week of the championship is week 6. The purposes of this training are as follows:

1. To gradually reduce the exercise load to allow the diver to feel progressively more rested and able to perform better in the pool.
2. To maintain the intensity of the exercise program at a reasonably high level in order to retain the strength and power gains of the previous training.
3. To change the emphasis of technical training to 50 percent competitive preparation and 50 percent retention and improvement of skills. Please refer to the section entitled "List Training" near the end of this chapter for directions on how to conduct this training effectively.

Variables

The variables that must be accounted for when developing the peaking plan are as follows:

- Technical training schedule—daily scheme
- Technical training volume—number of movements
- Technical training intensity—type and quality of movements
- Exercise training schedule—daily scheme
- Exercise training volume—number of repetitions
- Exercise training intensity—amount of resistance/speed

The peaking model presented here shows how these six variables can be organized and how they interact to provide high-performance results. There are certainly other models that can be successful, and experimentation is encouraged.

Weeks 1-4

A full six-day training week is maintained during this period; however, because the diver is spending considerable time doing lists of dives for a score, the training load is reduced.

Technical Training Schedule

Springboard or Platform Specialist

M	T	W	Th	F	Sa
Repetition/ Skills	Lists	Repetition/ Skills	Repetition/ Skills	Lists	Lists

Combination Springboard/Platform

M	T	W	Th	F	Sa
Lists	Lists	Repetition/ Skills	Repetition/ Skills	Lists	Lists

In both schedules Sunday is a rest day, unless a competition occurs; in that case, Monday becomes a rest day, and the rest of the week remains the same.

Technical Training Volume

Based on the previous daily schedule, the volume of training would be highest on the repetition/skills work days and lightest on the list training days. The coach should communicate with and monitor the diver on the high-volume days to determine the appropriate load. In both schedules, Wednesday would be the heaviest training day of the week because there is no list training the next day.

The weekly training volume does not change from week 1 to week 4. However, keep in mind that one of the purposes of the peaking program is to allow the diver to perform with high quality. If necessary, do not hesitate to reduce the training volume and/or intensity in any week to allow the diver to perform better.

Technical Training Intensity

The intensity of training is high on the list training days because the quality of diving is high. On the repetition/skills training days, the intensity of training would be the highest on Wednesdays, for the reason cited earlier, and moderate on the other days.

Exercise Schedule

The exercise program needs to interact with the training schedule so the diver is given the best opportunity to be successful in the pool, especially on list training days. In order to do this, the following schedule is suggested:

M	T	W	Th	F	Sa
Abdominal/ Trunk	Jumping	Weights Abdominal/ Trunk	Rest	Jumping	Weights Abdominal/ Trunk

This schedule places the heaviest exercise on Wednesday and Saturday, when there is no list training taking place the next day. The lack of exercises on Thursday allows a midweek recovery to occur before the two list training days to follow.

In the event that a competition occurs on Sunday in a given week, the Saturday exercise program would be done after the competition on Sunday. Monday becomes a rest day, and the rest of the week remains the same.

Exercise Training Volume

Beginning with the number of repetitions of each exercise done in the week preceding the peaking period, gradually reduce the percentage from week 1 through week 4. In week 1, the diver should perform 90 percent of the repetitions from the previous week, then reduce this by 5 percent in each of the succeeding three weeks.

Exercise Training Intensity

It is important to keep the intensity of the exercise program at a high level so deterioration of the training level does not occur. This means keeping the weight being used at 90 to 100 percent of the 1RM; the drop jumps remain at the same height and the abdominal/trunk power exercises remain the same.

Week 5

The schedule changes in the final week before departing for the championship to allow the diver added rest before travel and the pressure of the competitive week.

Technical Training Schedule

This schedule assumes that departure for the championship event would take place on either Saturday or Sunday.

M	T	W	Th	F	Sa
Lists	Repetition/ Skills	Repetition/ Skills	Lists	Rest	Rest

Technical Training Volume and Intensity

Training volume and intensity on the list training days would remain the same as in previous weeks. However, both volume and intensity should be moderate on the other days to allow the diver additional rest in preparation for the high-intensity championship week.

Exercise Schedule

This schedule is designed so the last day of weight training occurs approximately 10 to 14 days before the start of the championship event so the diver is well rested before departing.

M	T	W	Th	F	Sa
Weights	Abdominal/ Trunk	Rest	Jumping Abdominal/ Trunk	Rest	Rest

Exercise Training Volume and Intensity

The number of repetitions of the exercises should be reduced by 5 percent of that done in week 4, while the intensity of the exercises should remain the same.

Week 6

During the championship week, no exercise program takes place other than warm-up prior to diving. Upon arrival at the site, repetition training takes place first to allow the diver to adjust to the facility; then list training is done to prepare for the competition.

LIST TRAINING

When the diver is doing the lists of dives for score, it is extremely important to simulate the competitive environment as much as possible. If the training situation allows, the following conditions should be in place:

- All distractions should be eliminated from the area.
- One diver should be ready to dive, and one diver should be waiting. All other divers should be in their preferred spots between dives.
- The coach should announce the dive as in official competition, or even better, he or she can make a recording of someone else announcing the diver and the dive.
- Multiple judges (a minimum of three) should be used, if possible.

There are a few ways to analyze the scores achieved in list training to gain valuable insight into the diver's level of technical and competitive preparation. The following information can be determined:

- Average score for each individual dive (from these averages, the diver can learn which dives are weakest and work harder on them during repetitions)
- Average total judges' and point scores for the basic dives
- Average total judges' and point scores for the optional dives
- Average total judges' and point scores for all dives
- Highest single list total point score
- Potential highest total point list score (determined by compiling the highest score attained for each dive, regardless of the list in which it was achieved, into one list)
- Improvement in scores over time

PSYCHOLOGICAL CONSIDERATIONS

Moving from multiple repetitions of dives in the preseason routine to scoring the dives in the testing and peaking periods has a strong psychological effect. The way the diver thinks changes because the reward system changes. Also, the diver has an opportunity to play out various competitive scenarios.

When doing repetitions without scoring, the diver generally concentrates on a particular part of the dive and tries to make a specific correction. If the correction is made but the dive is not of high quality, that is frequently viewed as a successful attempt. The coach rewards the diver in the critique for making the correction. The diver's thought process is narrowly focused on one area of the dive. This is normal and as it should be for this period of training. Also, when doing repetitions without scoring, if the diver does the dive six to eight times and only one or two attempts are good, but the last attempt is one of the good dives, the diver moves to the next dive. The coach generally rewards the diver by saying something like, "That was an excellent dive. Let's move on." Again, that is acceptable for this period of training.

Introducing scoring in the testing period changes the reward system. The score received on each dive becomes the overriding objective. This forces the diver to change focus to the whole dive and to performing a good dive regardless of the circumstances. This is an interim step to list training, which is even more mentally demanding. In the repetition for score situation, if a poor score is received, the diver has numerous additional attempts to make up for it. When doing list training, a poor score cannot be improved on. The diver must learn to move on to the next dive and refocus, exactly as he or she would in competition.

Several scenarios occur in list training that simulate competitive situations. The diver may miss dives at various stages of the list, which will cause anxiety. The diver and coach need to work together through these situations as if in an actual competition. The correct mental response to each scene should be determined and then played out. By play-acting in this way, not only should the diver's ability to perform lists improve, but the ability to recover in each situation should also improve.

SUMMARY

Planning the training year by specific periods with a training program determined for each period gives the diver and coach a preparation edge. Devising an exercise program consistent with the requirements of the sport and the strengths and weaknesses of the individual improves the physical profile of the diver. This is reflected in improved diving performance. Using the peaking for competition program prepares the diver for a high-level performance.

Take the principles and guidelines presented here and adapt them to the training and competition schedule for your program.

ADDITIONAL READINGS

Bompa, T. O. (1994). *Theory and Methodology of Training* (3rd ed.). Dubuque, IA: Kendall/Hunt.

Bompa, T. O. (2000). *Total Training for Young Champions*. Champaign, IL: Human Kinetics.

Fleck, S. J., & Kraemer, W. J. (1997). *Designing Resistance Training Programs* (2nd ed.). Champaign, IL: Human Kinetics.

Kraemer, W. J., & Fleck, S. J. (1993). *Strength Training for Young Athletes*. Champaign, IL: Human Kinetics.

Zatsiorsky, V. M. (1995). *Science and Practice of Strength Training*. Champaign, IL: Human Kinetics.

Courtesy of Laurie Marchwinski

Effective Coaching and Mental Preparation

Technical knowledge and having a plan for preparing the athlete are the foundations of success in any sport, and diving is certainly no exception. However, the techniques used in teaching the diver and the manner in which the coach and diver relate and conduct themselves determine the effectiveness of the training process. Additionally, if the final preparations for a major competition are not well thought out and well planned, all the effort expended in training can still result in a poor performance.

COACH–DIVER INTERACTION

The way the coach and diver interact is extremely important in maximizing coaching and learning effectiveness. While the coach needs to be the leader and director of the program, there should be a feeling of cooperation between diver and coach. Both need to understand how the coaching and learning process takes place and feel that they are contributing to its success. This can be achieved through constant open communication. Just as feedback from the coach is helpful to the diver, feedback from the diver is helpful to the coach.

Learning Modes

There are four learning modes a diver may employ in the practice situation. It is important for the diver and coach to understand these modes so both can get the most out of the coaching process. Divers who are aware of the learning mode that works best for them can monitor the coach to ensure that he or she uses that mode consistently. Coaching a diver in the wrong mode can be very inefficient and can waste a lot of time. The learning modes are as follows:

- Visual
- Kinesthetic
- Cognitive
- Auditory

Visual learners rely heavily on mental pictures and images, videotape replays, and watching others. Kinesthetic learners need to feel the movement(s) they want to make by going through them in a dryland setting before reproducing them in the dive. They can practice the movements by themselves or with hands-on assistance from the coach. Cognitive learners strive to understand the concept or principle and then apply this knowledge to produce the desired results. Auditory learners get best results when hearing the information needed to perform the task.

Most divers are predominantly visual and kinesthetic, with some reliance on the cognitive and auditory modes. Knowing what mode(s) the diver uses in the learning process, the order of priority, and how much importance is given to each is very important. Once this is determined, the coaching style can be adapted to fit the diver's profile. The easiest way to find out the diver's learning process is to ask. Most divers, even younger ones, can give a pretty accurate assessment if the modes are explained properly. Psychological testing instruments are also available that can help coaches get a more accurate analysis.

If a diver relies heavily on one particular mode, this must be taken into account in the training process. A diver who is 85 to 90 percent kinesthetic should be trained to go through the correct movement patterns repeatedly before attempting the dive. Dryland training can also be emphasized with this type of learner. Divers who are primarily visual will benefit more from instant video replay between dives and video analysis in and out of the pool setting.

Many divers use three or four of the learning modes, although the visual and kinesthetic areas are strongest. For these divers, coaches should address all of the areas by doing the following:

1. Verbally describing the error and correction
2. Explaining the reason the movement should be done that way
3. Going through the correct movements for the diver to see
4. Having the diver go through the correct movements
5. Showing a videotape replay, when possible and feasible

Coaching the diver with the style best suited to that individual will eliminate a lot of frustration on the part of the diver and the coach and lead to faster, more effective learning.

Involving the Diver

The diver should be a part of the coaching process. For instance, the diver might be responsible for analyzing the dive while ascending to the surface. He or she should evaluate what happened in the various parts of the dive. With this information as a base, coaching can take any of the following courses:

1. The coach can ask questions and get feedback from the diver.
2. The diver can ask questions and get feedback from the coach.
3. A critique by the coach can be compared to what the diver feels.

This involvement makes the diver more attentive and accelerates the learning process. A consistent comparison of what the diver feels and what the coach sees facilitates the development of a plan for correcting the dive. Since the diver is part of the solution, he or she will likely assume more responsibility and put forth a greater effort in making the needed changes.

A dialogue between the diver and coach does not have to occur after every dive, nor should it. Following are critical times for diver involvement:

- When no progress is taking place
- When communication is not effective
- When the diver seems confused

COACHING TECHNIQUES

Every coach wants to do the best job possible to help an aspiring diver reach his or her potential. Sometimes, though, the coach does not understand the correct learning progression or uses an ineffective technique. Here are some tips to help the coaching process be focused, efficient, and positive. These are presented as do's instead of don'ts because the coach needs to be coached in a positive way also.

Learning Progressions

If at all possible, beginning divers should spend more time on out-of-pool activities than on in-pool activities. Teaching correct diving skills from the diving board without the aid of dryland equipment and training is extremely difficult. Due to lack of control and balance, plus the speed with which dives occur, beginners find it hard to perform the proper movements. When this type of poor performance is repeated over and over, bad habits are formed that are very difficult to change. In a controlled dryland setting, with the proper equipment, the opportunity for success is greatly increased. If this kind of training is not available, the best advice is to progress slowly in the pool, making sure that one skill is mastered before a new and more difficult one is introduced.

All dives, even the most difficult ones, consist of simple skills connected to form more complex movement patterns or skill chains. A forward four-and-a-half somersault consists of a good takeoff followed by four single somersaults that employ visual spotting, a come-out, and a lineup. When one of the component skills is incorrect or missing, performance of the difficult dive is reduced in quality or not possible. Remember, a chain is only as strong as its weakest link.

The learning process should begin with simple skills practiced correctly in a controlled situation until mastered. The skills can then be performed at a faster rate and connected to other skills. The ideal learning process is described as follows:

1. Slow, simple movement patterns on the floor
2. Gradually faster simple movement patterns on the floor
3. Slow, connected movement patterns on the floor
4. Gradually faster connected movement patterns on the floor
5. Skill progressions on the trampoline in the spotting belt
6. Skill progressions on the dryland board in the spotting belt
7. Skill progressions in the pool
8. Dive performance

An example of a skill chain for a forward one-and-a-half somersault tuck is as follows:

On the Floor

1. The diver walks through the forward approach to the preliminary takeoff position.
2. The diver repeats the previous step and connects to the throwing motion for a forward somersault takeoff.
3. The diver repeats the previous step to a forward roll tuck. A target placed on the mat in front of where the roll ends can help with visual spotting.
4. The diver repeats the previous step with a kick to a handstand following the forward roll. A second target can be placed at the entry point so the spot in front can be seen at the end of the roll and the entry spot can be seen as the handstand occurs.

On the Trampoline

1. The diver practices one step and hurdle.
2. In the belt, the diver performs one step and a hurdle to a forward somersault (this skill would have been learned effectively before beginning this progression). A visual target is placed where the diver should look prior to the come-out for the one-and-a-half somersault.

3. In the belt, the diver performs the previous step to a one-and-a-half somersault with a second visual spot placed at the entry point. The diver must spot both targets.

On the Dryland Board

1. The diver repeats the steps performed on the trampoline.

In the Pool

1. The diver repeats the steps from the dryland board using floating visual targets.
2. Prior to performing the one-and-a-half somersault, the diver does the lineup skill to practice the come-out phase.

The floating targets referred to in the previous skill chain can be a colorful raft or other object held in front of the board by another diver. The entry target could be a chamois dropped in the water where the entry should occur.

This skill chain represents the type of controlled learning process that will produce safe, effective progress. It allows controlled practice on all the component parts of the dive while the diver is preparing for performance.

Two other guiding principles should be followed when moving through the learning process. At the first sign that technique is breaking down when moving to a more complex skill, the diver should return to the previous step. Sometimes regressing is progressing! Second, even when the diver has mastered a complex skill, he or she should continue to practice the component parts in order to maintain mastery.

Indirect and Direct Transfer Training

When using dryland training equipment such as the trampoline or dryland board, two methods can help transfer training to the pool—indirect and direct. The indirect method is more commonly used, but the direct method, although more time consuming, can be very effective.

Indirect training involves practicing multiple repetitions of several different dives, or parts of dives, on the trampoline or dryland board. This training is followed by a move to the pool, where the diver performs the dives practiced on dry land. This process is time efficient, but there can be a considerable length of time between the dryland practice and the actual performance of the dive in the pool. This extended time period can make the transfer of skills from dry land to the pool less effective.

The direct training program focuses on one particular dive at a time, thus significantly reducing the time interval between dryland work and performance of the dive in the pool. The diver performs multiple repetitions of the selected dive or parts of the dive on the trampoline or dryland board and then moves to the pool and performs the dive. If successful transfer of skills does not occur, the process could be repeated several times until the desired improvement results.

The best training program should incorporate both types of training, as dictated by progress. If consistent use of the indirect transfer method offers no improvement, direct training should be used intermittently to increase the possibility for transfer of skills.

Coaching Methods

Four basic coaching methods can be used when explaining what the diver is supposed to do:

1. Incorrect/correct
2. Overcorrection
3. Analogy
4. Extremism

The incorrect/correct method entails pinpointing the incorrect technique(s) being done and then describing the correct movements to be substituted. This is the most common technique used.

Overcorrection involves instructing the diver to make a correction that is an error opposite the one presently being made. For example, if a diver's arms are above the head in a particular part of the dive and they are supposed to be at shoulder level, the coach may tell the diver to place them at hip level. The resulting performance should be somewhere in between and closer to the correct position.

When using analogy as the coaching technique, the desired movement to be made is related to something the diver can visualize or feel or has done before. The coach may say, for example, "Hold your arms as if wrapping them around a big beach ball" or "Start this dive as if you are rolling over a big ball." This method challenges the coach to be innovative and imaginative in creating scenarios to fit the situation.

If nothing else seems to work, especially in dives in which safe distance is the key factor, the coach may need to request extreme change. When a diver is doing a reverse dive too close to the board, the coach should not just ask him or her to move the dive out; rather, the coach should tell the diver to move the dive extremely far from the board. If possible, the coach may want to put a target in the area where he or she wants the dive to finish. Once the diver has accomplished the exaggerated dive several times, then he or she can begin working to slowly bring the dive back to good distance.

Of course, these coaching methods should be combined with the learning modes described earlier to structure overall coaching technique.

Coaching Effectively

During my many years of coaching and observing other coaches, I have developed a few very specific tips on how to be most effective and efficient in the coaching process. These relate to what the coach says and how he or she says it, and varying the practices so the coach and the diver don't get bored.

In many cases, coaches don't analyze their coaching habits. They respond in the same way time after time, sometimes not concentrating hard enough because of the repetitive nature of giving instructions for several hundred dives in a training session. I recommend that coaches not only analyze their divers on video, but also observe and listen to themselves. In so doing, they can find out what they like and don't like and can make the necessary changes. If you are a coach and you are not following some of the suggestions described here, maybe you should try to include them in your coaching repertoire.

Cause, Not Result

It seems useless to say "coach the cause, not the result" when referring to coaching diving. Everyone would agree that this is the goal, so why even bring it up? It is worth discussing because sometimes coaches are coaching the result without taking the time to realize it. When coaches are repeatedly giving the same instructions to a diver and no noticeable change occurs, one of three scenarios is in operation:

1. The diver is not listening or may be trying to do something other than what the coach is instructing.
2. The instructions are not phrased in a way that the diver can transfer into action.
3. The result, rather than the cause of the problem, is being coached.

In the first scenario, a discussion between the diver and coach is indicated. It must be determined if the diver is focusing on the instructions or trying to be his or her own coach. The second scenario requires that the coach find different words or analogies to coach the dive. If neither of these solutions works, it could be that the coach is missing the initial cause of the problem. In this case, the dive should be videotaped and studied in slow motion and with frame-by-frame analysis. The naked eye cannot always pick up movements that are occurring, especially at performance speed. After video analysis, if a new approach to the problem does not work, or is not found, it is time to consult another coach for an outside opinion. Only by pursuing the correct answer to the problem can progress result. The coach's ego should not stand in the way of this process, or the diver will pay the penalty.

Positive Bookends Critique

The style used in coaching a diver can have a great bearing on the response and results. The positive bookends method has proven to be very effective. The critique begins with a positive statement. Everyone likes to hear positive statements about their performance, so this gets the diver's attention. While the diver is still listening, the coach presents the information about what correction(s) needs to be made. Finally, the coach finishes the critique with another positive statement, to put the diver in a positive frame of mind for the next attempt.

Obviously, this coaching style cannot be used on every dive, but whenever possible, it will produce excellent results and help create a positive environment for training.

The Last Picture

Regardless of whether the positive bookends coaching style is used, the coach should make sure that the last statement made conjures up the correct picture in the diver's mind. This is because the last picture the coach presents to the diver is what the diver carries back onto the board. For example, if a final instruction relates to head position and the coach says, "Don't throw your head back," the diver will have the picture of the head thrown back in his or her mind. Instead, the coach should say, "Make sure you keep your head in line." Creating the positive, correct image will enhance the chance for successful performance.

Conciseness

Coaches should try to keep coaching comments to a minimum. They should say what has to be said as concisely as possible. Long, drawn-out explanations can bore the diver, turn off the listening mode, and slow down the training session. In many cases, the coach is critiquing too many points in the dive. Coaching no more than one or two points in a dive is a good policy. The chances that the diver can make three corrections in one dive are pretty slim. Also, the points being coached should not occur in the same part of the dive. The diver needs enough time to think about making the first correction, then switch to the second one. Time simply won't permit the diver to attempt two corrections in the takeoff, for example. A change in the takeoff followed by a change in the come-out will work much better.

Consistency

It is important to continue to coach the same point(s) in a dive from one attempt to another, from one day to another, and from and one week to another until improvement takes place. If the coach and diver are working on something in a specific part of the dive, the coach should stay focused on it until the diver makes the correction. Too often, coaches coach one thing on one attempt and something different on the next. When this occurs, the diver becomes confused about what to concentrate on. Coaches should instead work consistently on one or two corrections in a dive, over time, until the diver accomplishes the task. At that point, the coach can select the next most important correction or two and begin to work on those.

Getting Involved

Some coaches do the same thing every day in the practice situation. They come in, sit down in the same spot, and stay there the whole time. This can make for boring, uninspiring practices for the diver and coach. Instead, coaches should direct from different angles and move around the pool deck. Many things can be seen from the back, front, or top of the dive that cannot be seen from a profile view. The coach's activity level and involvement in the training process can have a positive, energizing effect on the diver.

GUIDELINES FOR DIVERS

In addition to coaching techniques and learning methods, divers can attend to other considerations in order to gain the most from their efforts.

Each diver needs to contribute positively to the learning and training process. Certain responsibilities and behavior patterns will make this possible and allow the diver to progress faster and more consistently. Some of these are not easy and require great discipline and concentration; however, for the diver to reach his or her full potential, they are essential.

1. Be on time or early to practice.

2. Be at practice consistently. Never miss training unless an exceptional circumstance arises. If you are sick but capable of doing some of the practice, be there.

3. Work hard every day. Some divers work hard two or three days a week and feel they are doing their best. Consistent hard work every day is the only way to achieve your goals.

4. Get adequate rest so you can work hard every day.

5. Follow the training plan your coach has designed; don't cut corners.

6. Don't balk unless you feel you are in danger on the takeoff.

7. Make every dive count. Do not break form or give up on a dive.

8. Listen carefully to your coach's comments.

9. If you don't understand the coaching critique, ask questions and discuss until you do understand.

10. Don't add your own coaching to what your coach is telling you without discussing this with the coach. If you go off on your own coaching direction, confusion between you and the coach will result.

11. Stay open to new suggestions, and be willing to experiment. Be like putty in your coach's hands. If you do what you are asked, progress will be accelerated.

12. Visualize the dive the way you want to do it, and practice the movements of the dive while waiting your turn for the next dive.

13. If you become frustrated with your performance, step back and take a minute to reframe your thinking. Make positive, encouraging comments to yourself; then start again with a new attitude.

14. When faced with adversity (e.g., wind, cold, rain, a noisy environment, a poor board, bad lighting, illness, etc.), consider it an opportunity to face a challenge and win. If you can perform well in adverse conditions, you are not only more efficient in training but also better prepared for competition. Remember, adversity is a challenge, not an obstacle.

15. If you suffer failure in training or competition, analyze the situation so you can learn from it. Ask yourself, What did I do that I shouldn't have done? and What didn't I do that I should have done? When you have the answer to these questions, you have positive information you can use to avoid the same mistakes the next time. You can now restart in a positive direction. Most people who have achieved great success have experienced great failure first.

GUIDELINES FOR COACHES

Just like the diver, the coach needs to do certain things not only to be a better coach but also to produce successful divers. Some of these guidelines may seem unnecessary or silly, but taken together they add up to a meaningful pattern of professional behavior. Following these guidelines and leading by example will go a long way toward getting the most out of yourself and your athletes. Most teams and athletes take on the characteristics of the coach. Be sure you are sending the right message, because *they will get it!*

1. Be early to practice.

2. Do your best to never miss practice, unless it is an emergency. If you are not feeling well, go to practice anyway. This is a great opportunity to provide an example to the divers of the level of commitment you want from them.

3. Work harder than your divers by putting in whatever time it takes to attend to every detail of preparation and planning.

4. Get adequate rest so you can attend to the details of preparation and planning.

5. Stay in good physical shape so you can not only work more efficiently but also demand a high level of fitness from your divers.

6. Dress in a professional way. Casual slacks, nice shorts, or a warm-up outfit with a collared shirt present a good appearance for the divers, parents, and unexpected visitors you may encounter (supervisors, administrators, community business leaders). Jeans, cutoffs, T-shirts, and so on, do not present a professional image to the observer.

7. Be prepared with a specific daily or weekly training plan as well as a more general monthly and seasonal plan. As much as possible, let the divers know what they will be doing ahead of time so they can be physically and mentally prepared to do their best.

8. Be flexible with the plan, and adapt it as circumstances warrant.

9. Pay strict attention to what is happening in the training session. Do your best not to miss dives performed. Control the pace of the practice so you can give adequate time to each dive and diver.

10. Listen carefully to divers' feedback on dives. You must match up what you see with what they feel in order to give them worthwhile directions.

11. Eliminate distractions during practice as much as possible. Do not take phone calls (turn off the cell phone!), keep the parents in a controlled area, do not engage in conversations unrelated to the training process, and if possible, restrict access to the training area to anyone but the team.

12. If a problem arises with a diver or divers (bad attitude, excessive emotion, lack of attention, playing around between dives, etc.), address the problem and resolve it right away. Do not let anyone have a negative impact on the other divers through their behavior, even if that means removing the offender(s) from the practice.

13. Help divers deal with the frustrating and adverse situations mentioned earlier. Constantly observe and analyze the mental frame of mind of your divers so you can intervene early when a problem begins. Give your divers an assessment of where you think they are, get their feedback, and give them directions as to how to reverse and eliminate the problem. Over time, divers who are coached and encouraged to act and react appropriately and healthfully in different situations establish healthy, effective behavior patterns.

14. Help your divers deal with failure. Assist them in answering the questions posed in guideline (for divers) #15. Help them find that positive spin that can be salvaged from the situation and direct them in setting new positive goals.

15. Spend as much of your out-of-pool time as possible educating yourself. Constantly be looking for new ideas from various fields such as sport science and sports medicine as well as from other sports and other coaches. You need to continue to improve, just as you expect your divers to improve.

16. When stressful situations occur, your divers will look to you for guidance. It is your job to stay calm and clearheaded so you can make good decisions.

By working hard to follow the preceding guidelines, both divers and coaches can make the most of the training program and preparation for performance.

CREATING A COMPETITIVE ADVANTAGE

Up to this point, you have studied the technical aspects of diving and learned how to plan the training program, conduct the training program, and interact as coach and diver. The final ingredient is gaining a mental edge for the championship competition.

There is a saying that being successful in competition is "90 percent from the neck up." There is a lot of truth to this, assuming the competitors are fairly even in ability. The difference between winning and losing is often determined by who has the mental edge. The ability to perform at the highest level in major competitions is based on confidence. Without supreme confidence, somewhere along the line, the athlete will falter. Confidence comes from feeling completely prepared, and feeling prepared comes from knowing that you did everything possible in the training process. In training, hard work is at the head of the list because without it, nothing else the athlete and coach do will be effective. The training program must also be carefully planned to cover all areas of preparation; it must be based on sound principles, and both diver and coach must attend to every detail. In addition to the training plan, the coach and diver must develop a specific competition preparation program and have a game plan in place for the competition.

Before describing what the coach and diver can do to create a competitive advantage, I want to emphasize the value of a good sport psychology program for the diver. The areas of relaxation, visualization, goal setting, anxiety control, and predive routines should be taught by a professional. If the coach can find someone in the local area to conduct this part of the program, the diver will have a great advantage. While this type of training is beyond the scope of my expertise, it is highly valuable. Whenever possible, it should be a part of the training process.

Role of the Training Plan

After reading the previous chapter, it should be evident that a great deal of time and attention goes into developing a training plan. Once the coach has developed the plan, the diver should be made a part of the plan. The coach and diver should discuss all aspects of the plan, and the diver's input should have weight. At the end of this interaction, the coach and diver should be on the same page, and the diver should feel a part of the decision-making process. Divers who feel included in the training plan not only cooperate with the plan, but also feel positive about their level of preparation.

Coaches have the task of instilling confidence in their divers so that they believe that (1) all the hard exercise work, followed by the six-week peaking period, will leave them totally physically prepared, and (2) all the work done on diving for score will help them handle any competitive situation.

Diver involvement and belief in the training and preparation process are the keys to building the high level of confidence responsible for success in major competitions.

Preparing for the Championship

With hard work and belief in the training plan as a foundation, other methods of preparing for the competition will help give the diver the proper mind-set and guidance to gain an edge. The coach and diver have roles and responsibilities to carry out prior to departure for the championship, at the site, prior to the start of competition, and on competition day(s). As a general rule, given divers with relatively equal ability, those with a plan usually beat those without a plan.

Prior to Departing

Prior to departure, the goals for the diver are to create an extreme feeling of confidence in performance, prepare mentally for any situation that may occur at the competition, and stay relaxed. The coach needs to build the diver's confidence through planning and positive input.

Diver

1. Create a best-ever videotape. Taking videos of practices and competitions prior to the championship affords the opportunity to put the best performance of each dive on one videotape. You can view your list of best dives frequently to instill confidence and improve your ability to visualize the dives effectively. If you'd like, you can add inspiring music to the tape to increase the positive impact of viewing. At the competition, you can view the tape on a portable, battery-operated VCR and monitor.

2. Visualize being at the competition site, doing the dives the way you did on your best-ever tape, and achieving the goals you set. Go as far as to see yourself at the award ceremony receiving the medal.

3. Think about every possible scenario that could happen to cause distraction or emotional stress, both in and out of the pool. Play the situations out and determine what the correct response would be for each. Program this to memory and be prepared to react that way, in the event any of those things happen at the competition. Review this process frequently.

4. Spend time putting the competition into a healthy perspective. It is not a life-or-death situation but an opportunity to be successful.

5. Watch some inspirational movies.

Coach

1. Prepare a day-to-day training and preparation plan for each diver while at the championship.

2. Go over the plan with the diver and, as in the training plan, get the diver's input, approval, and support. The diver will feel confident if there is a well-thought-out plan in place.

3. Assist the diver in selecting the best dives for the best-ever tape.

4. Keep the training and preparation atmosphere positive.

At the Site

The main objective of the training days leading up to the competition is for the diver to become adjusted to the new surroundings and diving equipment. The diver can accomplish this by doing more dives in the first few training sessions at the competition site. As he or she adjusts, the number of dives can be reduced to avoid fatigue prior to the start of the competition.

Diver

1. Do not train extra hard to improve at the last minute.

2. Do not make any last-minute major changes.

3. Follow the preplanned preparation schedule, but be flexible.

4. Continue to use the best-ever tape.

5. Continue to visualize the event unfolding, dive by dive, as you want it to happen.

6. If you have a poor practice, do not take this as an indication of not being ready. The hard training and preparation plan will override a poor practice.

Coach

1. Communicate frequently with the diver. Be observant of changes in mood or attitude. The diver should remain positive and energetic while preparing for the competition.

2. Stick to the preparation plan as much as possible, but alter it as needed on a day-to-day basis.

3. Keep the coaching on a general level. Resist the temptation to introduce new coaching tips and to overcoach. The work has already been done; let the diver do what he or she has been trained to do.

4. Stay positive.

On Competition Day

On competition day, the diver must accomplish two things: stay relaxed and be ready to perform when the competition starts, not before. It is here that the diver and coach can work together to keep the situation in perspective. They should be casual, tell some jokes, and talk about things other than diving.

Diver

1. Plan the day carefully so there is plenty of time to get from one place to another. Avoid having to rush. Follow the guideline "walk slow, talk slow." Controlling the pace of the day will help keep your anxiety level down.

2. In the initial warm-up practice, do not try too hard to dive well. This is merely a warm-up to get your body ready to perform. Build to a peak as the competition nears.

3. Determine ahead of time a strategy for whether you will watch other divers, their scores, and their places or occupy yourself in some other way. This is based on what has worked for you in past competitions. Once you have selected your strategy, stick with it.

4. Create a consistent pattern of what to do and when as you move to the diving area before each dive. This will help to create a rhythm to your performance.

5. Keep the same timing as far as how long you stand before starting each dive. This provides a consistent rhythm on each dive. Divers who go more quickly or wait longer on critical dives tend to miss them. Make all your dives the same.

Coach

1. Stay calm! Diving is not a sport in which a lot of emotion is helpful. Follow the first item of advice for the diver about controlling pace and reducing anxiety.

2. Don't give a pep talk, as the diver is already working to control his or her anxiety level.

3. Keep a keen eye on the look and body language of the diver. After working together on a close basis for an extended period of time, you know how he or she looks and acts when in the right frame of mind. If you observe any deviation from the diver's normal state, communicate with him or her immediately, find out what is going on, and make suggestions accordingly. Leading up to and during the competition, your job is to keep the diver on the right mental track.

SUMMARY

Coaches and divers should work together to determine the most effective techniques for learning, training, and preparing for competition. The information presented in this and the previous chapters is intended to help develop a complete diving program based on sound principles and concepts. Using them on a regular basis will make training more fun and productive and will put you on the road to success.

Glossary

backward press–A press in which the diver springs from the board or platform while performing a takeoff from a backward standing position.

backward save–An underwater motion in which the diver arches the body and bends the knees, drawing the heels toward the buttocks, to keep the legs entering the water vertically.

bottom of the press–The point in the forward and backward springing movements at which the diver fully flexes the legs and hips prior to extending the legs and jumping into the takeoff.

calling–Giving a verbal cue for the diver to *come out* of a dive.

checking–Using action–reaction movements or lengthening the body to slow somersault rotation.

circular closure–Method with which the diver accelerates backward and reverse somersaulting dives by moving the arms laterally and downward from the takeoff position, to grasp the legs.

C position–The general body shape the diver assumes to initiate backward and reverse somersaulting dives.

direct closure–Method by which the diver accelerates backward and reverse somersaulting dives by bringing the arms to the legs in a direct line of movement.

drive leg–The leg used in the hurdle to push the diver from the springboard.

dryland springboard–A diving stand and springboard installed in an area away from the pool, with a foam rubber landing pit.

failure–The point at which another successful repetition of an exercise cannot be performed.

forward approach–In springboard or platform diving, an approach that consists of a number of steps plus a hurdle from one foot to a two-foot landing at the take off point.

hollow position–A concave shape of the front side of the body.

hurdle–A jump from one foot to a two-foot takeoff from the end of the springboard or platform.

hurdle leg–The leg that is lifted into the air at the beginning of the hurdle.

intensity–The qualitative element of training, such as speed, power, or weight lifted. In dive training it refers to the number of somersaults and/or twists and the difficulty of the dive performed.

load–Amount of weight being lifted in one repetition.

opposition–The point in the backward press when the arms move upward and the heels move downward.

overhead spotting equipment–A system of pulleys and ropes attached to a belt around the diver's waist that allows the coach to safely control the diver's movements while in the air.

preliminary takeoff position–The position of the body when the springboard is at maximum depression.

press–The action of the diver depressing the springboard or, in platform diving, loading the body weight onto the legs prior to takeoff.

repetitions–The number of times an exercise is performed within a set.

repetition maximum–The maximal load that can be lifted in one attempt, also called "one-repetition maximum" (1RM).

rip entry–An entry into the water that creates little splash and is accompanied by a sound similar to fabric ripping.

set–The total number of repetitions performed before a rest interval is taken.

somersault save–An underwater somersaulting technique that aids the diver in controlling the angle of entry of the legs.

square-out–The method of stopping the twist in dives that combine somersaulting and twisting.

step length–The distance from the bottom of the kneecap (patella) to the ground, plus the foot length. This represents the length of the step, measured from the toes of the trailing leg to the toes of the lead leg, while the diver is performing steps at a moderate speed.

stuck–A diver's feeling that a somersaulting dive is not rotating very fast.

swimming the entry–A breaststroke-like movement of the arms used immediately after entry impact that aids the rip entry technique.

takeoff–The series of movements that take place from the beginning of the springing motion on the end of the springboard or platform until the feet leave the takeoff area.

top of the press–The point during the backward press technique when the diver is standing high on the toes, with the body straight and arms overhead, in preparation for dropping the body weight into the springboard or platform.

visual spotting–The technique by which the diver visually sees specific areas to aid in orientation in somersaulting dives.

Index

Note: The letters *f* and *t* after page numbers indicate figures and tables, respectively.